Crystal Xcelsius For Dummies®

Cheat Sheet

Index of Supported Excel Functions

ABS	DDB	HARMEAN	NORMDIST	SLN
ACOS	DEGREES	HLOOKUP	NORMINV	SMALL
ACOSH	DEVSQ	HOUR	NORMSDIST	SQRT
AND	DGET	IF	NORMSINV	STANDARDIZE
ASIN	DMAX	INDEX	NOT	STDEV
ASINH	DMIN	INT	NOW	SUM
ATAN	DOLLAR	INTERCEPT	NPER	SUMIF
ATAN2	DPRODUCT	IPMT	NPV	SUMPRODUCT
ATANH	DSTDEV	IRR	ODD	SUMSQ
AVEDEV	DSTDEVP	KURT	OR	SUMX2MY2
AVERAGE	DSUM	LARGE	PI	SUMX2PY2
AVERAGEA	DVAR	LEFT*	PMT	SUMXMY2
BETADIST*	DVARP	LEN*	POWER	SYD
CEILING	EDATE	LN	PPMT	TAN
CHOOSE	EOMONTH	LOG	PRODUCT	TANH
COMBIN	EQUALS	LOG10	PV	TEXT*
CONCATENATE	EVEN	LOOKUP*	RADIANS	TIME
COS	EXACT*	LOWER*	RAND	TIMEVALUE
COSH	EXP	MATCH	RANK	TODAY
COUNT	EXPONDIST	MAX	RATE	TRUE
COUNTA	FACT	MEDIAN	REPLACE*	TRUNC
COUNTIF	FALSE	MID*	REPT*	VALUE*
DATE	FIND*	MIN	RIGHT*	VAR
DATEVALUE	FISHER	MINUTE	ROUND	VDB
DAVERAGE	FISHERINV	MIRR	ROUNDDOWN	VLOOKUP
DAY	FIXED	MOD	⌐⌐⌐⌐	WEEKDAY
DAYS360	FLOOR	MODE		
DB	FORECAST	MONTH		
DCOUNT	FV	N*		
DCOUNTA	GEOMEAN	NETWORKDA		

D1530209

For Dummies: Bestselling Book Series for Beginners

Crystal Xcelsius For Dummies®

Index of Xcelsius Components Not Available in All Versions

Category	Component	Crystal Xcelsius Standard	Crystal Xcelsius Professional	Crystal Xcelsius Workgroup
Selector	List Builder			✓
Selector	Source Data Component		✓	✓
Selector	Ticker			✓
Selector	Accordion Menu		✓	✓
Selector	Sliding Picture Menu		✓	✓
Selector	Fish-Eye Picture Menu		✓	✓
Collaboration	Remote Scenarios Buttons			✓
Collaboration	People List			✓
Collaboration	Login			✓
Collaboration	Connection Light			✓
Other	Interactive Calendar		✓	✓
Web Connectivity	XML Data Button			✓
Web Connectivity	XML Map Refresh			✓
Web Connectivity	Web Service Connector			✓
Web Connectivity	External SlideShow		✓	✓

For Dummies: Bestselling Book Series for Beginners

Crystal Xcelsius™

FOR

DUMMIES®

Crystal Xcelsius™ FOR DUMMIES®

by Michael Alexander

Wiley Publishing, Inc.

Crystal Xcelsius™ For Dummies®

Published by
Wiley Publishing, Inc.
111 River Street
Hoboken, NJ 07030-5774
www.wiley.com

Copyright © 2006 by Wiley Publishing, Inc., Indianapolis, Indiana

Published by Wiley Publishing, Inc., Indianapolis, Indiana

Published simultaneously in Canada

For general information on our other products and services, please contact our Customer Care Department within the U.S. at 800-762-2974, outside the U.S. at 317-572-3993, or fax 317-572-4002.

For technical support, please visit www.wiley.com/techsupport.

Wiley also publishes its books in a variety of electronic formats. Some content that appears in print may not be available in electronic books.

Library of Congress Control Number: 2006920622

ISBN-13: 978-0-471-77910-0

ISBN-10: 0-471-77910-5

Manufactured in the United States of America

10 9 8 7 6 5 4 3 2 1

1B/QT/QU/QW/IN

WILEY

About the Author

Michael Alexander is a Microsoft Certified Application Developer (MCAD) with over 14 years experience consulting and developing office solutions. He is the author of several books and the principle contributor at www.datapig technologies.com, where he shares free Access and Excel tips to intermediate users. He currently lives in Frisco, Texas where he works as a Senior Program Manager for a top technology firm.

Dedication

For my wonderful family: Mary, Ethan, and Emma.

Author's Acknowledgments

Thank you to Kirk Cunningham for all his help in getting this project off the ground. Thank you to Jaime Zuluaga for all of the wonderful ideas, tips, and tricks. Thank you to the Crystal Xcelsius technical team for answering all my questions. Thank you to Santiago and Santi Becerra for creating this ground-breaking program. A big thank you to Loren Abdulezer, a superb Technical Editor who kept me honest and sparked some great ideas. Thank you to Greg Croy for taking a chance on this book about a new product. Many thanks to Chris Morris and the brilliant team of professionals at Wiley Publishing who helped bring this book to fruition. And a special thank you to my beautiful wife Mary for supporting all my crazy projects.

Publisher's Acknowledgments

We're proud of this book; please send us your comments through our online registration form located at www.dummies.com/register/.

Some of the people who helped bring this book to market include the following:

Acquisitions, Editorial, and Media Development

Project Editor: Christopher Morris

Executive Editor: Gregory S. Croy

Senior Copy Editor: Teresa Artman

Technical Editor: Loren Abdulezer

Editorial Manager: Kevin Kirschner

Media Development Manager: Laura VanWinkle

Editorial Assistant: Amanda Foxworth

Cartoons: Rich Tennant (www.the5thwave.com)

Composition

Project Coordinator: Michael Kruzil

Layout and Graphics: Andrea Dahl, Heather Ryan

Proofreaders: Jessica Kramer, Techbooks

Indexer: Techbooks

Publishing and Editorial for Technology Dummies

    Richard Swadley, Vice President and Executive Group Publisher

    Andy Cummings, Vice President and Publisher

    Mary Bednarek, Executive Acquisitions Director

    Mary C. Corder, Editorial Director

Publishing for Consumer Dummies

    Diane Graves Steele, Vice President and Publisher

    Joyce Pepple, Acquisitions Director

Composition Services

    Gerry Fahey, Vice President of Production Services

    Debbie Stailey, Director of Composition Services

Contents at a Glance

Table of Contents

Introduction

I like to pretend that I'm a young man, but then I remember that one of my first jobs was typing up orders on a Wang computer. For you spring chickens who don't remember Wang computers, let's just say they don't make them anymore. Anyway, my point is that I've been in the business world a long time. I remember the mad rush to invest in large data warehouses and enterprise reporting tools. These tools came with the promise of business intelligence, affectionately called *BI*. Business intelligence is what you get when you analyze raw data and turn that analysis into knowledge. BI can help an organization identify cost-cutting opportunities, uncover new business opportunities, recognize changing business environments, identify data anomalies, and create widely accessible reports. Unfortunately, data warehouse and enterprise tools of the past had analysis and reporting capabilities that were clunky at best and not very user-friendly. This left many business professionals using tools such as Lotus 1-2-3 and Excel to analyze and report data.

Fast-forward about a decade later, and you'll see that a lot has changed. The Internet is now a cornerstone of business, new technologies have emerged to enhance the quality and performance of Web reporting, and even the previously clunky BI tools can now provide analytical capabilities that are both robust and user-friendly. Nevertheless, even with all these advances in business intelligence capabilities, most of the data analysis and reporting done in business today is still done by using a spreadsheet: that's right, our old friend Excel, which has remained more or less unchanged for the last ten years. Make no mistake — no matter how advanced an IT manager thinks his enterprise system is, Excel is embedded somewhere in that organization's data pipeline.

This is where Crystal Xcelsius enters the scene. Unlike other enterprise solutions, Crystal Xcelsius doesn't try to replace Excel or to take away its need. Instead, Crystal Xcelsius works with Excel to create interactive visualizations by using Excel's data and functionality. With Crystal Xcelsius, users no longer have to feel bad about using Excel in an environment that touts high technology. Crystal Xcelsius allows Excel users to turn their spreadsheets into professional looking dashboards, scorecards, what-if visualizations, or even highly polished PowerPoint presentations. The best thing about Crystal Xcelsius is that with its user-friendly click-and-drag interface, anyone can create highly compelling dashboards in minutes. So ignore SAP for a while. Close out your Crystal Reports, and log off of your Panorama and Cognos portals. Fire up the stalwart Excel and take an in-depth look at this fabulous new program called Crystal Xcelsius.

About This Book

The chapters in this book are designed to be standalone chapters that you can selectively refer to as needed. These chapters provide you with step-by-step walkthrough examples as well as instruction on the wide array of functionality that Crystal Xcelsius has to offer. As you move through this book, you will be able to create increasingly sophisticated dashboards using more advanced components. After reading this book, you will be able to

- ✔ Create basic dashboards with charts, gauges, and sliders.
- ✔ Add advanced functionality to your dashboards such as alerts, maps, and dynamic visibility.
- ✔ Create interactive business calculators and what-if analysis tools.
- ✔ Integrate Crystal Xcelsius models into PowerPoint presentations.
- ✔ Create Crystal Xcelsius–based Web pages.

The three versions of Crystal Xcelsius are Standard, Professional, and Workgroup. In this book, I focus on the components and functionalities of Crystal Xcelsius Standard and Professional. If you use Crystal Xcelsius Workgroup, you will find that much of the information found here still applies to your version. However, this book doesn't cover the collaboration and the enterprise-level functionality of Crystal Xcelsius Workgroup.

Foolish Assumptions

I make three assumptions about you, the reader:

- ✔ Given that you're even reading this book, you've already bought and installed Crystal Xcelsius.
- ✔ You are a relatively experienced Excel user familiar with basic concepts, such as referencing cells and using formulas.
- ✔ You have enough experience with PowerPoint to add objects, resize objects, and run a presentation.

How This Book Is Organized

The chapters in this book are organized into five parts, each of which includes chapters that build on the previous chapters' instruction. As you go through each part, you will be able to build dashboards of increasing complexity until you're a Crystal Xcelsius guru.

Part I: Say Hello to Crystal Xcelsius

Part I is all about introducing you to Crystal Xcelsius. In Chapter 1, I share with you the various ways you can use Crystal Xcelsius as well as the core concepts that make Crystal Xcelsius components work. In Chapter 2, throw caution to the wind and create your first dashboard — without reading the instructions. At the end of Chapter 2, you will have a firm understanding of the fundamentals of using Crystal Xcelsius, including importing data, working with components, publishing your dashboard, and refreshing your data.

Part II: Getting Started with the Basics

In Part II, I take an in-depth look at some of the basic components that are key to any dashboard. In Chapter 3, I show you how Single Value components work and how to use them to build interactivity into your dashboards. In Chapter 4, I show you how to leverage alerts to enable conditional coloring in your components, allowing your audience to get an instant visual assessment on performance. Chapter 5 is all about creating charts in Crystal Xcelsius. I wrap up this part with Chapter 6, where I show you how to easily build menus and selectors into your dashboards with Selector components.

Part III: Getting Fancy with Advanced Components

In Part III, I go beyond the basics to take a look at some of the advanced components that Crystal Xcelsius has to offer. In Chapter 7, I demonstrate the different ways you can use Map components to add flair to your visualizations. In Chapter 8, I walk you through the basics of dynamic visibility and look at some examples of how dynamic visibility can help achieve focus on the parts of your dashboard that are important. Chapter 9 focuses on the advanced components and functions that are found only in the Professional version of Crystal Xcelsius, discussing how each can be used to enhance your visual models.

Part IV: Wrapping Things Up

Part IV focuses on the last two actions a user takes when wrapping up the production of a dashboard: formatting and distribution. Chapter 10 focuses on the functions and utilities that enable you to show off your artistic side and add your own style to your visual models. In Chapter 11, I show you just how easy it is to take your dashboards to market, and I share a few other tricks on how to share the data in a visual model.

Part V: The Part of Tens

Part V is the classic Part of Tens section found in every *For Dummies* title. The chapters here each present ten or more pearls of wisdom, delivered in bite-sized pieces. In Chapter 12, I share with you ten best practices that will help you design Excel models that allow you to go beyond simple dashboards. In Chapter 13, I share ten of my best Crystal Xcelsius tricks, making ordinary components do extraordinary things. Chapter 14 focuses on answering some of the questions that I hear most often. Chapter 15 covers real-world examples of Crystal Xcelsius in the workplace.

Lastly, the appendix at the end of the book contains an essay by Loren Abdulezer about the significance of the paradigm shift that Crystal Xcelsius represents.

Icons Used In This Book

Sometimes I have to talk about certain technical things in order to keep my guru mystique. These things are interesting but not crucial, so I mark them with this icon. You don't need to read them, but for some of the more tech-savvy of you, they may be useful.

Tips are suggestions to make your life easier. Skim these nuggets for time-savers, tricks, and just plain cool moves.

These notes denote info you ought to think about, but they're not going to cause a disaster if you don't pay attention.

Be sure to read text marked with this icon! If you do not follow a warning, bad things can happen: Puffs of black smoke might come out of your monitor, your workspace could be deluged by a plague of frogs, or your program simply won't work right.

This icon denotes subject matter about which you can find more on the World Wide Web. For the most part, the icon is used to point out examples you can download from this book's companion Web site at `www.dummies.com/go/xcelsius`.

Part I
Say Hello to Crystal Xcelsius

The 5th Wave   By Rich Tennant

@RICHTENNANT

"Frankly, I'm not sure this is the way to enhance our data presentation."

In this part . . .

In this part, you are introduced to Crystal Xcelsius. In Chapter 1, I share with you the various ways you can use Crystal Xcelsius as well as the core concepts that make the Crystal Xcelsius components work. In Chapter 2, throw caution to the wind and create your first dashboard — without reading the instructions. By the end of this part, you should have a firm understanding of the fundamentals of creating dashboards in Crystal Xcelsius.

Chapter 1

Introducing Crystal Xcelsius

In This Chapter

▶ Overcoming static cling

▶ Seeing beyond fancy graphics

▶ Checking out Crystal Xcelsius under the hood

So here you are with this new software application — Crystal Xcelsius — in your hand, ready to read this book, hoping to see how to make some really cool dashboards that organize and present your data in a brilliant new way. Little do you know that you are on the cusp of a revolution. It's true! I sit here writing one of the first chapters ever written about Crystal Xcelsius, which is fast becoming a force to be reckoned with in the world of business intelligence.

Using cutting-edge technology, Crystal Xcelsius bridges the gap between data analysis and data presentation, empowering anyone who can point and click a mouse to create professional and compelling dashboards. Gone are the days of deferring to the local Excel guru to help analyze your data or calling the local PowerPoint guru to help you build your presentations. Crystal Xcelsius simplifies even the most complex functionalities, enabling even a beginner to play the part of the guru, creating stunning presentations with just a handful of basic techniques. So as you sit there with your copy of Crystal Xcelsius, don't look so worried. Steady your hand, lift your head, and say with me, "I am the guru. I am the guru!"

This chapter is all about gaining some familiarity with Crystal Xcelsius before creating your first dashboard. Here, I give you an overview of the concepts behind Crystal Xcelsius, how Crystal Xcelsius works, and how you can use Crystal Xcelsius as an integral part of your daily operations.

Overcoming Static Cling

I love the TV show *Little House on the Prairie*. One of my favorite characters on the show is Doc Baker, who is the old country doctor fighting illness armed with nothing more than a stethoscope. (Sometimes I wonder just how effective he is with that stethoscope. I mean, how much information could he, or any other doctor in the 1880's for that matter, possibly gather with a stethoscope?) That's a long stretch from today, where technology provides doctors with an unprecedented amount of data with dynamic visualizations of the human body that are interactive, real-time, and 3-D. *Visualization* transforms data into a form that is comprehensible to the eye, allowing you to analyze data through the sense of sight. This allows surgeons and medical students to see the breathing patterns of an asthma patient or the beating human heart in rhythm with an EKG output.

However, these advances in visualization technology aren't limited to the medical field. Many industries have striven to move away from static data environments by using interactive visualization technologies. Consider some of the other industries that have taken advantage of interactive visualization technology:

- ✔ **Aviation:** In the early 1900s, pilots would spend the first weeks of flight training in a rocking fuselage with mock instruments. Pilots today train in flight simulators that use animation and interactive visualization to replicate a wide array of atmospheric scenarios.

- ✔ **Sports:** Professional athletes have the benefit of computer models that interactively capture their movements with animation, helping them pinpoint their problem areas and maximize their kinetic potential.

- ✔ **Meteorology:** Meteorologists use interactive visualization systems to model the effects of wind force from storms and hurricanes.

- ✔ **Toy industry:** Even popular board games that are inherently visual, such as chess, *Monopoly,* and *Risk,* have been augmented with technology that offers imaginative animations that enhance a player's gaming experience.

What's the point of all this visualization talk? Well, the question that you and I should be asking is what happened to the business world? Although tools like Excel and PowerPoint have brought us a long way from the days of using paper spreadsheets and overhead projectors, by no means have they come close to the interactive visualizations that other industries have benefited from. We still sit through hours and hours of boring meetings where we point to static charts like one you see here in Figure 1-1.

The question is, why are we still clinging to static technologies? Why hasn't anyone moved us forward? This is the same question that Santiago Becerra, Sr., and his son Santi Becerra, Jr., asked each other before they developed Crystal Xcelsius.

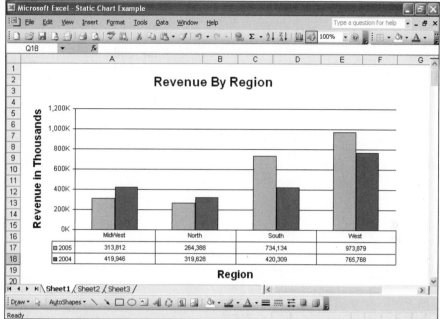

Figure 1-1:
Why are we
stuck in a
static world
of drab
static
spread-
sheets and
dull static
charts?

Like many of us in the corporate world, Santiago Becerra, Sr. has first-hand experience with the dull data environments that leave many managers and key decision-makers ill-equipped to manage their businesses. In his various roles in the business world, he knows that the problem he constantly faces is the same problem that many organizations suffer from — that too much information is lost in the transition between data analysis and data presentation. That is, after a presentation is put on paper, managers are automatically boxed into the thought processes of the presenter, often forcing them to either take the data analysis at face value or to ask for more analyses, which naturally takes up more critical company time. The question was how to provide a compelling presentation without losing the ability to interactively change the direction and scope of the data analysis behind the information being presented.

Becerra eventually joined forces with his son who had spent his career creating many popular video games such as *Midtown Madness* and *Midnight Club*. Together, they used video game technology in conjunction with practical business concepts to create Crystal Xcelsius. With Crystal Xcelsius, the Becerra father-and-son team provided business professionals with something few have had access to in the past: affordable, interactive visualization of business data that could be delivered in easy-to-create dynamic presentations. For the first time, managers could bridge the gap between data analysis and data presentation without the need for expensive enterprise solutions. Figure 1-2 illustrates this bridge.

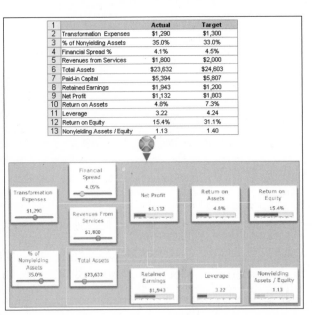

Figure 1-2:
Crystal
Xcelsius
bridges the
gap between
data analy-
sis and data
presentation,
converting
dull spread-
sheet tables
into inter-
active
dashboards.

More Than Just Fancy Graphics: The Benefits of Using Crystal Xcelsius

I've actually met people who use Crystal Xcelsius simply for the slick look and feel of the graphics. Face it: Many of us were initially attracted to Crystal Xcelsius because of the sleek graphical components, such as the gauges shown here in Figure 1-3.

And there is nothing wrong with that at all. The truth is that when many people see the slick and easy-to-use components in Crystal Xcelsius, they tend to lift some of the restrictions they have subconsciously placed on their presentations. For example, before Crystal Xcelsius, I would never even *have thought* about creating the gauge-based dashboard shown in Figure 1-3 because I didn't know how to create one in Excel or PowerPoint. Indeed, the stunning graphics alone undoubtedly fosters ideas about new and exciting ways you can present your data.

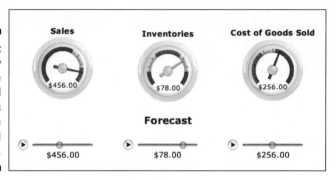

Figure 1-3:
Many people use Crystal Xcelsius for the sleek, fluid graphics.

Although you can easily get lost in the stunning graphics, remember that Crystal Xcelsius is a versatile tool that allows you to do more than just create fancy-looking presentations. Take a look at some of the other things that you can accomplish with Crystal Xcelsius that you might not have thought about.

Creating more robust presentations with interactive summary and detail layers

I exported a sample dashboard into a PowerPoint file called `Chapter1 - Example_A`, which you can find at the companion Web site for this book. To follow along with the demonstration in this section, go to this book's companion Web site. (The exact address appears in the Introduction.) Open the `Chapter1 - Example_A` PowerPoint presentation, found in the `C:\Xcelsius Sample Files\Chapter 1` directory, and run the slide show. Figure 1-4 shows the interactive dashboard that you see in the slide show. The idea is to select a Sales Rep from the list to see the key metrics for that Sales Rep.

To run the slide show in PowerPoint, go to the menu and choose Slide Show⇨ View Show. I show you how to export Crystal Xcelsius dashboards into PowerPoint in Chapter 12.

What is the point of this demonstration? Think about how much data is contained in this one-megabyte presentation. For 14 Sales Reps, you are showing the metrics around each rep's actual revenue, budget target, and revenue forecast. Not for 1 month, mind you, but for 12 months! Consider how many slides it would take to present something similar to this dashboard in a standard slide show. You can imagine that this would take, at a minimum, 14 slides to produce similar results — with less appealing graphics.

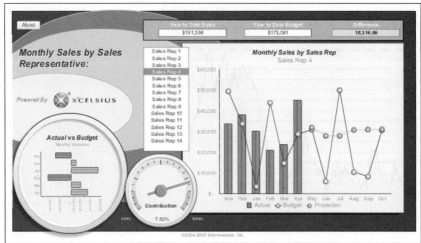

Figure 1-4: Select a Sales Rep from the list to see the metrics for that Sales Rep.

What about Excel? Could you fit all this information on an Excel spreadsheet? Sure, but as you can see in Figure 1-5, this data in an Excel spreadsheet is somehow not as compelling.

	November			December			January			Febr
	Revenue	BUDGET	Actual vs Budget	Revenue	BUDGET	Actual vs Budget	Revenue	BUDGET	Actual vs Budget	Revenue
Sales Rep 1	$ 48,230	$17,984	$30,245.8	$ 21,759	$15,809	$5,949.9	$ 29,430	$ 7,807	$21,622.9	$ 13,415
Sales Rep 2	$ 19,966	$27,274	($7,308.9)	$ 41,247	$49,713	($8,465.8)	$ 40,592	$41,422	($829.7)	$ 23,937
Sales Rep 3	$ 36,305	$24,371	$11,933.9	$ 16,826	$37,857	($21,031.1)	$ 31,274	$38,720	($7,445.8)	$ 24,823
Sales Rep 4	$ 33,574	$49,257	($15,682.4)	$ 38,094	$33,548	$4,545.9	$ 30,028	$ 3,381	$26,646.4	$ 20,876
Sales Rep 5	$ 20,175	$32,600	($12,424.9)	$ 41,948	$37,934	$4,014.3	$ 40,892	$15,263	$25,628.5	$ 41,007
Sales Rep 6	$ 34,748	$41,708	($6,959.6)	$ 15,487	$18,696	($3,209.3)	$ 16,352	$17,911	($1,559.2)	$ 28,800
Sales Rep 7	$ 18,791	$ 4,583	$14,208.6	$ 38,587	$30,478	$8,109.6	$ 44,985	$10,134	$34,850.4	$ 22,509
Sales Rep 8	$ 24,666	$13,450	$11,216.6	$ 12,772	$24,764	($11,992.9)	$ 35,382	$ 2,633	$32,748.9	$ 25,815
Sales Rep 9	$ 48,459	$48,194	$265.5	$ 26,478	$35,196	($8,717.4)	$ 43,564	$47,636	($4,072.4)	$ 25,578
Sales Rep 10	$ 19,080	$49,468	($30,387.4)	$ 18,167	$23,192	($5,025.0)	$ 43,179	$16,732	$26,447.3	$ 18,589
Sales Rep 11	$ 22,569	$25,778	($3,208.6)	$ 27,967	$29,766	($1,798.7)	$ 47,631	$45,147	$2,483.3	$ 46,232
Sales Rep 12	$ 20,687	$44,644	($23,957.8)	$ 25,649	$15,218	$10,430.9	$ 16,851	$30,380	($13,529.4)	$ 22,438
Sales Rep 13	$ 10,972	$28,180	($17,207.4)	$ 10,996	$13,951	($2,955.0)	$ 37,405	$45,019	($7,613.8)	$ 20,867
Sales Rep 14	$ 15,708	$42,962	($27,253.6)	$ 14,156	$17,969	($3,813.3)	$ 29,487	$17,682	$11,805.4	$ 32,829

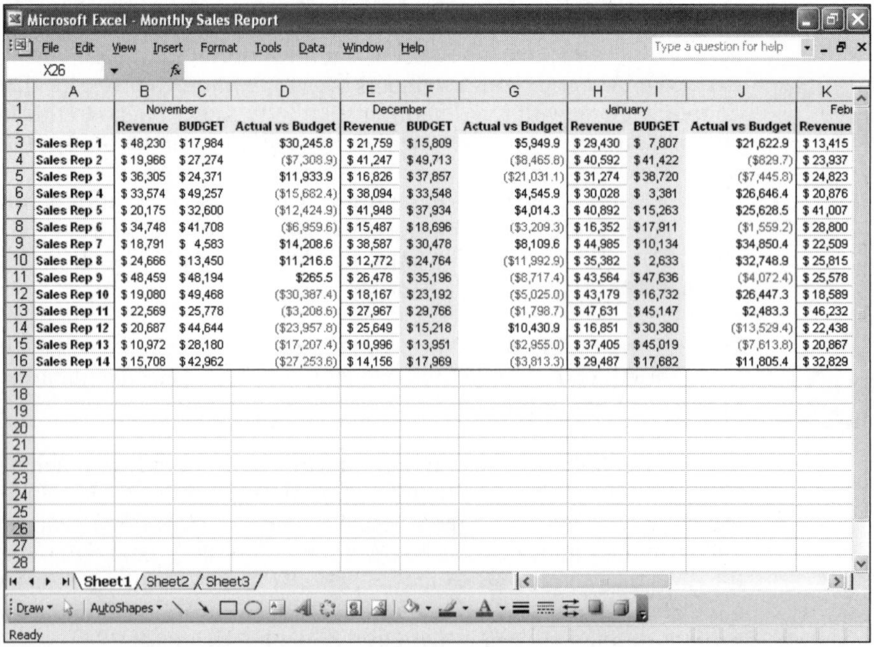

Figure 1-5: Showing the same data in an Excel spreadsheet is not as effective.

You can see that with Crystal Xcelsius, you can create multiple layers of summary and detail data in visually appealing dashboards. And because the average Crystal Xcelsius output is around 1.5 megabytes, you won't inundate clients with unnecessarily large files.

Because of Crystal Xcelsius's ability to produce presentations in relatively small files, you'll likely notice something different happening in your presentations. I bet you start consolidating information that you would normally parse into separate presentations. This not only gives your dashboards a more robust feel, but it also allows you to present lots of data without breaking the flow of your presentation. In addition, because you can easily build interactivity into your presentations, you won't have to worry about showing too much information at one time.

Building what-if analyses into your presentations

We all have an analytical side to us that feels compelled to question and analyze what we see. Everyone is a data analyst on some level. This is usually a good thing, but it can be a nightmare if you're the one giving a presentation to a roomful of inquisitive people playing the role of analyst. How many times have you given a presentation, only to be challenged with questions about the variables that you use in the analysis? In these situations, you probably do one of two things: fumble through papers as you try to answer the question, or turn to the ever-embarrassing standby, "I'll get back to you on that," followed by an awkward pause as you try to get back into the flow of your presentation.

Crystal Xcelsius can help you better prepare for these situations by enabling you to build what-if analyses directly into your presentation, allowing you to literally change your presentation on the fly. To demonstrate this, I exported a sample dashboard into a PowerPoint file called `Chapter1 - Example_B`, which you can find at the companion Web site for this book. To follow along with the demonstration in this section, go to this book's companion Web site. Open `Chapter1 - Example_B`, found in the `C:\Xcelsius Sample Files\ Chapter 1` directory, and run the slide show. Upon opening, you'll see the table shown in Figure 1-6.

Imagine that it's the end of FY (fiscal year) 2004 and you're presenting the budget plan for FY 2005, which is based on the assumption that gross sales will grow by 7 percent. When you present this plan, a few managers are disappointed at the fact that the planned net income for FY 2005 is less than the net income for FY 2004, so they ask you what the net income would look like if gross sales grew at a rate of 12 percent. In a standard presentation, this is where everything falls apart. Even if you are some mathematical genius who could quickly calculate the net income at the new growth rate, you wouldn't have visual backup for your explanation of how the change would ripple through the other parts of the budget.

In this situation however, I don't worry because I used Crystal Xcelsius to build myself a little insurance policy. Click the What If button to reveal a set of sliders that allow you to change the makeup of the analysis.

Now simply slide the vertical Gross Sales Growth Rate slider up to 12%, as illustrated in Figure 1-6. At this point, your presentation actually changes to reflect the new analysis!

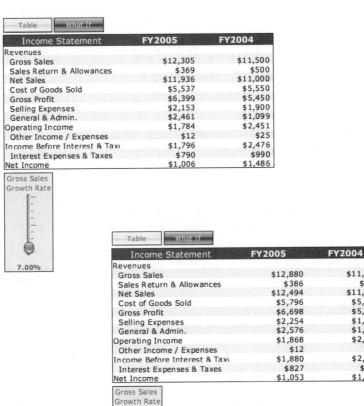

Income Statement	FY2005	FY2004
Revenues		
Gross Sales	$12,305	$11,500
Sales Return & Allowances	$369	$500
Net Sales	$11,936	$11,000
Cost of Goods Sold	$5,537	$5,550
Gross Profit	$6,399	$5,450
Selling Expenses	$2,153	$1,900
General & Admin.	$2,461	$1,099
Operating Income	$1,784	$2,451
Other Income / Expenses	$12	$25
Income Before Interest & Tax	$1,796	$2,476
Interest Expenses & Taxes	$790	$990
Net Income	$1,006	$1,486

Gross Sales Growth Rate

7.00%

Income Statement	FY2005	FY2004
Revenues		
Gross Sales	$12,880	$11,500
Sales Return & Allowances	$386	$500
Net Sales	$12,494	$11,000
Cost of Goods Sold	$5,796	$5,550
Gross Profit	$6,698	$5,450
Selling Expenses	$2,254	$1,900
General & Admin.	$2,576	$1,099
Operating Income	$1,868	$2,451
Other Income / Expenses	$12	$25
Income Before Interest & Tax	$1,880	$2,476
Interest Expenses & Taxes	$827	$990
Net Income	$1,053	$1,486

Gross Sales Growth Rate

12.00%

Figure 1-6: Crystal Xcelsius makes it possible to make on-the-spot changes to the analysis behind your presentation.

This is an unbelievable feat that would have been impossible without Crystal Xcelsius. The ability to make on-the-spot changes to the actual analysis behind a presentation is one of the most powerful and attractive functionalities of Crystal Xcelsius.

Building tools that help make decisions

A key benefit to building what-if analyses into your presentation is the ability to give managers a decision-making tool — a tool that allows them to test several scenarios and then choose the most appropriate scenario for the task at hand. For instance, open the PowerPoint presentation Chapter1 – Example C, found in the C:\Xcelsius Sample Files\Chapter 1 directory (at this book's companion Web site), and run the slide show. This presentation, as shown here in Figure 1-7, presents the budget plan for FY 2005, which is based on the assumption that gross sales will grow by 7 percent.

Income Statement	FY2005	FY2004
Revenues		
Gross Sales	$12,305	$11,500
Sales Return & Allowances	$369	$500
Net Sales	$11,936	$11,000
Cost of Goods Sold	$5,537	$5,550
Gross Profit	$6,399	$5,450
Selling Expenses	$2,153	$1,900
General & Admin.	$2,461	$1,099
Operating Income	$1,784	$2,451
Other Income / Expenses	$12	$25
Income Before Interest & Tax	$1,796	$2,476
Interest Expenses & Taxes	$790	$990
Net Income	$1,006	$1,486

Gross Sales Growth Rate	As a % of Sales	
	Sales Return & Allowances	3.0%
	Cost of Goods Sold	45.0%
	Selling Expenses	17.5%
	General & Admin.	20.0%
7.00%	Interest Expenses & Taxes	44.0%

Figure 1-7: Presenting the budget plan for FY 2005 and comparing it with actual revenue for FY 2004.

Suppose that when you present this plan, a few managers are disappointed that the planned net income for FY 2005 is less than the net income for FY 2004. In a knee-jerk reaction, they ask you to increase the gross sales until the net income for FY 2005 is more than FY 2004.

As you can see in Figure 1-8, the problem is that you will have to increase gross sales by 59 percent — yikes! — in order to beat FY 2004's net income. Needless to say, it is unrealistic to think that the company will increase gross sales by 59 percent.

Income Statement	FY 2005	FY 2004
Revenues		
Gross Sales	$18,285	$11,500
Sales Return & Allowances	$549	$500
Net Sales	$17,736	$11,000
Cost of Goods Sold	$8,228	$5,550
Gross Profit	$9,508	$5,450
Selling Expenses	$3,200	$1,900
General & Admin.	$3,657	$1,099
Operating Income	$2,651	$2,451
Other Income / Expenses	$12	$25
Income Before Interest & Tax	$2,663	$2,476
Interest Expenses & Taxes	$1,172	$990
Net Income	$1,491	$1,486

Gross Sales Growth Rate — 59.00%

As a % of Sales

Sales Return & Allowances	3.0%
Cost of Goods Sold	45.0%
Selling Expenses	17.5%
General & Admin.	20.0%
Interest Expenses & Taxes	44.0%

Figure 1-8: Use the sliders to present scenarios.

The solution is to use the other sliders, in conjunction with the gross sales slider, as levers to increase FY 2005 net income. You can test various scenarios to find one that is both realistic and conducive to your analysis. In this case, you can set your gross sales rate to 7%, reduce the Cost of Goods Sold to 42%, reduce Selling Expenses to 15%, and reduce General & Admin Costs to 18%. As you can see in Figure 1-9, this combination of sales growth and cost reduction helps to beat FY 2004's net income.

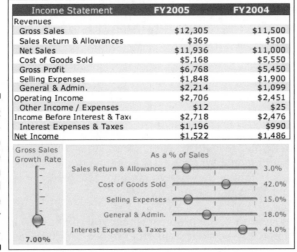

Income Statement	FY 2005	FY 2004
Revenues		
Gross Sales	$12,305	$11,500
Sales Return & Allowances	$369	$500
Net Sales	$11,936	$11,000
Cost of Goods Sold	$5,168	$5,550
Gross Profit	$6,768	$5,450
Selling Expenses	$1,848	$1,900
General & Admin.	$2,214	$1,099
Operating Income	$2,706	$2,451
Other Income / Expenses	$12	$25
Income Before Interest & Tax	$2,718	$2,476
Interest Expenses & Taxes	$1,196	$990
Net Income	$1,522	$1,486

Gross Sales Growth Rate — 7.00%

As a % of Sales

Sales Return & Allowances	3.0%
Cost of Goods Sold	42.0%
Selling Expenses	15.0%
General & Admin.	18.0%
Interest Expenses & Taxes	44.0%

Figure 1-9: Test scenarios to find one that is both realistic and conducive to your analysis.

Again, this analysis could be done in Excel, but you would have to take this back to your desk to create different scenarios on different tabs, effectively making everyone wait for your answers. With Crystal Xcelsius, you can have everyone in the room as you test out the various scenarios in real-time, allowing for on-the-spot decision making.

Crystal Xcelsius under the Hood

With your newly found perspective on Crystal Xcelsius and what it can do for you, you're probably chomping at the bit to get started building your first dashboard. But before I show you how to do that, you need to understand how Crystal Xcelsius really works.

In a nutshell, Crystal Xcelsius imports a snapshot of your Excel file, allows you to build a visual model by tying components to your data, compiles your final dashboard to a Flash SWF file, and then publishes your final dashboard to a chosen format. *SWF* (often pronounced *swiff*) is the vector-based graphics format designed to run in the Macromedia Flash Player. Figure 1-10 illustrates the basic workflow for a Crystal Xcelsius report.

Remember that Crystal Xcelsius is designed to work only with Excel XLS files. Therefore, you can not import other types of files such as text files (txt, csv, dbf) or Access MDB files. The good news, however, is that Excel spreadsheets of any size can be used in Crystal Xcelsius. Just keep in mind that the amount of data that is being moved and changed in your visualization can affect the performance of your dashboard.

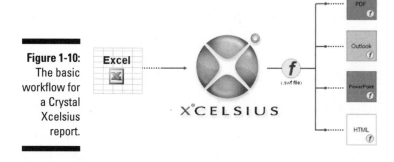

Figure 1-10: The basic workflow for a Crystal Xcelsius report.

When you install Crystal Xcelsius, it gives you the option to install the Macromedia Flash Plugin/Player. If you have not elected to install this *and* if you do not already have Macromedia Flash Player installed on your computer, you will not be able to use Crystal Xcelsius properly. However, you can easily get Macromedia Flash Player by downloading it free from www. macromedia.com.

As mentioned before, the three versions of Crystal Xcelsius are

- ✔ **Standard:** The Standard version is designed for those who are looking to get started with interactive visual analytics. It provides the basic features of Crystal Xcelsius.
- ✔ **Professional:** The Professional version is designed for large organizations that require dashboards that contain many layers of information.
- ✔ **Workgroup:** The Workgroup version is designed for environments where connections to live data are essential.

The components that are available to you depend on the version of Crystal Xcelsius you are using.

Importing data

All Crystal Xcelsius dashboards start with an Excel spreadsheet that typically contains data that has already gone through some analysis, massaging, and shaping. Crystal Xcelsius takes a snapshot of the Excel spreadsheet and imports that snapshot into memory. After the data is in memory, Crystal Xcelsius disconnects from the Excel spreadsheet.

This method of separating the data from the actual spreadsheet ensures two things. First, your final dashboard is a standalone object, independent of the location or status of the original spreadsheet. Second, it ensures that the size of your final dashboard is as small as possible, making for easy distribution.

Problems getting Crystal Xcelsius up and running?

There are three versions of Crystal Xcelsius: Standard, Professional, and Workgroup. No matter which version you have, getting Crystal Xcelsius up and running is a relatively intuitive process. However, if you find yourself having trouble getting started, help is at hand.

The Crystal Xcelsius team has a support desk that is willing to help you with any issues you may have. You can contact them by phone at 858-552-6674, or by e-mail at crystalxcelsius support@businessobjects.com.

Building the visual model

After the data you're using is in memory, you can start building your visual model. The visual model is essentially your dashboard in design mode. Much like a PowerPoint slide, your visual model starts off as a blank canvas on which you can add components. *Components* are those things that give your dashboard its utility and purpose: charts, gauges, menus, tables, and so on. The idea is to add individual components to your visual model, tying each component to the data that you import.

Compiling and publishing the dashboard

After you're happy with the functionality and look of your visual model, Crystal Xcelsius is ready to compile it.

First, Crystal Xcelsius compiles your visual model to a SWF file format. Compiling to a SWF file format ensures that your final dashboard plays back smoothly on any screen size and across multiple platforms. In addition, this ensures that your dashboard file size is small so as to not inundate your users with gigantic 40MB files.

After your visual model has been compiled to a SWF file, it is then published to a format of your choice. You can choose to publish your dashboard to PowerPoint, Outlook, an HTML Web page, an Adobe Acrobat PDF file, or a Macromedia Flash file. At this point, your dashboard is ready to share!

Chapter 2

Taking Crystal Xcelsius for a Spin

I confess that when I buy new software, I usually don't read the instructions first. I like to jump right in and see what it can do and how easy it is to use. As far as I'm concerned, all the nuances of the program can be learned later. So in that spirit, throw caution to the wind and just get right in there and build a dashboard. That's right, folks, we're going for it!

Is this irrational exuberance? No, not really. The purpose of this chapter is to demonstrate the intuitiveness of Crystal Xcelsius, and just how easy it is to create a professional-looking dashboard with no knowledge of programming or Flash. In the process, you will gain a firm understanding of the fundamentals of using Crystal Xcelsius, including importing data, working with components, publishing your dashboard, and refreshing your data.

To find the files I reference throughout this chapter, go to the companion Web site for this book. The site's address can be found in this book's Introduction.

Creating Your First Dashboard

For your first escapade with Crystal Xcelsius, I show you how to create a simple dashboard that provides information on the average daily temperature for 21 cities in Texas. The final dashboard will look similar to the one shown here in Figure 2-1.

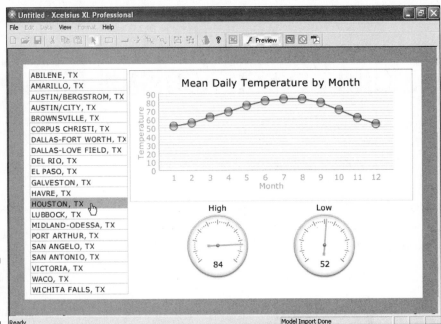

First things first. Open Crystal Xcelsius in either of the following ways:

✔ **Double-click its desktop icon.**

or

✔ **Choose it from the list of programs in your Windows Start menu.**

Upon opening, you immediately see several windows on your screen. These are highlighted in Figure 2-2. I talk about each of these windows a little later; for now, close them.

You are left with a white canvas. This is the starting point for your dashboard.

Step 1: Importing the Excel model

This is probably a good point to remind you that this chapter is dedicated to walking through the mechanics of Crystal Xcelsius. Thus, you are taking actions on components that you might not fully understand yet. Rest assured, each component and action you encounter in this chapter is covered in detail in subsequent chapters.

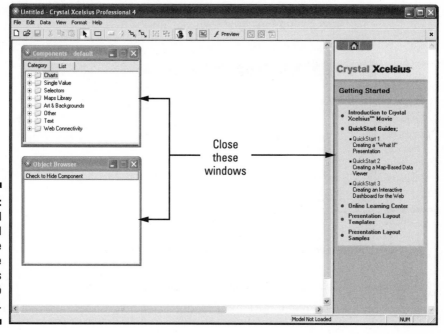

Close
these
windows

Figure 2-2:
Open Crystal
Xcelsius and
then close
the three
windows
that pop up
by default.

The first thing you need to do is to import the Excel model, which contains the data you are presenting with your dashboard. Again, any data you use in a Crystal Xcelsius visual model must be imported from an Excel file. This means that if your data is sitting in a text file or an Access database, you must transfer it to an Excel .xls file in order to import it into Crystal Xcelsius.

1. From the main menu, choose Data⇨Import Model.

This activates the Import Model dialog box, as shown in Figure 2-3.

You can also activate the Import Model dialog box by clicking the Excel icon on the Crystal Xcelsius taskbar.

Figure 2-3:
Activate the
Import
Model
dialog box.

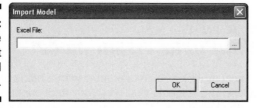

2. **Click the ellipsis button (the button with the three dots) to display the Open dialog box, as shown in Figure 2-4.**

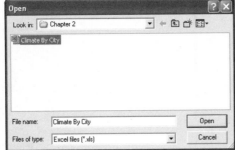

Figure 2-4:
Activate the Open dialog box and select the desired Excel model.

3. **Select the Excel file you want to use and then click Open.**

For this example, select the Climate By City Excel file found in the sample files folder on the companion Web site, and then click the Open button.

At this point, the Import Model dialog box contains the name and path of the Excel model you select.

4. **Click OK to start importing.**

In the lower-right corner of your screen is a progress meter in the Crystal Xcelsius status bar that shows you the percentage of data that has been imported. At the end of the process, the status bar reads `Model Import Done`.

At this point, your Excel model is stored in Crystal Xcelsius's memory, and you're ready to start adding components to your visual model.

Crystal Xcelsius takes a snapshot of your Excel model and imports only that snapshot into memory. After the data is in memory, Crystal Xcelsius *disconnects* from the original Excel file: That is, any changes you make to your source spreadsheet will not be captured until you reimport the model. I discuss keeping up with changes in your Excel model in detail later in this chapter.

Step 2: Building your visual model

After you import your Excel model, you are a painter with a blank canvas. From here, you can add the components that give your final dashboard its look, feel, and utility. To see the list of all the components available to you, go to the main menu and choose View⇨Components. This activates the Components window that you see in Figure 2-5.

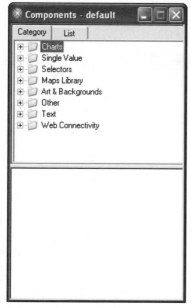

Figure 2-5:
Activate the
Components
window.

A word on terminology

Because Crystal Xcelsius is fairly new, some of the terminology in this book will likely be unfamiliar. Take a moment to familiarize yourself with some of the following terms:

✔ **Excel model:** The *Excel model* is the source spreadsheet that contains the data you want to represent in your final dashboard. This spreadsheet contains data that has typically gone through some massaging and shaping.

✔ **Visual model:** The *visual model* is essentially your dashboard in design mode. Much like a PowerPoint slide, your visual model starts off as a blank canvas on which you can add components that visually represent the data you import from your Excel model. When you save your visual model, it is saved as an XLF file.

✔ **Dashboard:** After you finish building your visual model, you can compile it to a SWF file and then export it to a document of a chosen format. The final document is your *dashboard*. Keep in mind that when I refer to a dashboard, I mean the finished product.

✔ **Canvas:** The *canvas* is the blank page you see each time you start a new Crystal Xcelsius document. This is the foundation of your visual model, where you add the components that make up your dashboard.

✔ **Components:** *Components* are the objects that give your dashboard its utility and purpose: charts, gauges, menus, tables, and so on. You build your visual model by adding individual components to the canvas, tying each component to the data that you import from your Excel model.

A word on the component categories

Crystal Xcelsius components are segregated into eight categories:

- ✔ **Charts:** Chart components allow you to add charting functionality to your dashboards.

- ✔ **Single Value:** Single Value components allow you to change or represent the value of a single cell in your data. These components include gauges, sliders, and progress bars.

- ✔ **Selectors:** Selector components are essentially menu providers. Components such as tables, list boxes, and radio buttons are used to offer options and capture the user selections.

- ✔ **Maps Library:** Map components allow you to tie geographically oriented data to a graphical map, enabling map-based dashboarding.

- ✔ **Art & Backgrounds:** These components are essentially formatting tools that control the look and feel of your dashboards.

- ✔ **Other:** The Other category comprises specialized components that don't necessarily fit into any other category. These include calendars, trending icons, scenario buttons, and data grids.

- ✔ **Text:** Text components allow for communication between Crystal Xcelsius and a user. These include input boxes (that a user can use to give Crystal Xcelsius a required argument) or labels (that Crystal Xcelsius can use to pass information back to the user).

- ✔ **Web Connectivity:** These components allow you to link to a URL and feed images from a URL.

Refer to Figure 2-2 to see the three windows that pop up by default when you first open Crystal Xcelsius. The Components window is one of them. It's a little annoying — you can't stop it from popping up by default — but you can easily get it out of your way by simply closing it. To reactivate the Components window after it's closed, simply choose View➪Components.

Select a component from the Components window and place it onto the canvas. After the component is on the canvas, you can configure it to look and behave the way you want it to.

For this running example, I start building the visual model by adding a Table component and then setting its display properties. Follow along with these steps:

1. **As illustrated in Figure 2-6, drill into the Selectors category, select the Table component, and then drag it onto the canvas.**

Crystal Xcelsius gives you a preview (as shown at the bottom of Figure 2-6) of the component when you click it. This default behavior is designed to give you an idea of what each component looks like without the need to drag it onto the canvas.

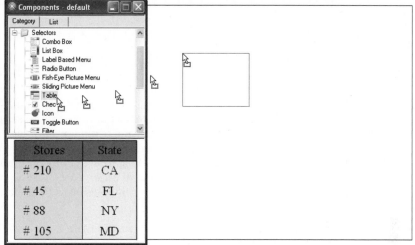

Figure 2-6:
Add
components
to your
visual model
by dragging
them onto
your
canvas.

A word on the Properties window tabs

In general, the Properties window has the same structure for all Crystal Xcelsius components, but the tabs that are available differ from component to component. For example, you can see in Figure 2-10 that the Properties window for the Table component contains three tabs: General, Behavior, and Appearance. However, there are actually five possible property tabs: General, Behavior, Alerts, Appearance, and Drill Down. The Alerts and Drill Down tabs do not apply to Table components; therefore, they are not shown.

The bottom line is that the number and types of tabs you see in the Properties window depend on the component with which you are working. Each tab controls different aspects of the component's attributes and functionality, as follows:

✔ **General:** The General tab controls the minimum required properties that enable the component to function properly. The General tab typically contains Data Source Link properties that tie the component to a range of cells, giving the component its basic functionality.

✔ **Behavior:** The Behavior tab controls properties that define how a component acts in run-time. This includes dynamic visibility, entry effects, zooming capabilities, and other options related to run-time interactivity.

✔ **Alerts:** The Alerts tab controls the properties that allow you to dynamically change the color scheme of a component based on it values. On this tab, you can define the number of alert levels, the color of each level, the color method, and the alert targets.

✔ **Appearance:** The Appearance tab controls properties that define the appearance and final look of each component. On this tab, you find options like font size, title location, and colors.

✔ **Drill Down:** The Drill Down tab contains a series of parameters for adding drill-down capability for charts. This tab is available only with Crystal Xcelsius Professional.

2. **Right-click the Table component and choose Properties from the shortcut menu.**

   You can also double-click the component to get to the Properties window. (See Figure 2-7.)

   You can see that the title bar on the Properties window includes the component's name. In Figure 2-7, the title bar reads Table 1 Properties; this means the name of this particular component is "Table 1." Every component that is added to the canvas is automatically assigned a name that consists of the component's type and a sequentially-assigned number. So if you were to add two Pie Chart components to your canvas, their names would be Pie Chart 1 and Pie Chart 2. Any additional pie charts would be numbered in sequential order. Later, I show you how to change and use the names of your components to help manage your visual models.

   You see the Properties window, as shown in Figure 2-7. The basic idea is to adjust each property of the component with which you are working in order to achieve the desired behavior. For this example, I start by adjusting the Display Data property of the Table component. This property tells the Table component what to display on the dashboard.

3. **Click the Cell Reference icon, shown in Figure 2-8, to identify the range of cells that contains the data you want the Table component to display.**

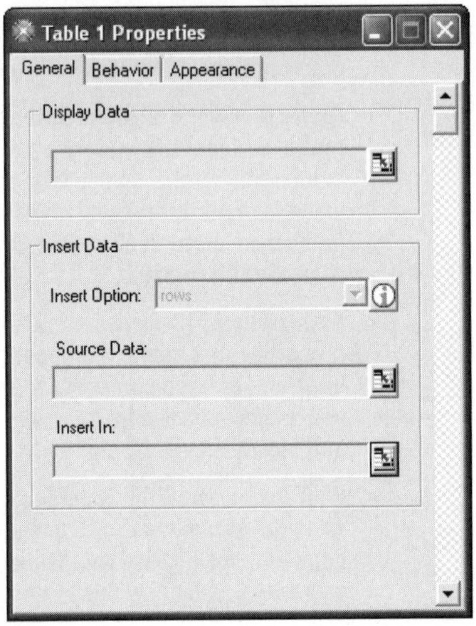

Figure 2-7:
Every
component
has
properties
that control
the way
they look
and behave.

Cell Reference icon

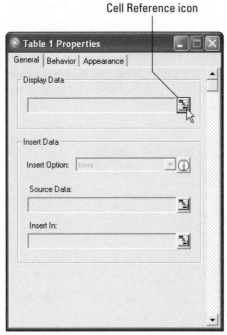

Figure 2-8:
Click the
Cell
Reference
icon for the
Display Data
property.

A representation of your Excel model activates along with a dialog box used to select the desired range. From here, simply select the cell, or range of cells, to which you want to tie your component's property.

4. **Because (in this example) I want the Table component to display each city in the dataset, I select all the cities illustrated in Figure 2-9 and then click OK in the Select a Range dialog box.**

	City	JAN	FEB	MAR	APR	MAY	JUN	JUL	AUG	SEP	OCT	NOV	DEC	Low	High
2															
3	City	JAN	FEB	MAR	APR	MAY	JUN	JUL	AUG	SEP	OCT	NOV	DEC	Low	High
4	ABILENE, TX	44	49	56	65	73	80	84	83	76	66	54	45	44	84
5	AMARILLO, TX	36	41	48	56	65	74	78	76	69	58	45	37	36	78
6	AUSTIN/BERGSTROM, TX														
7	AUSTIN/CITY, TX														
8	BROWNSVILLE, TX														
9	CORPUS CHRISTI, TX														
10	DALLAS-FORT WORTH, TX														
11	DALLAS-LOVE FIELD, TX	46	51	59	66	74	82	87	86	79	68	56	48	46	87
12	DEL RIO, TX	51	56	64	71	78	83	85	85	80	71	60	52	51	85
13	EL PASO, TX	45	51	57	65	74	82	83	81	75	65	53	45	45	83
14	GALVESTON, TX	56	58	64	70	77	82	84	84	81	74	65	58	56	84
15	HAVRE, TX	15	22	33	44	55	63	68	68	56	45	29	19	15	68
16	HOUSTON, TX	52	55	62	69	76	81	84	83	79	70	61	54	52	84
17	LUBBOCK, TX	38	43	51	60	69	77	80	78	71	61	48	40	38	80
18	MIDLAND-ODESSA, TX	43	49	56	64	73	80	82	80	74	64	52	45	43	82
19	PORT ARTHUR, TX	52	56	62	68	75	81	83	83	79	70	61	54	52	83
20	SAN ANGELO, TX	45	50	57	65	73	79	82	81	75	65	54	46	45	82
21	SAN ANTONIO, TX	50	55	62	69	76	82	84	84	79	71	60	52	50	84
22	VICTORIA, TX	53	57	64	70	77	82	84	84	80	72	63	55	53	84
23	WACO, TX	46	51	59	66	74	81	85	85	79	69	57	48	46	85
24	WICHITA FALLS, TX	41	46	54	62	71	80	85	84	76	65	52	43	41	85
25															

Select a Range

'Daily Mean Temperature'!$A$4:$A$24   OK   Cancel

Figure 2-9:
Select the
range of
cells to
display.

When Crystal Xcelsius imports an Excel model, it imports all tabs. This means that when you link components to a range of cells in your imported model, you're not limited to only the tab that is showing. You can select a range in any of the worksheet tabs that were imported.

As soon as you click OK, the Table component displays real data. Second, the Display Data property shows the reference to the worksheet and range of cells, as shown in Figure 2-10.

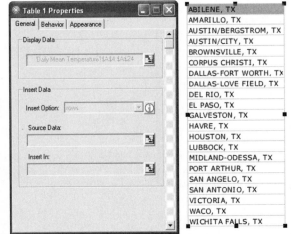

Figure 2-10:
Crystal Xcelsius provides live updates as you set component properties.

5. Repeat this process for the Source Data property.

As you can see in Figure 2-11, the Source Data property captures the actual data values that are bound to the Table component.

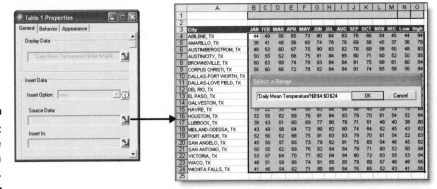

Figure 2-11:
Set the Source Data property.

6. **Repeat this process for the Insert In property, as shown in Figure 2-12.**

   This property identifies the destination cells that hold the selected data values.

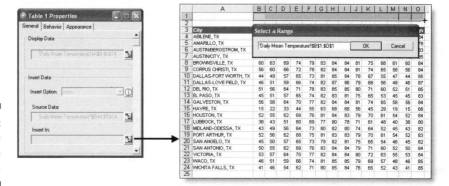

Figure 2-12: Set the Insert In property.

Again, don't concern yourself too much with what each property does. This is explained in subsequent chapters. The important thing is that you get comfortable with the mechanics of linking components to the imported Excel model.

7. **After the Table component is configured, I added a line chart to this visual model, as shown in Figure 2-13. Follow along to see how:**

   a. *Activate the Components window.*

   b. *Drill into the Charts category, select the Line Chart component, and then drag it onto the canvas.*

   c. *Right-click the Line Chart component that you just added and then choose Properties from the shortcut menu.*

8. **On the General tab of the Properties dialog box are a group of properties (under the heading Titles) that are dedicated to labeling various parts of your chart. Fill in these properties.**

   Figure 2-14 shows the properties for this example.

   The Titles properties also have the Cell Reference icon. This means that you can capture a value from a cell to use as a title instead of entering the title manually. Keep in mind that most property settings allow you the option of either manually entering a value or using the Cell Reference icon. Those that don't give you this option have a disabled input box, allowing only values that come from a cell reference.

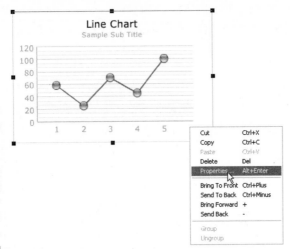

Figure 2-13:
Add a line
chart
component
to your
visual
model.

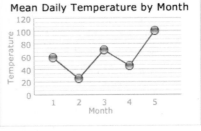

Figure 2-14:
Enter the
appropriate
titles for
your chart.

9. **Still on the General tab, assign a data range to the line chart. (See Figure 2-15.)**

   a. *Select the Data Range radio button to activate the Data Range section.*

   b. *Click the Cell Reference icon.*

   c. *Identify the range of cells that contain the data you want captured in the Line Chart component and then click OK.*

   You have a configured Table component and a Line Chart component in your visual model.

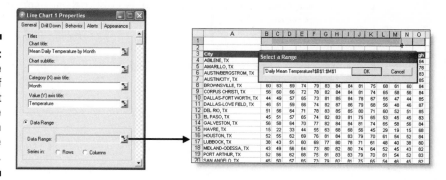

Figure 2-15: Identify the range of cells that are to be captured in your line chart.

I continue by adding a Gauge component. Here's how:

1. **Activate the Components window and drill down into the Single Value category and then into the Gauge category. From there, select Gauge-1 and drag it onto the canvas, as illustrated in Figure 2-16.**

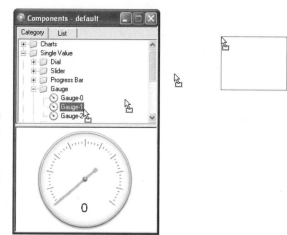

Figure 2-16: Add a Gauge component to your visual model.

There is no difference between Gauge-0, Gauge-1, and Gauge-2 other than aesthetics. All three Gauge components function and behave the same way.

2. **Configure the Gauge component, as shown in Figure 2-17.**

   a. *Right-click on the Gauge component and activate the Properties window.*

     *b. Type **Low** in the Title property input box. This gauge displays the low temperature for each city.*

     c. Link the Data property to cell N1.

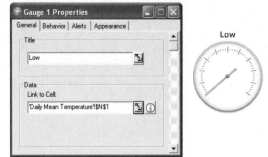

Figure 2-17:
Configure
the Gauge
component.

3. **Add a second Gauge component (repeat Step 1) and configure the newly added gauge, as shown in Figure 2-18.**

     a. Activate the Properties window.

     *b. Type **High** in the Title property input box. This gauge displays the high temperature for each city.*

     c. Link the Data property to cell O1.

Figure 2-18:
Add a
second
Gauge
component
and
configure
the
properties.

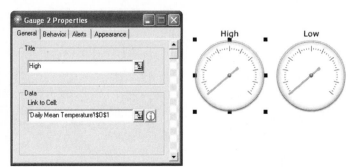

That's it! All the hard work (if you can call it that) is done. All that's left to do is rearrange the components on your visual model by dragging them around the canvas just as you would on a PowerPoint slide. Figure 2-19 shows the final arrangement.

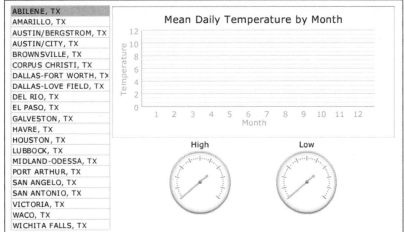

ABILENE, TX
AMARILLO, TX
AUSTIN/BERGSTROM, TX
AUSTIN/CITY, TX
BROWNSVILLE, TX
CORPUS CHRISTI, TX
DALLAS-FORT WORTH, TX
DALLAS-LOVE FIELD, TX
DEL RIO, TX
EL PASO, TX
GALVESTON, TX
HAVRE, TX
HOUSTON, TX
LUBBOCK, TX
MIDLAND-ODESSA, TX
PORT ARTHUR, TX
SAN ANGELO, TX
SAN ANTONIO, TX
VICTORIA, TX
WACO, TX
WICHITA FALLS, TX

Figure 2-19:
Arrange the
components
by moving
them
around your
canvas.

At this point, do the smart thing and save your visual model. To do this, choose File➪Save. This activates the Save As dialog box. Name this visual model `FirstDashboard` and save it in the following directory: `C:\Xcelsius Sample Files\Chapter 2`.

You can also activate the Save As dialog box by clicking the floppy disk icon on the Crystal Xcelsius taskbar.

Time to test your visual model and publish it to a dashboard.

Step 3: Testing and publishing your visual model

Before publishing and distributing your dashboard, you want to test it in order to ensure that all the components are working the way you intended. Not surprisingly, Crystal Xcelsius allows you to easily test your dashboard with a click of a button. That button is the Preview button, shown in Figure 2-20.

Figure 2-20:
Click the
Preview
button to
test your
visual
model.

When you click the Preview button, Crystal Xcelsius compiles your visual model into a SWF file.

After your visual model is finished compiling, you will be working with a Flash preview of your visual model. This preview allows you to validate your visual model and to test out the look and feel of your dashboard. The preview mode is also useful when you want to experiment with components, colors, and layouts before exporting the final dashboard.

As you can see in Figure 2-21, you can test the components on your dashboard by clicking a few cities in the Table component.

The Preview button is a *toggle* button (either on or off). You are in Preview mode when most of the menu commands are disabled and the Preview button looks depressed (pressed down, not sad). Exit Preview mode by clicking the Preview button again.

When you're satisfied that everything is working as it should, publish the final dashboard. When you publish your dashboard, Crystal Xcelsius takes two actions:

- ✔ **It compiles your visual model into a SWF file.**
- ✔ **It embeds that file into a document or format of your choice.**

Here's how you publish a dashboard in Crystal Xcelsius:

1. **Choose File⇨Export.**

   As you can see in Figure 2-22, you have a choice of formats to which you can publish your dashboard, including Flash, HTML, PowerPoint, PDF, and Outlook.

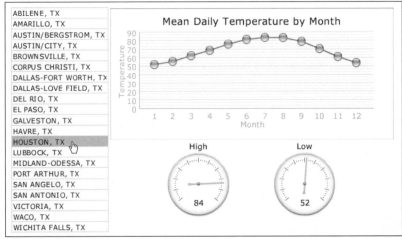

Figure 2-21: In preview mode, test how the final dashboard will look and feel when published.

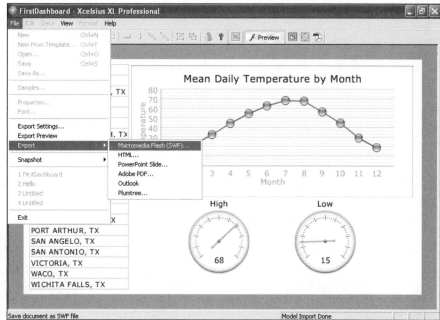

Figure 2-22:
Choose your
publishing
format.

2. **For this example, I publish the dashboard to a Macromedia Flash file, as shown in Figure 2-22.**

   After you make your choice, an Export dialog box activates, asking you to enter the name and location of your final dashboard.

   I cover exporting Crystal Xcelsius dashboards in detail in Chapter 12.

3. **Name your dashboard `FinalDashboard` and save it in the following directory: `C:\Xcelsius Sample Files\Chapter 2`.**

4. **Close Crystal Xcelsius and open the directory `C:\Xcelsius Sample Files\Chapter 2`.**

   You should see the following files, as shown in Figure 2-23:

   • An XLS file, which is the original Excel model from which you imported the data

   • The XLF file, which is the saved visual model

   • The SWF file, which is the document containing the final dashboard

Figure 2-23:
Each one of
these files
played a
role in the
develop-
ment of your
dashboard.

Figure 2-23:
Each one of
these files
played a
role in the
develop-
ment of your
dashboard.

5. **Double-click the `FinalDashboard.swf` file to view your final dashboard.**

   Because this file is a SWF file, it will open in your default Web browser. For many of you, this is Internet Explorer. Figure 2-24 illustrates what the final dashboard looks like in Internet Explorer.

   If you've followed this chapter to this point, I hope you're really excited. Take a moment and think about what you did. In a matter of just a few mouse clicks, you took a drab-looking, static spreadsheet and transformed it into a dynamic, interactive dashboard. Figure 2-25 shows a side-by-side comparison that shows the stunning difference.

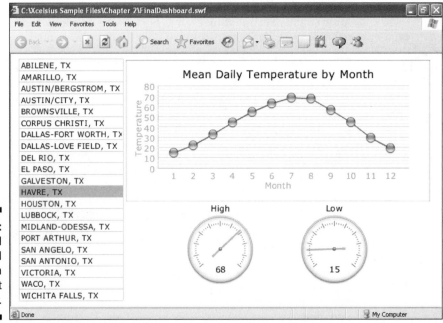

Figure 2-24:
Your final
dashboard
shown in
Internet
Explorer.

Enabling active content

Some of you might receive the following security message when you try to open the `Final Dashboard.swf` file:

> To help protect your security, Internet Explorer has restricted this file from showing active content that could access your computer. Click here for options.

This is a security setting that disables ActiveX content, preventing you from viewing your dashboard. You can permanently enable Internet Explorer to view active content on local files by taking the following actions:

1. **Choose Tools⇨Internet Options in Internet Explorer.**

2. **Click the Advanced tab in the Internet Options dialog box and then scroll down to the Security section.**

3. **Select Allow Active Content To Run In Files On My Computer.**

Note: Although this change enables only files that are local, you should do this only if you feel confident in your computer's security measures.

Figure 2-25:
In just a few steps, you transformed a dull spreadsheet into an eye-catching, interactive dashboard!

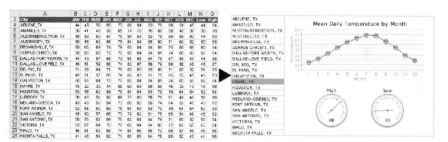

Getting Fresh with your Dashboard

No matter how effective and visually appealing your dashboard presentations are, the world will not stand still for you; things change, and data gets updated. Your job is to ensure that the dashboards you create have the freshest, most appropriately up-to-date data.

As I mention earlier, neither your final dashboard nor your Crystal Xcelsius visual model is connected to your original Excel model. This means that any changes to the data in your Excel model will not be captured by Crystal Xcelsius until you take action. Here's how to refresh your dashboards when there is a change in data.

Imagine that your Excel model gets updated with new data. As a result, you need to update your dashboard. The first step is to open your previously saved visual model.

1. **Open the saved visual model.**

   If you followed the earlier running example in this chapter, you can use the `FirstDashboard.xlf` visual model that you saved in the `C:\Xcelsius Sample Files\Chapter 2` directory.

2. **After your visual model is open, reimport the Excel model that contains the updated data. From the main menu, choose Data⇨Import Model.**

   This activates the Import Model dialog box, as shown in Figure 2-26.

Figure 2-26:
To refresh dashboard data, activate the Import Model dialog box.

The Import Model dialog box looks different from earlier in this chapter. Not only are a file and file path already specified, but you now have three choices:

- **Refresh Data Sources:** This option is typically used when changes to the Excel model originally used are limited to data changes — that is, when the Excel model itself has not changed due to structural changes such as rows and columns being inserted or deleted.

- **Clear Data Sources:** This option is useful when the structure of your original Excel model is significantly different and you need to delete all the links and start the model again. This essentially imports the Excel model and clears all previously established component links.

- **Refresh Spreadsheet Format:** This option comes in handy when you want to update some of the spreadsheet formatting that persists in the Label and Table components of your dashboard: for example, numeric format (number, percent, currency), cell width/height, cell colors, cell borders, and so on.

Crystal Xcelsius components use static references to link to imported Excel models. This means that if you change the structure of your original Excel model (insert, delete, or modify rows or columns), you might risk the links that you created. For example, imagine that you originally linked a Chart component to range A2:G2, and then you decided to insert a row below row 1. You need to manually adjust the Chart component to link to range A3:G3 after reimporting the Excel file. Crystal Xcelsius continues to use the range A2:G2 until you manually change the link.

In this scenario, I want to refresh only the data sources.

3. **Make sure that the Refresh Data Sources radio button is selected, and then click OK.**

   A confirmation dialog box appears.

4. **When the confirmation message pops up (see Figure 2-27), click the Yes button to confirm.**

Figure 2-27:
Click the Yes
button to
confirm the
reimport.

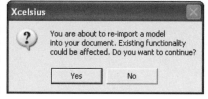

This refreshes the data in your visual model.

In order to get these changes to your final dashboard, you have to recompile the visual model and export a new dashboard:

1. **For this example, choose File⇨Export⇨Macromedia Flash (SWF).**

2. **Replace the previously saved file (FinalDashboard.swf, in this example), as shown in Figure 2-28.**

Figure 2-28:
Replace the
previously
saved file.

Export Macromedia Flash (SWF)

C:\Xcelsius Sample Files\Chapter 2\FinalDashboard.swf already exists.
Do you want to replace it?

Yes   No

Part II
Getting Started with the Basics

The 5th Wave   By Rich Tennant

"Nifty chart, Frank, but not entirely necessary."

In this part . . .

In this section, I take an in-depth look at some of the
basic components that are important to the creation of
any dashboard. Here I show you how to use Single Value
components to build interactivity into your dashboards,
how to leverage alerts to enable conditional coloring in
your components, how to create charts in Crystal Xcelsius,
and how to easily build menus and selectors into your
dashboards with Selector components.

Chapter 3

Interacting with Single Value Components

....

In This Chapter

▶ Understanding Single Value components

▶ Working with sliders and dials

▶ Using Gauge components

▶ Building a loan payment calculator

....

As their name suggests, *Single Value components* are components that link to a single cell, allowing you to modify or represent the value in that cell. Although these components are some of the easiest to understand and work with, Single Value components provide your dashboards with some of the slickest, most interactive functionality of all the components. In this chapter, I take a closer look at Single Value components to give you an understanding of how they work and how these versatile components can be used to build interactivity into your dashboards.

Managing Interactivity: Input vs. Output

Before you begin, open Crystal Xcelsius and find the Single Value components in the Components window. As you can see in Figure 3-1, the Single Value components category includes

✔ Dials

✔ Sliders

✔ Progress bars

✔ Gauges

✔ Value boxes

✔ Spinners

✔ Play buttons

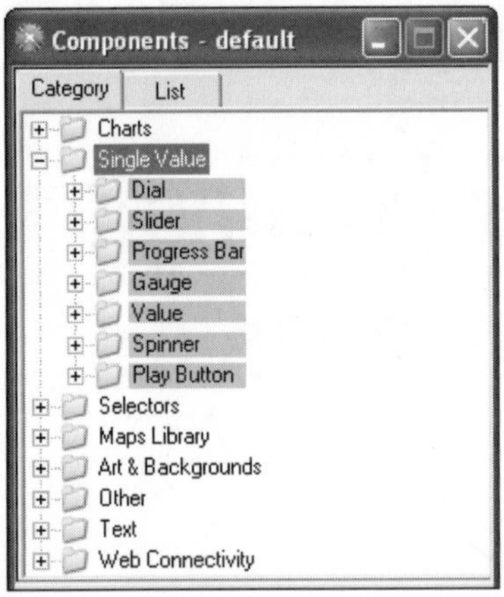

Figure 3-1:
Single Value
components
comprise
seven types.

Although each one of these components functions in similar ways, they can be classified into two groups:

✓ **Input components:** Input components are designed to take information from the user. These components allow users to adjust dashboard variables at run-time, empowering them to interactively analyze various scenarios.

✓ **Output components:** Output components are designed to pass information to the user.

Table 3-1 details the typical uses for each of these components.

Table 3-1		Single Value Components
Component	*Component Type*	*Description*
Dial	Input	Typically used to allow a user to modify the value of a cell in order to affect the results of other components. Dials are considered to be input components because they are used to feed specified values to a linked cell.
Slider	Input	Like the Dial component, used to modify the value of a cell. Sliders are considered input components because they are typically used to directly change the values in a linked cell.

Component	Component Type	Description
Progress Bar	Output	Used to provide users with a visual measure of the linked value as compared with a maximum target value. This component is considered to be an output component because it is typically used to report a cell's value as opposed to changing its value.
Gauge	Output	Used to measure the result of changes in a linked cell. Like Progress Bar components, Gauge components are considered output components because they are typically used to report a cell's value as opposed to changing its value.
Value	Output/Input	The only Single Value component routinely used as both an input component and an output component (for example, an input box or a dynamic label).
Spinner	Input	Input component used to directly change the values in a linked cell, typically affecting the results of other components.
Play Button	Input	Used to incrementally change the value of a linked cell until it reaches a predetermined value, giving the dashboard an animated feel. Because the Play Button component modifies its linked cell, it is considered an input component.

The classification of these components as *input* or *output* seems based on whether the component is used to change values or not. In reality, however, this classification has more to do with the type of cells to which these components are typically linked. What do I mean by that? This classification comes down to whether the component is typically linked to a formula or a value. To show you what I mean, follow along and conduct this test that links two gauges to our Excel model. One gauge will be linked to a value while the other will be linked to a formula. This test demonstrates how cell types dictate whether the component becomes an input component or an output component.

Note: Gauges aren't the only thing you can test. You can perform this test with any Single Value component and get the same results.

You can find the example files on the companion Web site for this book. The address for this site can be found in this book's Introduction.

1. **From the main menu, choose Data⇨Import Model, and then import the `SingleValues.xls` file from the `C:\Xcelsius Sample Files\Chapter 3\` directory, as shown in Figure 3-2.**

Figure 3-2:
Start by
importing
this file.

2. **Activate the Components window and drag a Gauge component onto the canvas.**

Activate the Components window by choosing View⇨Components.

3. **Set the component's Title property.**

Double-click the Gauge component to activate the Properties window and then adjust the Title property. Here, I use the title Linked to a Value, as shown in Figure 3-3.

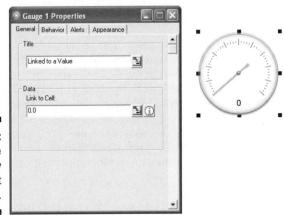

Figure 3-3:
Change the
Title property
for the first
component.

4. **Link to your reference data.**

In this example, click the Cell Reference icon and link to cell B11, as shown in Figure 3-4. This particular cell contains a hard-coded value that is used as a variable in the formula found in cell B12.

The term *hard-coded* means that the value you see in the cell has been entered manually and is not dependent on other cells to achieve that value. Unlike hard-coded cells, formula-based cells have values that are reached as a result of a mathematical operation.

Figure 3-4: Adjust the Link to Cell property to link to the hard-coded value.

5. Add a second Gauge component to the canvas.

6. Set the second Gauge component Title property.

Double-click the Gauge component to activate the Properties window and then adjust the Title property to read Linked to a Formula, similar to Step 3.

7. Link to your reference data.

Click the Cell Reference icon and link to cell B12, as shown in Figure 3-5. This particular cell contains a formula.

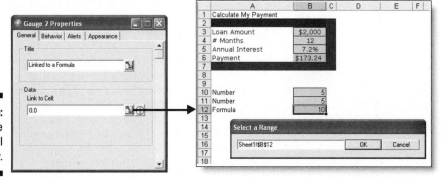

Figure 3-5: Adjust the Link to Cell property.

Your visual model should look similar to the one shown in Figure 3-6. You should have two gauges: one containing a value of 5, and the other with a value of 10. Keep in mind that the gauge that contains a 5 is linked to a hard-coded cell and the gauge that contains a 10 is linked to a formula-based cell.

Linked to a Value   Linked to a Formula

5   10

Click the Preview button on the taskbar to switch to Preview mode to conduct a few tests.

✔ **Test 1:** Hover you mouse over both gauges. (Don't click, just hover.) When you hover your mouse over the gauge linked to a value (on the left in Figure 3-6), your cursor turns into a hand. Meanwhile, when you hover your mouse over the gauge linked to a formula (on the right in Figure 3-6), your cursor does nothing.

✔ **Test 2:** Try to move the needle within the gauge that is linked to a formula (on the right in Figure 3-6). It doesn't move. This is because the value you see in the gauge (the number 10) is not a value that you can incrementally change; it's the result of a formula that returns the outcome of a mathematical operation.

✔ **Test 3:** Try to move the needle within the gauge that is linked to a value (on the left in Figure 3-6). Not only does the needle move, but the needle in the second gauge moves as well. This is because the value that is linked to the needle you're moving is a variable in the formula used in the second gauge. You are essentially changing the value of a cell and affecting the other component in the visual model as a result.

It may feel strange that you move the needle on a gauge to change the results of another gauge. In this scenario, you essentially use a gauge as an input tool: using it to modify data. However, this never happens in real-world situations. A gauge is typically a tool that you use to see results or an outcome. Following that logic, it makes sense that Gauge components are typically linked to cells that contain formulas because by nature, formulas return the outcome of an operation. Progress bars are also outcome-oriented tools measuring results; those, too, are typically used with cells containing formulas.

On the other hand, feeding inputs with tools such as Slider and Dial components feels natural. However, as you can see with Test 2 in the earlier bulleted
list, *you can't change the value of a cell when it contains a formula.* These tools
need to be linked to cells that contain hard-coded values that can be modified.

Given this new perspective, go back and replace the gauge that is linked to a
value with something more appropriate. A Slider component is a perfect candidate. Sliders are traditionally input tools seen in many real-world scenarios.

1. **Delete the Gauge component that is linked to a value.**

2. **Activate the Components window and drag a Slider component onto
   the canvas.**

3. **Repeat Steps 3 and 4 of the preceding list to set properties for the
   slider.**

4. **Click the Preview button on the taskbar to switch to Preview mode.**

   Your dashboard should look similar to the one shown in Figure 3-7.
   The slider, which is an input component, is linked to the value that
   can be modified. The gauge, which is an output component, is linked to
   the formula that returns the outcome of a mathematical operation.

   Test the slider to feel the difference in performance and usability. It's
   important to remember that an important part of creating an effective
   dashboard is providing components that feel natural.

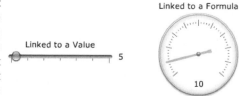

Figure 3-7:
The input
component
(the slider)
is linked to a
value; the
output
component
(the gauge)
is linked to a
formula.

If the cell to which the component is linked contains a formula of any type,
you can't interact with that component: The component effectively becomes
an output-only component. However, if the cell to which the component is
linked does not contain any formula, it effectively becomes an input component, allowing you to interactively modify its value.

Understanding Scale Behavior

The functionality of your Single Value components depends heavily on the parameters that you set around them. The limits and attributes that you give your Single Value components are largely determined by their purpose and how they fit in the larger dashboard. For example, the slider in Figure 3-8 has an upper limit of 10,000, preventing the user from inputting a value greater than that number.

Figure 3-8:
This slider
is limited
by your
parameters.

$5,556
$0 $10,000

The parameters and behavior of a Single Value component are governed by a set of properties that Crystal Xcelsius calls *Scale Behavior*. In this section, I take a closer look at Scale Behavior to show you how Scale Behavior properties can help shape the look and feel of your Single Value components.

Figure 3-9 shows the Scale Behavior properties. You find Scale Behavior properties on the Behavior tab of the Properties dialog box of any Single Value component.

Figure 3-9:
Set Scale
Behavior
here.

As you can see in Figure 3-9, Scale Behavior is defined by seven properties:

- ✔ Initial Limits Calculation
- ✔ Lower Limit Behavior
- ✔ Upper Limit Behavior

✔ Minimum Value

✔ Maximum Value

✔ Increment

✔ Snap to Scale

Initial Limits Calculation

The *Initial Limits Calculation property* controls the method used by the component to determine the initial upper and lower limits; that is to say the maximum and minimum values that can be represented in the component. These methods include

✔ **Manual:** The Manual method is used when you want to manually set the minimum and maximum values. This is the default, and most commonly used, method.

✔ **Value Based:** With the Value Based method, the minimum and maximum values are automatically assigned by Crystal Xcelsius, comprising a tight range around the component value.

✔ **Zero Based:** In the Zero Based method, the component limits are composed of zero as the upper or lower limit and the component value at the opposite end. Again, these limits are automatically assigned when you select the Zero Based method.

✔ **Zero Centered:** With the Zero Centered method, the minimum and maximum values are automatically assigned by Crystal Xcelsius, comprising of a range that has zero at the center.

The term *component value* refers to the value that is displayed through the component based on the cell it is referencing.

Figure 3-10 demonstrates the difference in these methods. Although all these gauges are linked to the same value, the Initial Limits Calculation setting in each gauge affects how the data is presented.

Figure 3-10: These gauges all link to the same value but use different Initial Limits Calculations.

Lower Limit Behavior and Upper Limit Behavior

The Lower Limit Behavior property allows you to control the flexibility of the lower limit, and the Upper Limit Behavior property allows you to control the flexibility of the upper limit. Both properties allow you three options:

- ✔ **Fixed:** This is the default setting as well as the most common. In the Lower Limit Behavior property, a Fixed setting ensures the linked value cannot be less than the Minimum Value. In the Upper Limit Behavior property, a Fixed setting ensures that the linked value cannot be more than the Maximum Value.

- ✔ **Adjustable:** The Adjustable setting has essentially the same effect as the Fixed setting. However, this setting actually allows you to adjust the lower and upper limits at run-time.

- ✔ **Open:** This setting allows either the lower or upper limit to be set to any number that does not conflict with the other.

Minimum Value and Maximum Value

The Minimum Value property is used to set the lower limit of the component, and the Maximum Value property is used to set the upper limit of the component. If these values are based on cell references, changes to the value of the cell are reflected in the component's limits.

You have the option of setting this property only if the Initial Limits Calculation is set to Manual.

Increment and Snap to Scale

The Increment property is used to define the rate that a component increases or reduces in value when a user interacts with it at run-time. For example, if the Increment property is set to 5, each click increases or decreases the value by 5.

The Snap to Scale property forces the graphical representation of the component to match the value. This property is useful when you are working with values that go into two or more decimal places.

Building a Loan Payment Calculator

Calculator? What about a calculator? Crystal Xcelsius is all about creating dashboards, right? Well, Crystal Xcelsius is a versatile tool with plenty of functionality that promotes interactive analysis. You can do many things with this functionality, including build visually interactive calculators. Single Value components are perfect for creating these types of interactive calculators. After you get the fundamentals of Single Value components under your belt (see the earlier sections of this chapter), you can create a simple loan payment calculator. Stick with me as I show you how.

Step 1: Import the Excel model

You can't have a visual model without an Excel model. (For background on an Excel and a visual model, visit Chapter 2.) In that light, import an Excel model, starting with a new visual model.

1. **Open Crystal Xcelsius. Or, if Crystal Xcelsius is already open, choose File⇨New from the main menu.**

2. **From the main menu, choose Data⇨Import Model and then import the** `SingleValues.xls` **file from the** `C:\Xcelsius Sample Files\ Chapter 3\` **directory.**

Step 2: Add a Value component to capture the loan amount

You have to give the user a way to capture the amount of the loan. Because the loan could literally be for any amount, use a Value component so that your users can specify any loan amount they want, up to $500,000.

1. **Activate the Components window and drag a Value component onto the canvas.**

2. **Double-click the Value component to activate the Properties window and then adjust the Title property to read Enter Loan Amount.**

3. **Click the Cell Reference icon and link to cell B3, as shown in Figure 3-11.**

   This particular cell contains a hard-coded value, not a formula. Linking to a hard-coded value ensures that the component becomes an input component, allowing you to interactively modify its value.

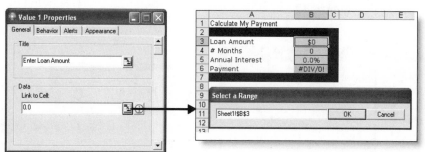

Figure 3-11: Adjust the Link to Cell property to link to the value in cell B3.

4. **While still in the Properties window for the Value component, click the Behavior tab and then adjust the Maximum Value property to 500,000 (as shown in Figure 3-12).**

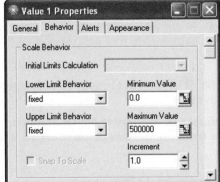

Figure 3-12:
Adjust the
Maximum
Value
property.

Step 3: Add a Slider component to capture the number of months

Focus now on building a component that captures the number of months for the loan. You can assume that the greatest number of months given for any loan is 360 (a 30-year loan). Because you can safely build limits into this component, use a Slider component to allow for the selection of the number of months.

1. **Activate the Components window and drag a Horizontal Slider component onto the canvas.**

2. **Double-click the Horizontal Slider component to activate the Properties window and then adjust the Title property to read Select Number of Months.**

3. **Click the Cell Reference icon and link to cell B4, as shown in Figure 3-13.**

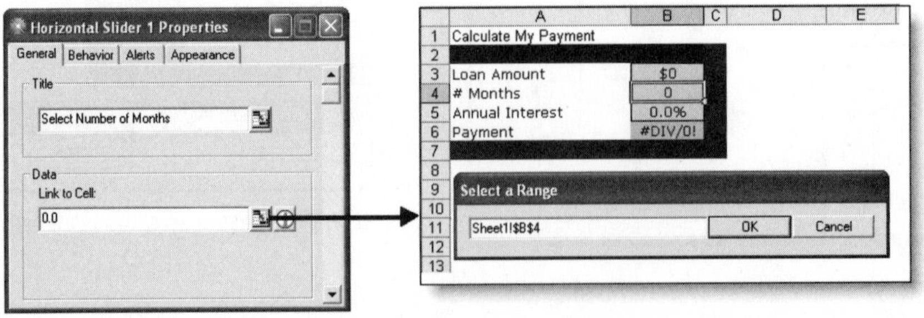

Figure 3-13:
Adjust the
Link to Cell
property
to link to
the value
in cell B4.

4. **While still in the Properties window for the slider, click the Behavior tab.**

5. **As shown in Figure 3-14, adjust the Maximum Value property to 360.**

   360 months/payments — get it?

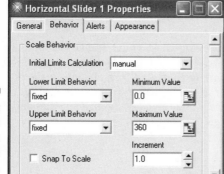

Figure 3-14:
Adjust the
Maximum
Value
property.

Step 4: Add a Dial component to capture the interest rate

Next, add a Dial component to capture the interest rate for the loan. You know that the interest rate for a loan rarely goes above 30%, so you can safely build limits into this component.

1. **Activate the Components window and drag a Dial component onto the canvas.**

2. **Double-click the Dial component to activate the Properties window and then adjust the Title property to read Select the Interest Rate.**

3. **Click the Cell Reference icon and link to cell B5, as shown in Figure 3-15.**

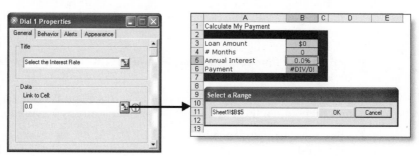

Figure 3-15:
Adjust the
Link to Cell
property
to link to
the value
in cell B5.

4. **While still in the Properties window for the Dial component, click the Behavior tab.**

5. **As shown in Figure 3-16, adjust the Maximum Value property to .30 and the Increment property to .01.**

   Setting the Maximum Value property to .30 ensures that the user cannot select an annual interest rate greater than 30%. Setting the Increment property to .01 allows the user to increase the annual interest rate by 1%.

   When you work with percentages, you have to use decimals to set the Scale Behavior properties. When you use decimals, Crystal Xcelsius sometimes translates your settings to a format that you won't recognize. For example, if you enter **.01** as a property setting, Crystal Xcelsius automatically translates it to *1.e-002*. This behavior is normal and is built into Crystal Xcelsius by design.

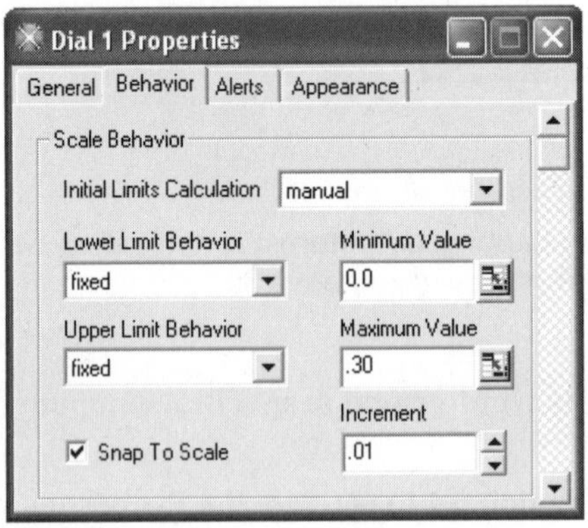

Figure 3-16:
Adjust the
Maximum
Value and
Increment
properties.

Step 5: Add a Gauge component to display the monthly payment

Almost done! The final component displays the monthly payment based on the variables given with the other components. Because this component will be tied to a cell that contains a formula, use a Gauge component.

1. **Activate the Components window and drag a Gauge component onto the canvas.**

2. **Double-click the Gauge component to activate the Properties window and then adjust the Title property to read Monthly Payments.**

3. **Click the Cell Reference icon and link to cell B6, as shown in Figure 3-17.**

4. **While still in the Properties window for the Gauge component, click the Behavior tab.**

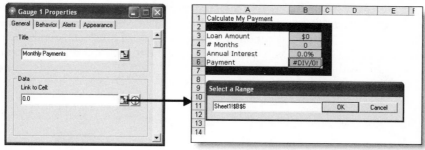

Figure 3-17:
Adjust the
Link to Cell
property
to link to
the value
in cell B6.

5. **As shown in Figure 3-18, adjust the Maximum Value property to 5,000
(our maximum acceptable monthly payment).**

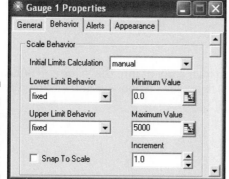

Figure 3-18:
Adjust the
Maximum
Value
property.

Step 6: Test your loan payment calculator

After a little arranging, your visual model should look similar to the one you
see in Figure 3-19.

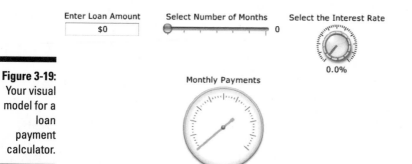

Figure 3-19:
Your visual
model for a
loan
payment
calculator.

Test your newly created loan payment calculator. Switch to Preview mode by clicking the Preview button on the taskbar. After you're in Preview mode, play around with the components to get a sense of how each component plays a part to come up with the monthly payment. Figure 3-20 is one scenario I came up with for a payment on a minivan.

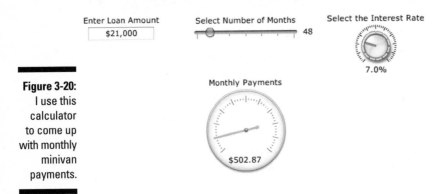

Figure 3-20:
I use this calculator to come up with monthly minivan payments.

If you have trouble entering a loan amount into the Value component, double-click the Value component to enter the component first and then start typing.

Chapter 4

Calling Attention to Alerts

· ·

In This Chapter

▶ Understanding alerts and the alert tab

▶ Configuring alert levels

▶ Applying a percent alert

▶ Applying a value alert

· ·

*T*hose of you who are Excel power-users will no doubt be familiar with the concept of conditional formatting. *Conditional formatting* is functionality where Excel dynamically changes the color or formatting of a value, cell, or range of cells based on a set of conditions that you define. This allows a user to look at a spreadsheet and make split-second determinations on which values are "good" and which are "bad," based on formatting. In Crystal Xcelsius, the analogous functionality is called *alerts*.

In this chapter, I show you how to leverage alerts to enable conditional coloring in your components, allowing your audience to get an instant visual assessment on performance.

The Anatomy of the Alert Tab

The wonderful thing about alerts is that Crystal Xcelsius handles all the formulas and validations internally so you can focus on enhancing your dashboards — and not focus on the programming. Figure 4-1 demonstrates how alerts can enhance the utility of your dashboards.

In this example, we are using the standard red, yellow, and green colors to measure performance — red means poor performance, yellow means satisfactory performance, and green means good performance. As you can see, the alerts that have been applied to the gauge on the right give you a visual determination of what 54% means in terms of performance. The needle is not only in the yellow portion of the gauge, but it is barely past the red portion. This quickly tells you that 54% is just marginally satisfactory.

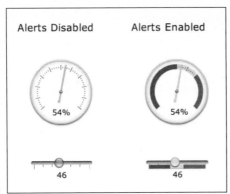

Figure 4-1:
Alerts
show users
instant
visual
assess-
ment on a
metric's per-
formance.

Although alerts aren't available for use with all components, you can enable alerts in a wide range of commonly used components, including most charts, maps, Single Value components, grids, and icons.

Like all functionality in Crystal Xcelsius, configuring your components with alerts is a delightfully simple point-and-click endeavor. This process starts with the Alert tab, shown in Figure 4-2, which can be found in the component's Properties window.

There are two ways to get to the Properties window. You can double-click on the component to activate the Properties window, or you can right-click on the component and the select Properties.

The Alerts tab is broken into five sections:

- ✔ Alert Method
- ✔ Alert Definition
- ✔ Alert Levels
- ✔ Alert Level Display
- ✔ Target

All the properties in the Alerts tab are disabled by default. You have to select the Enable Alerts check box in order to enable them.

Follow along as I walk you through each of these sections to get a firm understanding of the different parts that make up an alert.

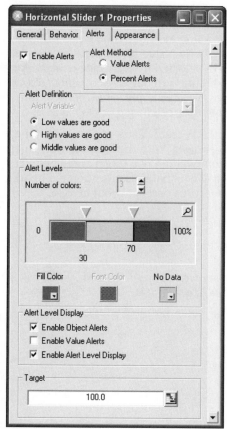

Figure 4-2:
The Alerts
tab is found
in the
Properties
window.

Alert Method

The Alert Method section, shown in Figure 4-3, specifies the method by which the alert levels are defined.

Figure 4-3:
The Alert
Method
section
of the
Alerts tab.

You can choose one of two methods:

- ✔ **Value Alerts:** Choose the Value Alerts method when the values being evaluated are integers. With the Value Alerts method, the alert levels are either manually entered or selected from a range of cells. For example, suppose your dashboard reports the number of units sold by each of your sales representatives. You can apply Value Alerts to turn the Number of Units metric red, yellow, or green based on its value.

- ✔ **Percent Alerts:** Choose the Percent Alerts method when the values being evaluated are percentages. With the Percent Alerts method, the levels are defined by a combination of a target and a number of percentages. Examples include a gauge that measures percent of quota achieved or a progress bar that measures percent profit margin.

Alert Definition

The Alert Definition section, shown in Figure 4-4, defines the calculation method by which the alert levels are allocated.

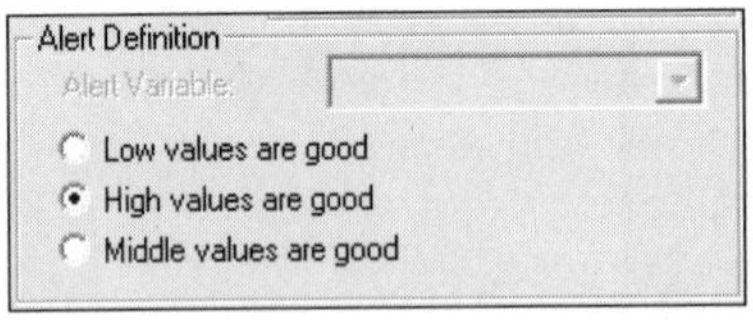

Figure 4-4:
The Alert
Definition
section
of the
Alerts tab.

Alert Definition

Alert Variable:

○ Low values are good
● High values are good
○ Middle values are good

Each method is based on a different way to measure the performance of the actual values against the target values:

- ✔ **Low Values Are Good:** Choose this option when values that are less than the target represent the desired performance. For example, if you're measuring labor cost as a percent of revenue, low values are good.

- ✔ **High Values Are Good:** Choose this option when values that are greater than the target represent the desired performance. For example, if you're measuring revenues as a percent of budget, high values are good.

- ✔ **Middle Values Are Good:** Choose this option when the objective is to get as close to the target as possible. For example, if you're measuring On-Time performance — where being consistently late or consistently early is unacceptable behavior — middle values are good.

As you can see in Figure 4-5, the selection you make determines the position of the *acceptable* color: the color that represents good, which is usually green. For example, when you specify that middle values are good, the acceptable color is located at the center of the component.

The colors for the alert levels in the Alerts tab default to red, yellow, and green. This is because red, yellow, and green are traditionally the colors that are used to measure performance. Red typically means poor performance, yellow means satisfactory performance, and green usually means good performance. However, you are not locked in to these colors — you can choose colors to fit your needs.

Figure 4-5:
Use the Alert
Definition
section to
dictate how
the color
levels are
employed.

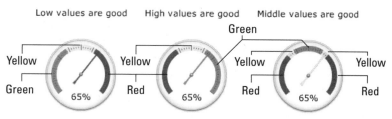

Alert Levels

The Alert Levels section allows you to define the number of alerts, the trigger points for each alert, and the color for each alert.

The process of configuring the Alert Levels section is different for those components that use the Percent Alerts method versus those that use the Value Alerts method. Look at each method separately.

Configuring alert levels when using the Percent Alerts method

As I mention earlier, the Percent Alerts method is used for those components where you are evaluating percent values. For the Percent Alerts method, the process for setting the alert levels is fairly straightforward.

First, set the number of colors that you want via the Number of Colors property, as shown in Figure 4-6.

Figure 4-6:
The Alert
Levels sec-
tion of the
Alerts tab
when using
the Percent
Alerts
method.

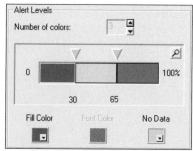

The Number of Colors property essentially defines how many alert trigger points you have in your component. You can select anywhere from two colors to ten colors by clicking the up and down arrows.

Next, you can adjust the trigger points for each alert level by dragging the gray arrows above the alert color selector. After the trigger points are set, you can change the colors by clicking each color and adjusting the Fill Color property via the Color palette, as shown in Figure 4-7.

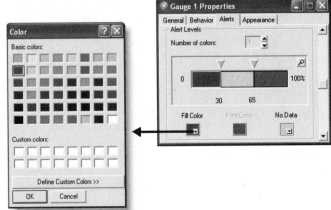

Figure 4-7:
Change
alert colors
by adjusting
the Fill Color
property.

Configuring Alert Levels when using the Value Alerts method

Use the Value Alerts method for those components where you are evaluating integers. The process for setting the alert levels when using Value Alerts is a little different.

For Value Alerts, alert levels are defined in the Alert Numbers window, as shown in Figure 4-8. As you can see, you click the ellipsis button to activate this window.

After you're in the Alert Numbers window, you can add as many alerts as you need, specifying their trigger values as you go.

Click the plus and minus buttons to add and remove alert levels in the Alert Numbers window.

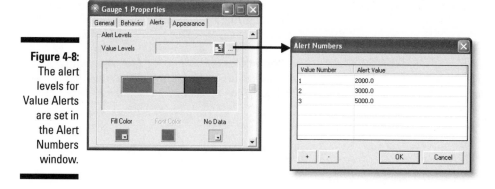

Figure 4-8:
The alert
levels for
Value Alerts
are set in
the Alert
Numbers
window.

Alert Level Display

The Alert Level Display section, shown in Figure 4-9, allows you to apply the alert colors to various parts of Single Value components.

Figure 4-9:
The Alert
Level
Display sec-
tion of the
Alerts tab.

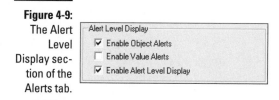

You can select one or more of the following options:

- ✔ **Enable Object Alerts:** This option activates the alert color display of the component. For example, for Gauge components, this option enables the needle to change colors. Meanwhile, in Slider components, this option enables the slider itself to change color.

- ✔ **Enable Value Alerts:** This option activates an alert value box around the component value. In other words, the actual value is wrapped in a box that changes colors based on an alert level.

- ✔ **Enable Alert Level Display:** This option activates a representation of all the alert limits, allowing you to evaluate the current value against the alert limits.

Figure 4-10 shows how each of these options can enhance the visual effects of the target component.

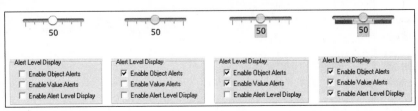

Figure 4-10:
Enhance the
visual effect
of your
components
by selecting
Alert Level
Display
options.

Target

When you use the Percent Alerts method (refer to Figure 4-3), a target must be specified in order to define a reference point for the percentage levels. The Target property, shown in Figure 4-11, allows you to define this reference point. For example, if you set the Target property to 1000 and you create an alert level at 90%, that alert level is triggered at a value of 900.

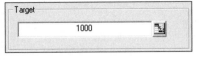

Figure 4-11:
The Target
section
of the
Alerts tab.

Applying Your First Percent Alert

It's time for some hands-on action. In this scenario, I show you how to apply alerts to the gauge in the visual model you see in Figure 4-12. This example uses the Percent Alerts method described in the section, "Configuring Alert Levels when using the Percent Alerts method," earlier in this chapter.

The purpose of this dashboard is to determine how many sales calls a sales rep has to make in order to hit a quota of $5,000 given the following variables:

- The average close rate is 20%.
- The price per unit is $295.

The idea is to move the slider, increasing the number of sales calls until the gauge shows that revenue is 100% of quota. Your objective is to create three alerts levels: one at 95% of quota, one at 90% of quota, and one at 85% of quota.

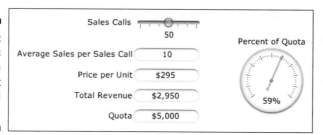

Figure 4-12: Apply alerts to the Gauge component in this visual model.

You can find these example files online at this book's companion Web site. Check out the Introduction for the exact address.

1. **Double-click the `Alerts Example.xlf` file in the `C:\Xcelsius Sample Files\Chapter 4\` directory.**

   This opens Crystal Xcelsius and the Alert Example visual model.

   For more on the visual model, see Chapter 2.

2. **Double-click the Gauge component to activate the Properties window, and then click the Alerts tab.**

   Just as in Figure 4-13, all the properties in your Alerts tab are disabled.

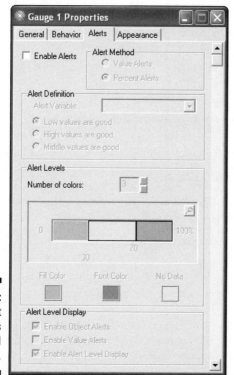

Figure 4-13: The alert properties are disabled by default.

3. **Select the Enable Alerts check box to activate the alert properties.**

   The Alert Method property is set to Percent Alerts by default. (For more on Percent Alerts, see the earlier section, "Alert Levels.") For this example, leave that property as-is.

4. **Set the percentage.**

   In this scenario, the bigger the percentage, the better the performance. In that light, change the Alert Definition property to High Values Are Good, as shown in Figure 4-14.

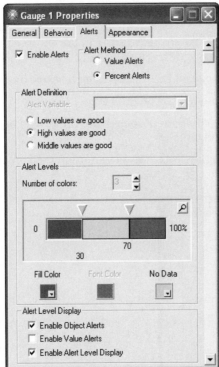

Figure 4-14:
Set the Alert
Definition
property.

5. **Adjust the Alert Levels property.**

   In this scenario, you need three alert levels:

   - Less than 85% of quota

   - Between 85% and 95% of quota

   - 95% of quota or greater

6. **Given the level requirements, adjust the trigger points for each alert level by dragging the gray arrows above the alert color selector.**

   Your Alert Levels property should look similar to Figure 4-15.

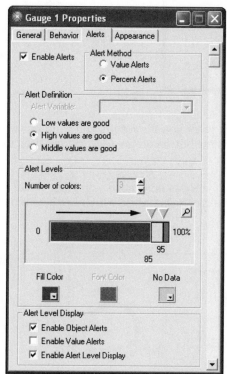

Figure 4-15:
Adjust
the trigger
points in the
Alert Levels
property.

7. **Set the Alert Level Display property.**

   The Alert Level Display property is set appropriately for this scenario, so leave that property as-is.

8. **Set the Target property.**

   The default value for the Target property is 100. However, that needs to be changed for this example because you're dealing with percentages here. Set the Target property to 1 in order to represent 100%, as shown in Figure 4-16.

   You successfully applied your first alert!

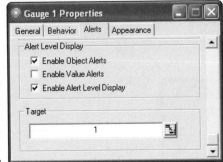

Figure 4-16:
Set the
Target prop-
erty to 1.

See whether your handiwork gives you the results you want by switching to Preview mode. Click the Preview button on the taskbar, and then use the slider to increase the number of sales calls.

As you can see in Figure 4-17, you can now make an instant visual assessment on the performance level that can be achieved with a certain number of sales calls.

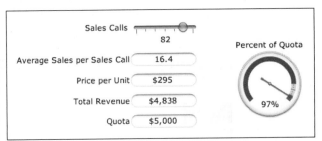

Figure 4-17:
You
successfully
applied your
first alert!

Applying Your First Value Alert

In the visual model shown in Figure 4-18, the Total Revenue Value component shows the total revenue that would be achieved with the number of sales calls identified by the Slider component. As the number of sales calls increases and decreases, so does the Total Revenue.

Apply a Value Alert to Total Revenue so that the Value component gives you a color determination of good versus bad revenue. This example uses the Value Alerts method described in the section, "Configuring Alert Levels when using the Value Alerts method," earlier in this chapter.

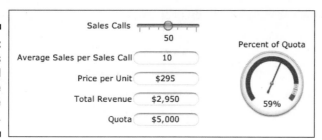

Figure 4-18:
Apply alerts
to the Total
Revenue
Value
component.

1. **If it's not already open, double-click the `Alerts Example.xlf` file in the `C:\Xcelsius Sample Files\Chapter 4\` directory.**

2. **Double-click the Value component titled Total Revenue. This activates the Properties window, where you click the Alerts tab.**

3. **Select the Enable Alerts check box to activate the alert properties.**

4. **Set the Alert Method property.**

   For this example, set the Alert Method property to Value Alerts.

5. **Set the Alert Definition property.**

   In this scenario, the bigger the revenue amount, the better the performance. In that light, change the Alert Definition property to High Values Are Good.

   Your Alerts tab should look similar to the one shown in Figure 4-19.

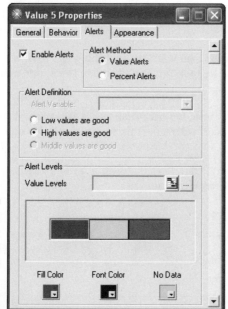

Figure 4-19:
Set the Alert
Method
and Alert
Definition
properties.

6. Define the alert levels for this component.

> *a. In the Value Levels property, click the ellipsis button to activate the Alert Numbers window, as shown in Figure 4-20.*
>
> *b. Adjust the alert values, as shown in Figure 4-20.*

Note: The numbers you see in Figure 4-20 are the limits that make up the alert levels for this component. The numbers you use depend on the levels appropriate for your situation.

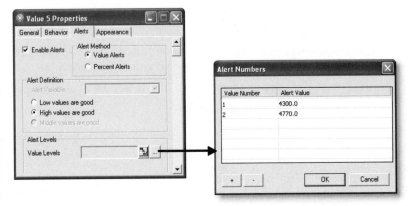

Figure 4-20: Activate the Alert Numbers window and adjust the alert values.

7. Set the Alert Definition property.

The Alert Level Display property is set appropriately for this scenario, so leave that property as-is.

See whether you get the results you want by switching to Preview mode. Click the Preview button on the taskbar, and then use the slider to increase the number of sales calls.

As you can see in Figure 4-21, you can now make an instant visual assessment on the revenue dollars achieved with a certain number of sales calls.

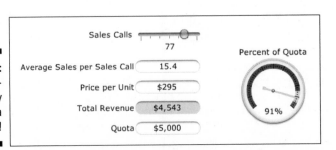

Figure 4-21: You successfully applied a value alert!

Chapter 5

Getting Graphic with Charts

In This Chapter

▶ The basics of charts in Crystal Xcelsius

▶ Creating your first chart

▶ Common chart formatting

▶ Understanding combination charts

*N*o other tool is more synonymous with visualization than a chart. Charts have been used to graphically represent data long before Excel came about. Over the years, fast-paced business environments and new technologies have helped moved charts from a "nice-to-have" to a vital part of most organizations' business analyses. Managers today want to absorb data as fast as possible, and nothing delivers that capability faster than a chart.

Because it is a visualization tool, Crystal Xcelsius certainly has charting capabilities, which I cover in this chapter. In addition, I show you here how to work with combination charts, how to apply formatting charts, and how to leverage some techniques from preceding chapters to create charts that are both dynamic and interactive.

The Basics of Crystal Xcelsius Charts

Creating a chart in Crystal Xcelsius is not only delightfully easy but surprisingly similar to creating a chart in Excel. Indeed, many charting methods and concepts that you use when creating charts in Excel apply to Crystal Xcelsius. Thus, if you know how charts work in Excel, you'll have a relatively easy time creating charts in Crystal Xcelsius. Begin by going over some of the basics of Crystal Xcelsius charts.

If you haven't been exposed to charts in Excel, you might want to pick up a copy of *Excel Charts For Dummies* (by Ken Bluttman, Wiley). This book provides an excellent introduction to every aspect of charting with Excel.

Understanding the chart types

Open Crystal Xcelsius and find the Charts component in the Components window. As you can see in Figure 5-1, Crystal Xcelsius offers 13 chart types.

Figure 5-1:
The avail-
able chart
types.

Deciding which chart type to use is entirely up to you. This decision, more often than not, is governed by the function of the chart and the role you want it to play in your final dashboard. Take a moment to look at the different chart types offered.

Line Chart

The line chart is one of the most common types of charts, typically used to show trends over a period of time. Figure 5-2 demonstrates how you could use a Line Chart to show revenue by quarter.

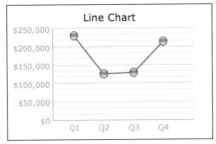

Figure 5-2:
Line charts
are ideal for
showing
trends
over time.

Pie Chart

A pie chart represents the distribution or proportion of each data item over a total value that is represented in the overall pie. For example, in the Pie Chart shown in Figure 5-3, you can easily see how much of the total value is made up by the brands A, B, and C.

Figure 5-3: Pie charts show the distribution of values within an overall value.

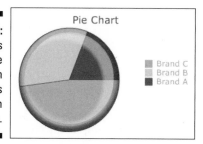

Column Chart

Column charts are typically used to compare several items in a specific range of values. Figure 5-4 demonstrates how a column chart could be used to compare the performance of different products.

Figure 5-4: Use a column chart to visually compare the values of items.

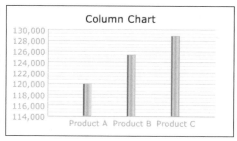

Stacked Column Chart

A stacked column chart allows you to compare items in a specific range of values as well as show the relationship of the individual sub-items to the whole. For instance, the stacked column chart in Figure 5-5 shows not only the revenue for each quarter but also the proportion of the total revenue made up by each product.

Figure 5-5:
Use stacked
column
charts to
show the
relationship
of sub-items
with the
total value.

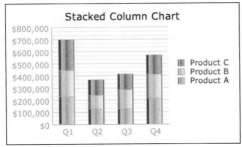

Bar Chart

A bar chart is most commonly used for illustrating the comparisons between data items. For instance, Figure 5-6 shows a very simple bar chart that compares the Brands A, B, and C.

Figure 5-6:
Bar charts
are ideal
for showing
differences
between
data items.

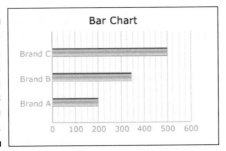

Stacked Bar Chart

Like a bar chart, the stacked bar chart is used for illustrating the comparisons between data items. The difference is that a stacked bar chart allows you to show the relationship of individual sub-items in the overall bar that is compared with other bars. For instance, the column chart in Figure 5-7 shows not only the revenue for each quarter but also the proportion of the total revenue made up by each product.

Figure 5-7:
Stacked bar
charts show
the rela-
tionship of
sub-items
with the
total value.

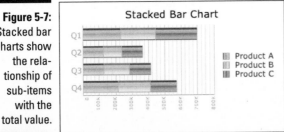

Combination Chart

A combination chart typically consists of a column and a line stacked on top of each other to show variances and magnitude of change. For instance, the chart in Figure 5-8 illustrates the year-over-year variance between 2000 and 2005.

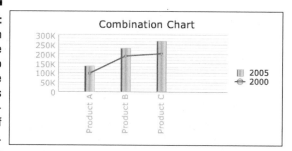

Figure 5-8: Combination charts are perfect to illustrate variances and magnitude of change.

Bubble Chart

Bubble charts allow you to compare data series based on three different parameters, the x axis, the y axis, and the z value. The x and y axes work together to represent the item location on the chart based on the intersection of x values and y values. The z value determines the bubble size based on the comparison of the data item with other data items. For example, the center bubbles in the chart shown in Figure 5-9 represent the number of applicants. With this chart, you can see how the number of applicants is affected by the starting salary for an advertised position.

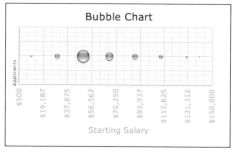

Figure 5-9: Bubble charts use bubble size to illustrate comparisons between data items.

XY Chart

The XY chart (also known as a *scatter plot chart*) is ideal for showing relationships between two sets of values. The x and y axes work together to represent the item location on the chart based on the intersection of x values and y values. For example, Figure 5-10 illustrates the correlation between employee performance and competency, demonstrating that employee performance rises as competency improves.

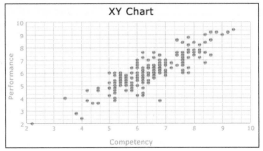

Area Chart/Stacked Area Chart

Area charts are ideal for illustrating the magnitude of change between two or more data points. For instance, the chart in Figure 5-11 illustrates the magnitude of the change between 2000 and 2005. The difference between a Stacked Area chart and a basic Area chart is the number of data series that are displayed. A basic Area chart plots one data series, but a Stacked Area chart plots two or more data series and shows the variance between them.

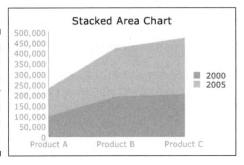

Radar Chart/Filled Radar Chart

A radar chart is commonly used to illustrate the differences between the aggregate values of a data series. Figure 5-12 illustrates a Radar chart and a Filled Radar chart, demonstrating the look and feel of both. Both of these charts are plotting the same data: the vitamin content of three different brands of supplements. In this example, you can see that Brand C covers the largest area. This means that at an aggregate level, Brand C has the highest vitamin content.

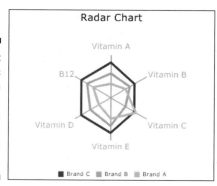
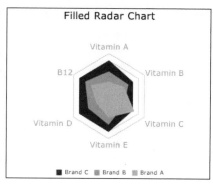

Figure 5-12:
Area charts
are useful to
illustrate
differences
between
aggregate
values.

Creating Your First Chart

For your first chart, create a simple column chart that shows revenue by region. Then tie a Slider component to it so you can perform some what-if analyses around the price per unit. Your final chart will look similar to the one shown in Figure 5-13.

Although this example focuses on a column chart, the techniques you use here apply to all chart types.

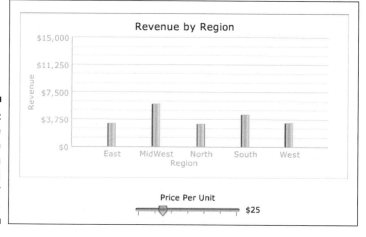

Figure 5-13:
Create
a simple
column
chart tied
to a Slider
control.

1. **From the main menu, choose Data⇨Import Model.**

2. **Import the `Charts.xls` file from the `C:\Xcelsius Sample Files\ Chapter 5\` directory.**

3. **Activate the Components window and drag a Column Chart component onto the canvas.**

   For a refresher on this, see Chapter 2.

4. **Double-click the Column Chart component to activate the Properties window.**

   On the General tab, shown in Figure 5-14, are three sections:

   - **Titles:** The Titles section is the standard place where you can name the various parts of your chart.

   - **Data Range/Series:** The Data Range and Series sections both perform the same function: to define the data that is to be displayed. Just like in Excel, you can use the Data Range property to define the various data series in your chart, or you can define each series one at a time with the Series section.

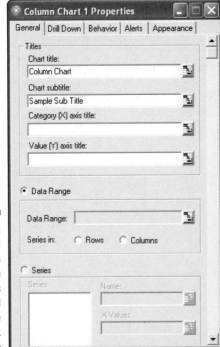

Figure 5-14:
The General tab contains the minimum properties required to create a chart.

As a general rule, if the data you want to plot in a chart is in a range of contiguous cells, using the Data Range section is easiest. On the other hand, the Series section is best for data series that are segregated or one-offs.

In this example, the data you're working with is in a contiguous range, so use the Data Range property.

5. Click the Cell Reference icon and link to cells A3:B8, as shown in Figure 5-15.

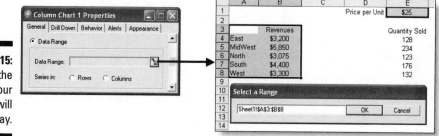

Figure 5-15:
Select the data your chart will display.

6. Label the parts of your chart.

For this example, set the following:

- **Chart Title:** Revenue by Region
- **Category (X) Axis Title:** Revenue
- **Value (Y) Axis Title:** Number of Units

Your Titles Section should look like Figure 5-16.

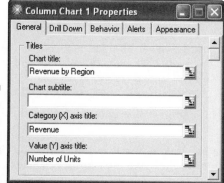

Figure 5-16:
Adjust the properties in the Titles section.

As you can see in Figure 5-17, the final chart looks pretty basic.

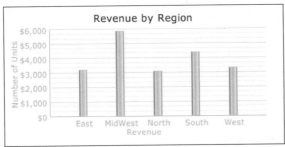

Figure 5-17:
You created
your chart
with just a
few mouse
clicks!

Now add some interactivity by tying a Slider control to the price per unit for-mula that feeds the chart.

1. **Activate the Components window and drag a Horizontal Slider compo-nent onto the canvas.**

2. **Double-click the Horizontal Slider component to activate the Properties window and then adjust the Title property to read** `Price per Unit`**.**

3. **Click the Cell Reference icon and link to cell E1, as shown in Figure 5-18.**

Figure 5-18:
Adjust the
Link to Cell
property
to link to
the value
in cell E1.

	A	B	C	D	E	F	G	H	I
1				Price per Unit	$25				
2									
3		Revenues		Select a Range					
4	East	$3,200		Sheet1!$E$1			OK	Cancel	
5	MidWest	$5,850							
6	North	$3,075							
7	South	$4,400			176				
8	West	$3,300			132				

Cell E1 (price per unit) is used as a variable in the formulas that make up the revenue figures for each region. The idea here is that the Slider com-ponent will change the price per unit variable. This causes the values in the chart's data range to recalculate, effectively changing the chart.

Note: For a refresher on how Single Value components work, check out Chapter 3.

4. **Switch to Preview mode by clicking the Preview button on the taskbar; then use the slider to increase the number of sales calls.**

At this point, your visual model should look similar to Figure 5-19. Now, as you adjust price per unit, your chart changes to reflect the new values.

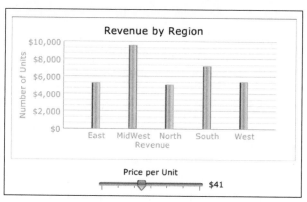

Figure 5-19: Your chart is now interactive, reflecting the impact of the changes in price per unit.

Understanding scale behavior

One of the tricky things about having an interactive chart is that the *scales* for the chart — that is, the reference of relative magnitude represented by the numbers in the x and y axes — have to keep up with the changes you interactively apply at run-time. This sometimes leads to the scales having an erratic feel. The good news is that you can set Scale Behavior options to give your chart scales a smoother, more predictable feel.

If you've followed this chapter to this point and created the sample chart, view it in Design mode. (If you're in Preview mode, click the Preview button on the taskbar to return to Design mode.) After you're there, double-click the chart to get to the Properties window. The Scale Behavior options, shown in Figure 5-20, are found on the Behavior tab of the Properties window.

TIP

The default Scale Behavior option for all chart types is Auto Scale.

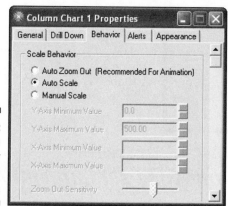

Figure 5-20: Find Scale Behavior options here.

You have essentially three Scale Behavior options to choose from:

✔ **Auto Zoom Out:** This option is ideal for charts that are interactive or animated. This setting ensures that the axis scale grows only as data changes and does not shrink, thus minimizing rescaling and giving the chart a smoother feel. Selecting this option also enables the Zoom Out Sensitivity parameter (slider) — you can see this slider grayed-out in Figure 5-20. The Zoom Out Sensitivity parameter determines how much an axis scale grows as the data changes. Moving the slider to the extreme left causes the scale to increase by a small factor as the data changes, and moving the slider to the extreme right causes the scale to increase by a large factor as the data changes.

✔ **Auto Scale:** Choose this option when the data that feeds your chart changes but not through animation. For example, imagine that you have a list of products in a list box. When you click a product, your chart changes to reflect the data for that product. In this case, each product might have a different minimum and maximum value, so you would want Crystal Xcelsius to determine the scale range automatically.

✔ **Manual Scale:** The Manual Scale option is used when the data in the chart doesn't require the scales to change. When you select Manual Scale, the four input boxes (shown in Figure 5-21) become enabled. These input boxes allow you to manually adjust and lock in the minimum and maximum scale values.

The X-Axis Minimum Value input box and the X-Axis Maximum Value input box are available only when you are working with charts where the x-axis displays a scale (such as XY charts, bubble charts, and bar charts).

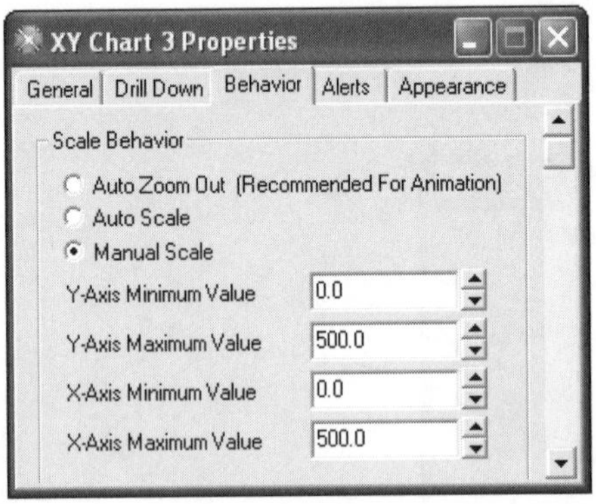

Figure 5-21:
Select the
Manual
Scale option
to manually
adjust your
scale
ranges.

> **XY Chart 3 Properties**
>
> General | Drill Down | Behavior | Alerts | Appearance
>
> Scale Behavior
>
> ○ Auto Zoom Out (Recommended For Animation)
> ○ Auto Scale
> ● Manual Scale
>
> Y-Axis Minimum Value `0.0`
> Y-Axis Maximum Value `500.0`
> X-Axis Minimum Value `0.0`
> X-Axis Maximum Value `500.0`

Leveraging the run-time scaling options

Also on the Behavior tab is the Run Time Options section. These options, shown in Figure 5-22, allow users to decide how the chart's scales behave.

Figure 5-22:
The Run
Time Options
empower
users to
change
scale
behavior
dynamically.

Each option represents some functionality that you can add at run-time.

- ✔ **Show Focus Button:** Adding this option provides the users with the ability to force rescaling of the chart axes based on the data that's visible at the time.

- ✔ **Show Reset Scale Button:** Adding this option provides the users with the ability to reset the scales to the original values seen when the dashboard was first loaded.

- ✔ **Show Scale Behavior Options:** Adding this option provides users with the ability to change scale behavior at run-time.

When one or more of these run-time options are selected, a special icon becomes visible in the upper-left corner of the Chart component. Passing your mouse over this icon causes a menu to appear with all or some of the scaling options, depending on the options you selected. Figure 5-23 demonstrates how the run-time options look in action.

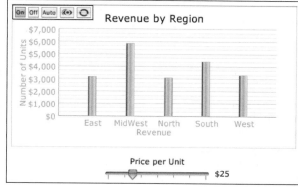

Figure 5-23:
This column
chart has all
three Run
Time Options
enabled.

Changing Chart Appearance

After you create your chart, you can change its look and feel by modifying its colors, font size, background, and so on. In Excel, you typically make changes to each object within the chart by right-clicking that object and pulling up its properties. For example, to change the color of a data series, you right-click that series and go to its properties.

In Crystal Xcelsius, however, there is no such thing as a data series object or an x axis object. Instead, a Crystal Xcelsius Chart component is essentially one big object that has properties that you can set. What this means is that you can't right-click individual parts of a Crystal Xcelsius chart and expect to find individual properties that you can change. Instead, a set of properties within the component itself determine the formatting and appearance of the chart. These can be found on the Appearance tab of the Properties window.

Appearance tab options

As you can see in Figure 5-24, the Appearance tab is a rather robust tab with five embedded sub-tabs: Series, Y-Axis, X-Axis, Titles, and Layout.

Figure 5-24:
The Appearance tab contains all the properties that define the formatting and appearance of your chart.

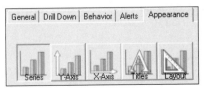

✔ **Series:** This tab is where you find all the properties that handle the formatting of a data series. This sub-tab has 11 sections (sets of properties) that make themselves available based on the type of chart with which you're working. These properties control such data series formatting as color, width, size, marker type, transparency, and highlights.

✔ **Y-Axis:** This tab controls the look of the Y-Axis category. This includes the format of the Y-Axis title, the Y-Axis labels, and the major and minor tick marks on the y axis.

✔ **X-Axis:** This tab controls the look of the X-Axis category, including the format of the X-Axis title, the X-Axis labels, and the major and minor tick marks on the x axis.

✔ **Titles:** This tab controls the formatting for the chart's title.

✔ **Layout:** This tab handles the formatting of the chart's background and plot area. The properties found here control such formatting as color, borders, and gridlines.

The idea is that when you need to format certain parts of your chart, you know exactly where to go. For example, if you need to format your data series, go to the Series sub-tab. If you need to change the font for the categories in the x axis, go to the X-Axis sub-tab.

To illustrate the intuitiveness of formatting a chart in Crystal Xcelsius, continue this chapter's running column chart example and apply some basic formatting to your chart.

1. **Double-click the Column chart to open the Properties window and then select the Appearance tab.**

2. **Change the color and width of the columns to give them more definition.**

3. **Because this action requires formatting the data series, go to the Series sub-tab (just click it).**

4. **In the Plot Settings section, change the Bar Width property.**

   In this example, I change it to 30.

   The formatting changes you make to your charts are made in real time so you can immediately see the impact of your adjustments. Watch your chart as you adjust each property in the Appearance tab.

5. **In the Plot Settings section, change the Bar Color property.**

   a. Enable the Use Custom Color check box.

   b. Click the Bar Color property and select a color.

   Orange sounds good to me.

At this point, the properties in the Series sub-tab should look similar to the ones shown in Figure 5-25.

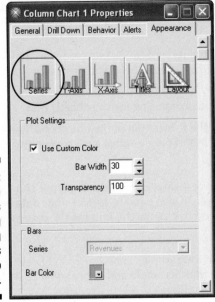

Figure 5-25:
Change
series
formatting
by adjusting
the Series
sub-tab
properties.

6. Accentuate the chart's title by adding a border around it.

Because you're formatting the title, you can find the appropriate properties under the Titles sub-tab. Seeing a pattern here?

a. Click the Titles sub-tab.

b. In the Chart Title section, select both the Show Border and Show Fill check boxes.

This applies formatting around the chart title, as shown in Figure 5-26.

7. Add texture to the plot area by adjusting a few properties in the Layout sub-tab.

a. Click the Layout sub-tab.

b. In the Chart Area section, deselect the Show Background check box.

c. In the Plot Area section, select the Show Fill check box.

The Layout sub-tab should look similar to Figure 5-27.

Figure 5-26:
Apply some
formatting
around the
chart title.

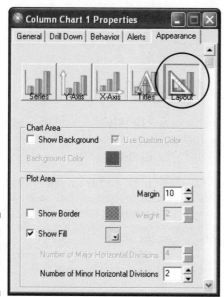

Figure 5-27:
Add texture
to the
plot area.

8. **Close the properties window and take a look at your chart.**

You successfully enhanced the look and feel of your chart with just 12 clicks and 2 keystrokes. Figure 5-28 shows a before and after comparison.

Before

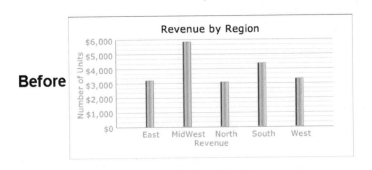

After

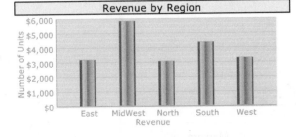

Figure 5-28: Your column chart before and after formatting.

Sub-tab sections by chart type

The properties that you encounter in each sub-tab greatly depend on the chart type with which you are working. This means that the make-up of your sub-tabs will differ from chart type to chart type.

For example, when you work with a pie chart, you see a section called Slices in the Series sub-tab. This section contains properties that allow you to adjust the color for each slice in the pie. Because other chart types don't represent data points as slices, it stands to reason that the Slices section is visible only when working with a Pie Chart component.

Table 5-1 highlights each of the sections that are available in the five sub-tabs and describes the purpose of each section. This table also specifies the chart types to which each section applies.

Table 5-1   Index of Appearance Property Sections by Sub-tab

Sub-tab	Section	Applicable Chart Types	Description
Series	Bars	Column, bar	Changes the formatting of bars used to identify each series in a column or bar chart.
Series	Bubble	Bubble	Allows you to change the color of the bubbles in a bubble chart.
Series	Column Plot Settings	Combination chart	Controls how columns are displayed. This section allows you to set the width and transparency of each data series.
Series	Line Plot Settings	Combination chart	Controls how the line markers for each data series are displayed.
Series	Lines & Markers	Line, area, radar	Changes the formatting of lines and markers used to identify each series.
Series	Plot Settings	Line, column, bar, pie, XY, radar, bubble	Controls the formatting tied to the data series. This includes color, size, width, transparency, and highlights.
Series	Series Markers	Combination chart	Allows you to specify whether a series is represented by a column or a line.
Series	Series Settings	Area	Controls the transparency of all series in an area chart.
Series	Slices	Pie	Changes the color of each data series in a pie chart.
Series	Symbols	XY	Changes the markers used to identify each series. Your choices are a circle, diamond, star, triangle, or an X.
Series	Values	All but area charts	Controls how values are displayed. This includes color, font size, and numeric format.

(continued)

Table 5-1 *(continued)*

Sub-tab	Section	Applicable Chart Types	Description
Y-Axis	Vertical Axis Titles	All but pie charts	Allows you to adjust the formatting of the y axis title.
Y-Axis	Vertical Axis	All but pie charts	Controls the formatting of the y axis itself.
Y-Axis	Vertical Axis Labels	Line, column, bar, XY, area, bubble, combination	Allows you to adjust the formatting of the y axis labels.
X-Axis	Horizontal Axis Titles	Line, column, bar, XY, area, bubble, combination	Allows you to adjust the formatting of the x axis title.
X-Axis	Horizontal Axis	Line, column, bar, XY, area, bubble, combination	Controls the formatting of the x axis itself.
X-Axis	Horizontal Axis Labels	Line, column, bar, XY, area, bubble, combination	Allows you to adjust the formatting of the x axis labels.
X-Axis	Vertical Axis Labels	Radar	Controls the formatting of the axis itself.
Titles	Chart Title	All chart types	Allows you to specify whether and how the chart title is displayed.
Titles	Legend	All chart types	Allows you to specify whether and how the chart legend is displayed.
Layout	Chart Area	All chart types	Controls the look and feel of the chart area.
Layout	Plot Area	All chart types	Allows you to add color and texture to the chart's plot area.
Layout	Horizontal Gridlines	All but pie charts	Controls whether and how the horizontal gridlines are displayed.
Layout	Vertical Gridlines	All but pie charts	Controls whether and how the vertical gridlines are displayed.

Understanding Combination Charts

A *combination chart* is a special kind of Chart component that enables you to plot your data using columns and lines in the same chart. These powerful charts allow you to plot multiple groups of data together in one chart, visually displaying variances and magnitudes of change.

Although combination charts are powerful, building a combination chart is not as intuitive as building other chart types. This causes many first-time Crystal Xcelsius users to shy away from using them. In the next section, I show you that combination charts are actually very easy to build after you know a few of the ground rules.

Combination chart ground rules

Before you get started, you need to understand the few rules and limitations that come with combination charts.

- **You're limited to columns and lines.** When Excel power-users hear the term *combination chart,* they think of a chart in which multiple chart types (XY, area, pie, line, column, and so on) are plotted into a single chart. In Crystal Xcelsius, however, combination charts are limited to columns and lines. As of Crystal Xcelsius 4, there is no way to plot chart types other than columns and lines in a combination chart.

- **Only the second data series is defaulted to a line.** When building a combination chart, Crystal Xcelsius plots your data and assigns a chart type to each data series automatically. The first data series in your range is always a column, and the second is always a line.

- **All data series after the second are defaulted to columns.** If you have three or more data series, all data series after the second one are automatically assigned as columns. What happens when you delete the second data series? The third series moves to the second position and is automatically changed from a column to a line. In many cases, this default behavior just won't do. The good news is that you can easily reassign chart types manually.

Creating a combination chart with three data series

Suppose you were asked to create a chart that shows 2005 revenues and how each month's revenues compare with 2004 *and* the average monthly revenue in 2005. You need a chart that looks similar to the one shown in Figure 5-29 — essentially, a combination chart with three data series: a column and two lines.

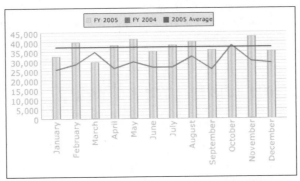

Figure 5-29: You need a combination chart with three data series: a column and two lines.

Start by opening Crystal Xcelsius and creating a new visual model.

The *visual model* is essentially your dashboard in Design mode. It is the blank canvas on which you add components that visually represent the data you imported from your Excel model. When you save your visual model, it is saved as an .xlf file. Chapter 2 covers more Crystal Xcelsius terminology.

1. **From the main menu, choose Data⇨Import Model and then import the ComboChart.xls file from the C:\Xcelsius Sample Files\ Chapter 5\ directory.**

2. **Activate the Components window and drag a Combination Chart component onto the canvas.**

3. **Double-click the Combination Chart component to activate the Properties window.**

4. **On the General tab, clear the Chart Title input box and the Chart Subtitle input box.**

   You won't need titles for this example.

5. **On the General tab, click the Cell Reference icon for Data Range and link to cells A2:M5, as shown in Figure 5-30.**

   After you select your data range, you should be left with a combination chart that looks similar to the one shown in Figure 5-31.

Figure 5-30:
Select the
data your
chart will
display.

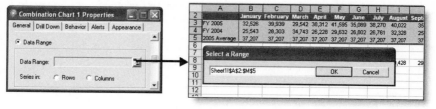
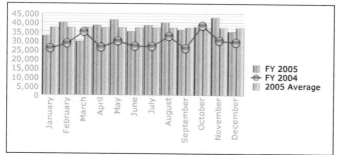

Figure 5-31:
You created
a basic
combination
chart, but
it's not quite
right yet.

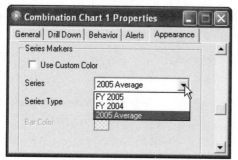

The problem is that the 2005 Average data series needs to be a line — not a column. Remember that all data series after the second one default to a column. You have to adjust this manually.

1. **Double-click the Combination Chart component to activate the Properties window, and then go to the Appearance tab.**

2. **On the Appearance tab, make sure that the Series sub-tab is selected.**

3. **In the Series Markers section, click the Series drop-down list box, shown in Figure 5-32, and find the one you want to change.**

   In this case, it's 2005 Average.

Figure 5-32:
Select the
series you
want to
change from
the Series
Markers
section.

4. **Change the Series Type property to Line, just as you see in Figure 5-33.**

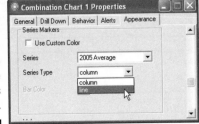

Figure 5-33:
Adjust the
Series Type
property to
change the
data series
to a line.

As you can see in Figure 5-34, a few more properties become visible as soon as you choose Line.

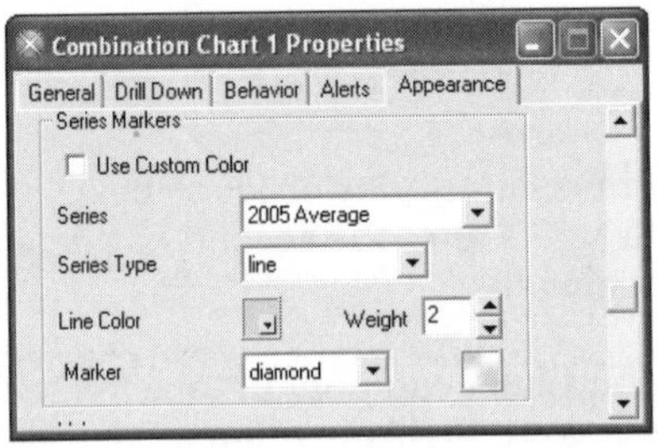

Figure 5-34:
The
formatting
properties
for the
line auto-
matically
become
visible.

Now it's just a question of formatting:

5. **Change the Line Color property to something noticeable.**

I chose red.

6. **Click the Series drop-down list box and choose the second data series.**

In this example, choose FY 2005.

7. **Change the Bar Color property.**

I chose yellow.

8. **In the Line Plot Settings section, deselect the Show Markers check box.**

This removes the markers on the lines in your chart.

9. **Switch to the Titles sub-tab and set formatting in the Legend section, as shown in Figure 5-35.**

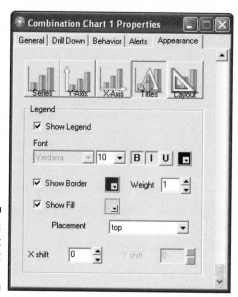

Figure 5-35:
Format the chart legend.

10. **After you make all the formatting changes, close the Properties window to reveal your final chart.**

If all went well, your chart should look like the one in Figure 5-36.

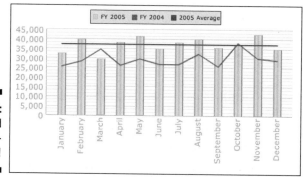

Figure 5-36:
You created your combination chart!

Adding a series to a combination chart

Undoubtedly, your manager was so happy with the chart you created in the preceding section that he wants more. (Imagine that.) Now he wants to add a line to the chart that represents the average monthly revenue for 2004 so he can compare it with the other data points on the chart. What does this mean for you? You simply have to add a series to the combination chart that you already built.

For the purposes of this book, the data series is already in the Excel model you imported for the first combination chart. Therefore, you don't need to reimport the model. Keep in mind, however, that in a real-life scenario, you would have to add this data series to your Excel model and then reimport the model.

1. **Double-click the combination chart to activate the Properties window.**

2. **On the General tab, find the Series section and click the Add button, as shown in Figure 5-37.**

   This adds a new data series called Series1.

Figure 5-37:
Add a new
series by
clicking the
Add button
in the Series
section.

3. **Give the series an appropriate name; you can rename the series in the Name input box.**

   As you can see in Figure 5-38, after you press Enter on the keyboard, the name also changes in the Series list.

4. **Click the X Values Cell Reference icon and link to cells B8:M8, as shown in Figure 5-39.**

   When referencing data for a single series, as in Figure 5-39, all you need to reference is the actual data that will be plotted by that series. You don't need to include the name of the series or data from other series in the range.

Figure 5-38:
Rename the
new series
to some-
thing more
appropriate.

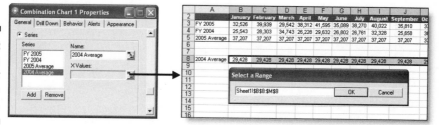

Figure 5-39:
Assign data
to your
newly cre-
ated series.

5. **Switch to the Appearance tab and make sure that the Series sub-tab is selected.**

6. **On the Series sub-tab, go to the Series Markers section and choose 2004 Average from the Series drop-down box. After the 2004 Average series is selected, change the Series Type to Line.**

7. **Close the Properties window to reveal your final chart.**

   If all went well, your chart should look like the one in Figure 5-40.

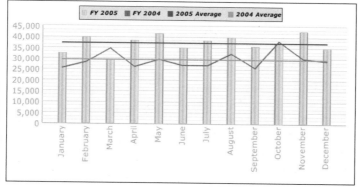

Figure 5-40:
You added
a series to
your combi-
nation chart!

Chapter 6

May I Please See the Menu?

To most managers, an *interactive dashboard* basically means one thing — choices. Gone are the days of static Web reports that provide only one view of a dataset. Today's managers increasingly want to be empowered to switch from one view of data to another with a simple selection from a menu of choices. Unfortunately, with most dashboard and report building platforms, adding menu functionality generally requires some level of programming skill or at least power-user status. In contrast, Crystal Xcelsius allows you to design and build menu functionality into your dashboard by simply linking a Selector component to your data. In this chapter, I show you how to easily build menus and selectors into your dashboards with Selector components.

Delivering Choices with a Selector Component

In very basic terms, think of a Selector component as a delivery truck. You fill the Selector component with data by linking it to a table. Based on that data, the Selector component displays the choices available to you as menu items. When you select one of these menu items, the Selector component delivers a predefined attribute or value to a destination range (a cell or a range of cells). The destination range to which you deliver the data is typically linked to other components that use the data in a predefined way.

To get a solid understanding of this concept, walk through the creation of a menu in a visual model.

ON THE WEB

1. **Open the `BasicSelector.xlf` visual model from the `C:\Xcelsius Sample Files\Chapter 6` directory.**

   When the visual model loads, you see one Gauge component that displays a value representing units sold.

2. **Double-click the Gauge component to get to the Properties window.**

   As you can see in Figure 6-1, this Gauge component is linked to cell D2.

Figure 6-1:
This Gauge component is linked to cell D2.

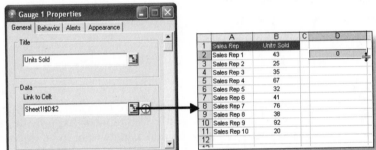

The idea here is that you don't want to hard-code the units sold in cell D2. Instead, you want to be able to select a sales rep from a menu and have the data value for that selection populate cell D2 interactively. And because the Gauge component is linked to cell D2, this causes it to react to your selection.

To accomplish this, we use a Combo Box component.

3. **Activate the Components window, drill into the Selectors category, and drag a Combo Box component onto the canvas.**

4. **Double-click the Combo Box component to activate the Properties window.**

   Note the two sections on the General tab: Titles and Insert Data. Work on the Titles section first. This section is dedicated to the labeling and displaying of the menu items. Here, you identify the values that display as the menu choices within the component.

5. **Click the Labels Cell Reference icon to identify the range of cells that contains the labels you want the Combo Box component to display.**

   Figure 6-2 illustrates this action.

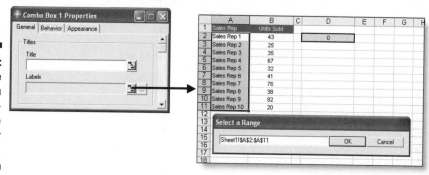

6. **Define how the component behaves by adjusting the properties in the Insert Data section. These properties are**

   - **Insert Option:** The Insert Option property allows you to define which of the attributes you want the component to deliver. I cover the Insert Option property in detail in this chapter.

   - **Source Data:** The Source Data property defines the data values for the Selector component.

     The Source Data property is visible only when the Insert Option property is set to Value, Rows, or Columns.

   - **Insert In:** The Insert In property defines the cell or range of cells into which you want the selected data to be delivered.

7. **Select Value from the Insert Option drop-down list, as shown in Figure 6-3.**

   In this scenario, you want a single value to be delivered to cell D2, feeding the Gauge component.

   After you set the Insert Data property to Value, the Source Data property becomes visible.

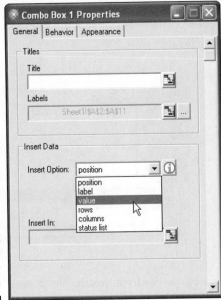

Figure 6-3:
Define the attribute you want delivered to the destination cell.

8. **Click the Source Data Cell Reference icon, shown in Figure 6-4, and select the cells that contain the data values you want passed to the destination range.**

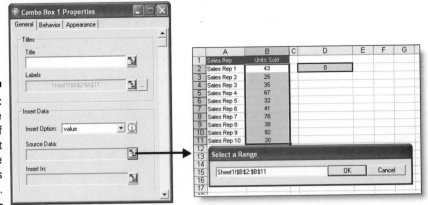

Figure 6-4:
Select the range of cells that contain the data values in your table.

9. **Click the Insert In Cell Reference icon to select the destination range, as shown in Figure 6-5.**

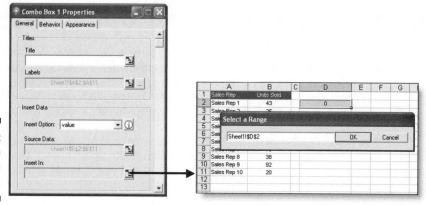

Figure 6-5:
Select the
destination
range.

10. **Switch to Preview mode by clicking the Preview button on the taskbar and Combo Box component as a drop-down Selector to change the value of the Gauge component.**

Figure 6-6 illustrates the final effect.

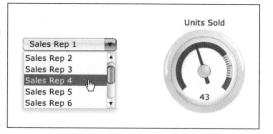

Figure 6-6:
You built
your first
dashboard
menu!

Take a moment and think about what you accomplished. Because ten sales reps are listed in your newly created Combo Box component, you essentially packaged ten dashboards into one visual model.

Although this is a very basic example that uses the Combo Box component, the same fundamental steps taken here apply to all Selector components in Crystal Xcelsius.

1. Define the label names for the menu items in your component.

2. Define the delivery method with the Insert Option property.

3. Specify the source data to be used with the Source Data property.

4. Specify the destination range with the Insert In property.

Understanding the Insert Option Property

In the example of the preceding section, I show you how to deliver a single value to the destination range. That is to say, when you select a sales rep from the menu, one data value is inserted into the destination range (the units sold). This happens because you set the Insert Option property to Value in Step 7, effectively telling the Selector component to deliver a single value.

The Insert Option essentially defines the attribute or value that is to be delivered. *Attributes* are the characteristics that make up an object. For example, you can think of height, weight, hair color, and eye color as attributes of a person. Every object has attributes, including data tables. Some of the attributes of a data table are

- **Row Count:** The number of rows or records in the data table

- **Column Count:** The number of columns or fields in the data table

- **Row Index:** The integer-based catalog that identifies each row in the data table as a number

- **Column Index:** The integer-based catalog that identifies each column in the data table as a number

- **Data Values:** The actual values that reside in the data table

When you link a Selector component to a data table, the Selector component stores these attributes into memory. From there, the Insert Option property is used to define the attribute that is delivered to the destination range, giving the Selector component its functionality.

The six possible settings in the Insert Options property are

- Position
- Label
- Value
- Rows
- Columns
- Status List

Take a moment and look at each setting.

Position

The Position setting allows you to use the row index attribute for the menu item selected. For example, the table shown in Figure 6-7 contains four rows. Each row has an index number that is interpreted by the Selector component as a position number.

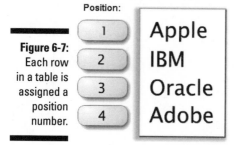

Figure 6-7: Each row in a table is assigned a position number.

When a menu item is selected, as in Figure 6-8, the Selector component delivers the position number for that selection.

Figure 6-8: The position number for the selected item is delivered to the destination range.

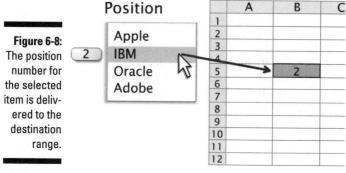

 Although the images shown here might not look like the Selector component you are working with, the concepts discussed in this section apply to all Selector components.

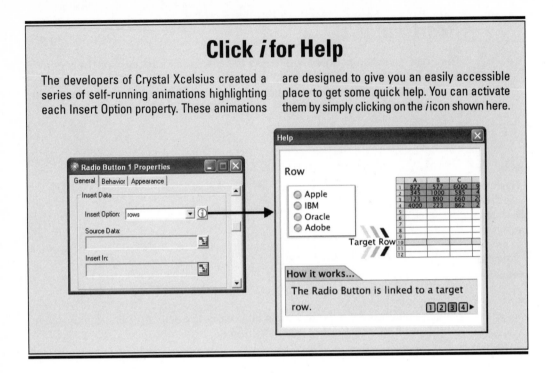

Click *i* for Help

The developers of Crystal Xcelsius created a series of self-running animations highlighting each Insert Option property. These animations are designed to give you an easily accessible place to get some quick help. You can activate them by simply clicking on the *i* icon shown here.

Label

The Label setting allows you to deliver the menu items themselves to the destination range. For example, when you select IBM from the Selector component in Figure 6-8, the actual word *IBM* is delivered to the destination range. Figure 6-9 illustrates this concept.

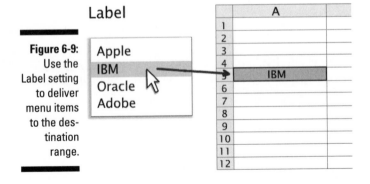

Figure 6-9: Use the Label setting to deliver menu items to the destination range.

Both the Position and Label settings are ideal when you're working with Excel models that use IF formulas or VLOOKUP formulas. These settings are also effective when they are used in conjunction with the dynamic visibility functionality that I talk about in Chapter 8.

Value

The Value setting allows you to deliver a single value to a destination range. This setting tells the Selector component to deliver a single value based on the row index of the item that you select. For example, if you select the second item in the menu, the second data value in the source table is delivered to the destination range. Figure 6-10 demonstrates how this works.

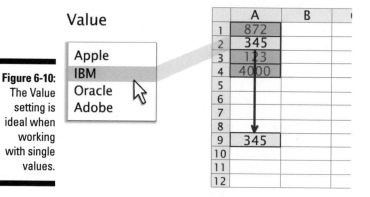

Figure 6-10: The Value setting is ideal when working with single values.

The Value setting is perfect for feeding Single Value components such as gauges or progress bars.

Rows

The Rows setting tells the Selector component to deliver a row of data based on the row index of the item that you select. For example, if you select the second item in the menu, the second row in the source table is delivered to the destination range. Figure 6-11 demonstrates how this works.

The Rows setting is ideal for delivering data to cells that are used as the source cells for Chart components.

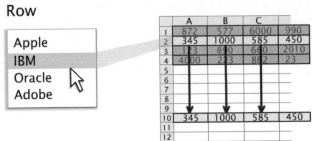

Columns

The Columns setting tells the Selector component to deliver a column of data based on the column index of the item that you select. For example, if you select the second item in the menu, shown in Figure 6-12, the second column in the source table is delivered to the destination range.

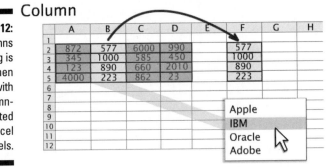

The Columns setting is ideal for delivering data to cells that are used as the source cells for column-oriented dynamic charts.

Status List

With the Status List setting, the Selector is linked to a contiguous range of cells in the spreadsheet. When an item is selected, the application inserts the number 1 into the corresponding cell. All other cells contain the number 0 (zero). Figure 6-13 illustrates how the Status List setting works.

Figure 6-13:
The Status List setting delivers a 0 or 1 for all items in the source data. Only the selected item is tagged with a 1.

	A	B	C
1			
2		0	
3		1	
4		0	
5		0	
6			
7			

Status List

Apple
IBM
Oracle
Adobe

The Status List setting is designed to be used specifically with the dynamic visibility functionality I talk about in Chapter 8.

Working with the Filter Component

The Filter component stands apart from the other Selector components because it does something that the other components don't do. It allows you to create multiple filter menus that interact with one another, giving you the ability to drill through multilayered hierarchies. To get a better idea of what this means, open the `FilterExample.xlf` visual model from the `C:\Xcelsius Sample Files\Chapter 6\` directory.

As you can see in Figure 6-14, there are three filter menus in this visual model. However, if you try to move one of them, you will quickly realize that they are connected. (Although the drop-down menus here look like separate components, they are actually part of the same Filter component.)

Figure 6-14:
Filter menus.

REGION	MARKET	STORE	Revenue Last Year
North ▼	Great Lakes ▼	14010010 ▼	

These filter menus are actually one Filter component that represents the hierarchy of Region, Market, and Store. The idea is to select a region in the Region selector and see only the markets that belong to that region in the Market selector. Then select a market and see only the stores that are located in that market. To see this Filter component in action, switch to Preview mode by clicking the Preview button on the taskbar.

As you play around with the selections, notice that each selector is automatically filtered based on the item chosen in the selector to the left of it. Figure 6-15 illustrates how this allows you to easily drill through the hierarchy.

Figure 6-15:
Each selector is filtered based on the item chosen in the selector to the left of it.

Creating Your First Filtered Dashboard

If you've followed this chapter to this point, you have an idea of what a Filter component is designed to do. Time to build a visual model that leverages a Filter component to give you a dynamic menu of choices.

1. **Start a new visual model by choosing File⇨New from the main menu.**

2. **Import the `FilterSelector.xls` file from the `C:\Xcelsius Sample Files\Chapter 6\` directory.**

3. **Activate the Components window, drill into the Selectors category, and drag a Filter component onto the canvas.**

4. **Double-click the Filter component to activate the Properties window.**

   The first thing you should notice is that the Filter component automatically places two filter menus onto the canvas. You might need to add filter menus depending on how many levels are in your hierarchy. You can do this by adjusting the Number of Filters property, as shown in Figure 6-16.

Figure 6-16:
The Number of Filters property specifies how many filter menus you want in your Filter component.

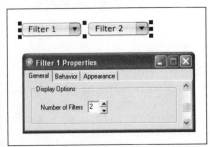

The default number of filter menus in a Filter component is 2. The maximum number of filter menus a Filter component can have is 10.

In this scenario, you have only two levels in your hierarchy (Region and Market), so the default is okay.

5. Click the Titles Cell Reference icon and select titles for the filter menus, as shown in Figure 6-17.

Figure 6-17: Select titles for the filter menus in your Filter component.

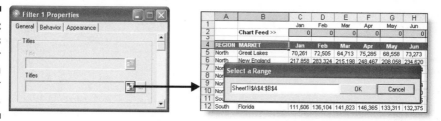

The Filter component uses the column index to determine the menu items in each filter menu. This means that the first filter menu is automatically tied to the first column in your data table, the second filter menu is tied to the second column, the third to the third column, and so on. All properties of the Filter component adhere to the column index as well. For example, when you select range A4:B4 as the source for the Titles property, the first label in the selection is automatically assigned to the first filter menu.

6. Click the Source Data Cell Reference icon, shown in Figure 6-18, and select the source data for the Filter component.

Figure 6-18: Select the data source for your Filter component.

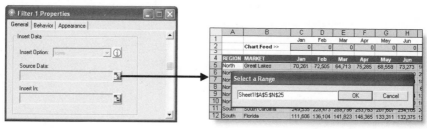

Don't include the column labels in the Source Data property. Doing so includes a selection in your filter menus for the column header.

7. **Click the Insert In Cell Reference icon and select the destination range (cells C2:N2), as shown in Figure 6-19.**

Figure 6-19:
Select the
destination
range for
the Filter
component's
output.

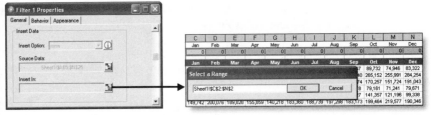

Keep in mind that any column that is not tied to a filter menu is included in the row data that is delivered to the destination cells. This means that if you have 14 columns in your data table and 2 of them are tied to filter menus, 12 columns are included in the delivered row. Given this fact, you want to make sure that the delivery range you specify via the Insert In property is large enough to hold 12 columns of data.

8. **Click the Appearance Tab and go to the Labels section.**

Although there are many properties you can work with to change the appearance of the Filter component, adjust just two:

- The label fonts
- The number of menu selections that are displayed at one time

9. **Adjust the Font property to 10 and then adjust the Rows Displayed property to 10.**

When finished, the Labels section of your Filter component should look like Figure 6-20.

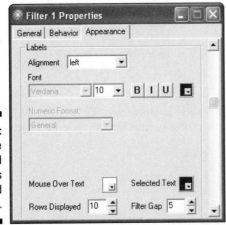

Figure 6-20:
Adjust the
Font and
Rows
Displayed
properties.

At this point, your Filter component is ready to go!

The next step is to tie a column chart to the range where the Filter component's data is delivered.

10. **Activate the Components window and add a Column Chart component to the canvas.**

11. **Double-click the Column Chart component to activate the Properties window and then clear the chart titles in the Titles section.**

12. **Click the Data Range Cell Reference icon, shown in Figure 6-21, and select the source data for the Filter component.**

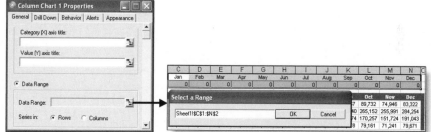

Figure 6-21:
Select the range of cells to feed your newly added column chart.

That's all you need to do on the Column Chart component for now.

Take a step back and think about what you created. You have a Filter component that allows you to drill into a region and select from a list of markets specific to that region. After you select a market, the Filter component delivers a row of 12 data points to cells C2:N2. This range of cells is also used to feed the Column Chart component you added to this visual model. The resulting effect is that the column chart displays the data for the selected market. Simply click the Preview button on the taskbar to switch to Preview mode. Your dashboard should look like the one in Figure 6-22.

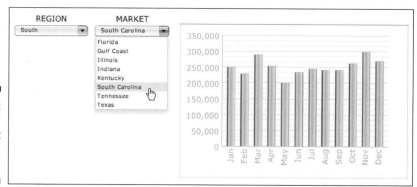

Figure 6-22:
You created your first filtered dashboard!

Part III

Get Fancy with Advanced Components

The 5th Wave   By Rich Tennant

"The top line represents our revenue, the middle line is our inventory, and the bottom line shows the rate of my hair loss over the same period."

In this part . . .

In this section, go beyond the basics to take a look at some of the advanced components Crystal Xcelsius has to offer. First, explore the use of Map components and look at the different ways you can use those components to add flair to your visualizations. Next, walk through the basics of dynamic visibility and look at some examples of how it can help achieve focus in your dashboards. Finally, focus on the advanced components and functions found in the Professional version of Crystal Xcelsius.

Chapter 7

Getting Geo-Graphic with Maps

. . . .

. . . .

I can hear those MapPoint gurus now just waiting to take this chapter apart. To you distinguished professionals, I say relax. Crystal Xcelsius is not mapping software: It's a visualization program. The Map components in Crystal Xcelsius aren't designed to do hardcore mapping tasks like assign data by ZIP code, create layers of maps, or measure distances. Instead, Map components are designed to select and display the geographic-oriented data in your visual mode by region.

In this chapter, I show you how to use Map components to add flair to your visualizations. I also cover some of the different ways you can use Map components in your dashboards.

Understanding the Concept of Regions

Think of Map components as visual selectors that allow you to tie geographic data to selections in a map. So, for example, instead of having your users select a state from a list in a Combo box, visual selectors allow you to provide them an interactive map from which they can select a state. This enables you to add elements to your dashboard that are both interactive and visually appealing.

In this section, we explore the concept of *regions*, and how regions are used to tie data to a Map component.

Open Crystal Xcelsius and activate the Components window. You can do this by selecting View⇨Components from the main menu. Drill into the folder called Maps Library to find the Map components, as shown in Figure 7-1.

Figure 7-1:
Crystal
Xcelsius has
nine default
Map com-
ponents.

As you can see in the Components window, Crystal Xcelsius comes with nine default Map components. Each Map component comes with a predefined set of Regions that are used to map data:

✔ **United States by State:** Each state in the U.S. represents a Region that can be mapped to data. The U.S. map holds 49 Regions, including the District of Columbia but excluding Alaska and Hawaii.

✔ **World Map by Continent:** Each continent in the world map represents a Region. The eight Regions that can be mapped to data are Africa, Antarctica, Asia, Australia, Europe, North America, Oceania, and South America.

✔ **California Map by County:** Each of the 58 counties in California is a Region that can be mapped to data.

✔ **Africa Map by Country:** Each of the 59 countries in Africa is a Region that can be mapped to data.

✔ **Asia Map by Country:** Each of the 53 countries in Asia is a Region that can be mapped to data.

✔ **Central America Map by Country:** Each of the eight countries in Central America is a Region that can be mapped to data.

✔ **Europe Map by Country:** Each of the 50 countries in Europe is a Region that can be mapped to data.

✔ **North America Map by Country:** Each of the 37 countries in North America is a Region that can be mapped to data.

✔ **South America Map by Country:** Each of the 14 countries in South America is a Region that can be mapped to data.

To see the list of Regions available to you in a particular Map component, drag the United States by State component, shown in Figure 7-2, onto the canvas.

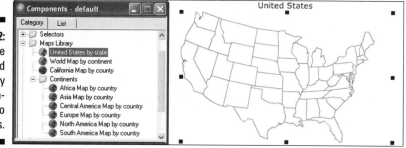

Figure 7-2:
Add the United States by State component to the canvas.

Double-click the map to activate the Properties window. On the General tab, set the Region Names property. Click the ellipsis button, as shown in Figure 7-3.

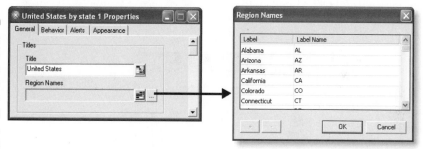

Figure 7-3:
Click the ellipsis button to see the predefined list of Regions.

In the Region Names dialog box, there are two columns:

- **Label:** This column shows you the actual Region that is programmed into the component.

- **Label Name:** This column shows you the Region Code that the component uses to match data to the Region.

The United States map uses the standard postal two-digit state abbreviations (such as AL and MN) as default Region Codes. Thus, in the data table shown in Figure 7-4, the line with the state code of AZ will be mapped to Arizona in the Map component.

So what happens when the states in your data aren't labeled with two-digit state names? You can easily edit the code associated with each Region by simply showing Crystal Xcelsius the list of names that you are using.

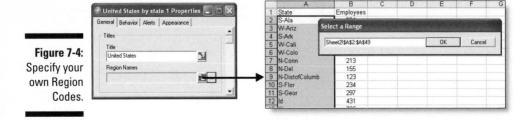

Figure 7-4:
Specify your
own Region
Codes.

To do this, click the Region Names Cell Reference icon, as shown in Figure 7-4, and link the component to the list of codes you'd like to use.

Figure 7-4 demonstrates that the Region Codes you use don't even have to be conventional names. You can use any crazy name you come up with. The only rule is that the order of your codes must be the same as the order of the Regions in the Map component. For example, the code for Alabama must come first in your list because it's the first Region in the US Map component. Arizona must come second; Arkansas must come third, and so on.

You can also change individual Region Codes manually by simply double-clicking the code and typing in the new name, as shown in Figure 7-5.

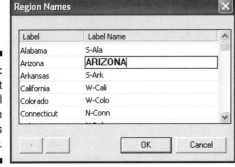

Figure 7-5:
You can edit
individual
Region
Codes
manually.

Creating a Basic Map-Based Dashboard

If you've followed this chapter to this point, you have a solid understanding of the concept of Regions. Time to build your first map-based dashboard!

The idea for this dashboard is to use your Map component as a menu selector that feeds data to a Chart component. For example, when a user clicks the state of Texas, the Map component delivers the data for Texas to the cells that feed your Chart component. This gives users the feeling that the Chart component is reacting to their selection.

1. **Start a new visual model by choosing File⇨New from the main menu.**

2. **Import the `MapData.xls` file from the `C:\Xcelsius Sample Files\ Chapter 7\` directory.**

3. **Activate the Components window, drill into the Maps Library, and drag the United States by State component onto the canvas.**

4. **Double-click the Map component to activate the Properties window.**

   In this example, you're using the full state names, so the first thing you need to do is to tell the Map component to use your state names as the Region code for each Region.

5. **Click the Region Names Cell Reference icon, shown in Figure 7-6, and link your Map component to the Region Codes you will use.**

Figure 7-6:
Select the Region Codes to match and map data to each Region in the Map component.

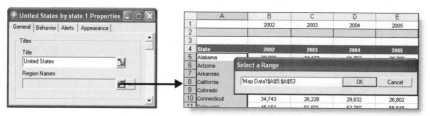

REMEMBER

The United States map uses the two-digit abbreviations as the default Region Codes. If your list of state names is already in the two-digit format, you can skip Step 5.

6. **Click the Source Data Cell Reference icon and select the source data for the Map component, as shown in Figure 7-7.**

Figure 7-7:
Select the source data.

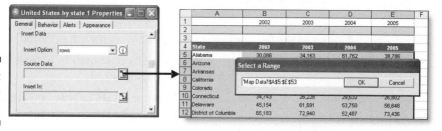

7. **Click the Insert In Cell Reference icon and select the destination range (cells A2:E2), as shown in Figure 7-8.**

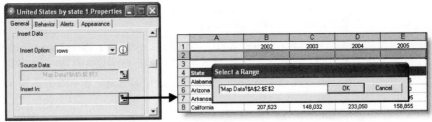

Figure 7-8:
Select the destination range for the Map component's output.

At this point, your Map component is ready to go. The next step is to tie a column chart to the range where the Map component's data will be delivered. Here's how:

1. **Activate the Components window and add a Column Chart component to the canvas.**

   For the lowdown on column charts, see Chapter 5.

2. **Double-click the Column Chart component to activate the Properties window.**

3. **In the Titles section, link the Chart Title property to cell A2, as shown in Figure 7-9.**

Figure 7-9:
Link the Chart Title property to cell A2.

This ensures that the chart title changes with each selected state.

4. **Click the Data Range Cell Reference icon, shown in Figure 7-10, and select the source data for the Map component.**

5. **In the Series section, click the Category Axis Labels Cell Reference icon, shown in Figure 7-11, and select the labels that will be displayed in your chart's x axis.**

Figure 7-10:
Select the range of cells that will feed your newly added column chart.

Figure 7-11:
Select the range of cells that contain the x axis labels for your chart.

6. **Click the Preview button on the taskbar to switch to Preview mode. Your dashboard should look like the one in Figure 7-12.**

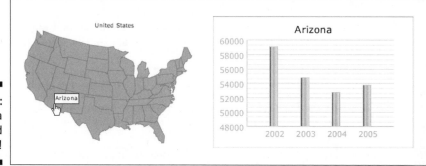

Figure 7-12:
You have a map-based dashboard!

You have a map-based dashboard that allows you to see data for a state by simply clicking that state in the map.

Why can't you use index numbers to match data?

You must always include your Region identifiers (in this case, the State names) in a Map component's source data. Unlike other Selector components, Map components don't use index or position numbers as a matching mechanism. Map components locate and select data by performing a literal match between the Region codes you define in the Region Names property and the Region identifiers that are in your source data. In this scenario, leaving the state names out of the Source Data reference causes the Map component to fail.

Applying Alerts to Map Components

Take an extra step and add another layer of visualization to your map-based dashboard by applying alerts to your map.

The concept of using alerts with a Map component is simple. You first assign a value to each Region, and then you compare that value with a target for that Region. In that light, you need two data tables in order to apply alerts:

✔ One that defines the actual value for each Region
✔ One that defines the target for each Region

Coincidentally, the model that you imported for your map-based dashboard does indeed have these two tables. Start by assigning a value to each Region.

Assigning a value to each Region

Each Region in a Map component can have a single value assigned to it. This value is also called the *Display Data*. You can assign Display Data by adjusting the Display Data property.

1. **Double-click the Map component to activate the Properties window.**

2. **Click the Display Data Cell Reference icon, shown in Figure 7-13, and select the data table that defines the value for each Region.**

   The Region identifiers (in this case, the State names) must always be represented in the first column of the data table.

3. **Switch to the Appearance tab and enable the Show Values check box, as shown in Figure 7-14.**

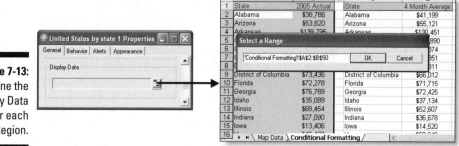

Figure 7-13:
Define the
Display Data
for each
Region.

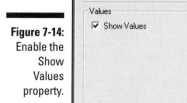

Figure 7-14:
Enable the
Show
Values
property.

4. Click the Preview button on the taskbar to switch to Preview mode.

At this point, you're testing to make sure that the Display Data works
properly. You'll know that all went well if you see the 2005 actual revenue amount in a ToolTip box when you hover over each state, as
shown in Figure 7-15.

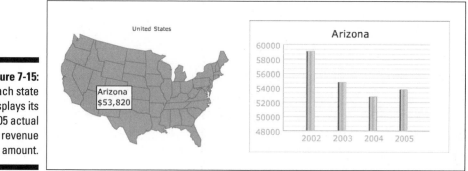

Figure 7-15:
Each state
displays its
2005 actual
revenue
amount.

Assign a target to each Region

As you can glean from this chapter, an *alert* essentially compares a baseline value with a target. For this running example, I show earlier in this chapter how to assign a baseline value to each Region by setting the Display Data property. All that's left to do is assign targets to each region. Start by switching back to design mode by clicking the Preview button again.

1. **Click the Alerts tab of the Properties dialog box.**

2. **Select the Enable Alerts check box to activate the alert properties.**

   By default, the Alert Method property is set to Percent Alert, so leave that property as is.

3. **Change the Alert Definition property to High Values Are Good.**

   In this scenario, the bigger the percentage, the better the performance.

4. **Adjust the Alert Levels property.**

   In this scenario, you need three alert levels:

   • Less than 85% of quota

   • Between 85% and 95% of quota

   • 95% of quota or greater

5. **Given the level requirements, adjust the trigger points for each alert level by dragging the gray arrows above the alert color selector.**

   After you do this, your Alert Levels property should look similar to Figure 7-16.

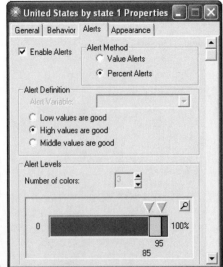

Figure 7-16:
Adjust the trigger points in the Alert Levels property.

6. **Click the Target Cell Reference icon, shown in Figure 7-17, and select the data table that defines target values for each Region.**

   In this case, the target is the four-month average revenue.

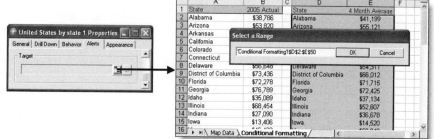

The Region identifiers must always be represented in the first column of the data table. I know it looks redundant to keep listing each state over and over, but that's the way it goes.

7. **Click the Preview button on the taskbar to switch to Preview mode.**

   As you can see in Figure 7-18, you add another layer of analysis by applying alerts to your Map component. In addition to being able to drill into the yearly revenue by clicking a state, you can now quickly determine the states whose 2005 revenues are below their four-month average revenue.

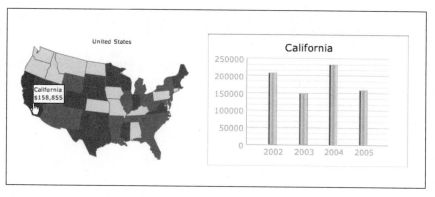

Figure 7-18:
Applying
alerts to this
map-based
dashboard
provides
another
layer of
analysis.

Dynamically Feeding Data to Map Components

Because Map components are typically used as selectors, they are often used to feed other components. However, you can create some interesting visual models by going the other way and actually feeding your Map component. That is to say, instead of selecting data from your Map component, you dynamically assign values to the map at run-time. For instance, the visual model shown in Figure 7-19 is a simple utility that allows you to select an area code and pinpoint the state to which that area code belongs.

Figure 7-19:
In this visual model, data is dynamically fed to the Map component based on the selected area code.

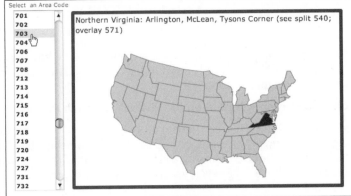

To get a firm understanding of the concept of feeding data to a Map component, build a visual model similar to the one shown here.

1. **Start a new visual model by choosing File⇨New from the main menu.**

2. **Import the `FeedingAMap.xls` file from the `C:\Xcelsius Sample Files\Chapter 7\` directory.**

3. **Activate the Components window, drill into the Selectors category, and drag a List Box component onto the canvas.**

   A List Box component is a type of Selector component. Feel free to review Chapter 6 to get a refresher on Selector components.

4. **Double-click the List Box component to activate the Properties window.**

   The purpose of this list box is to give the user a menu of area codes from which to choose. After an area code has been selected, this list box delivers a row of data to a range of cells that feed a Map component.

5. Click the Labels Cell Reference icon and then select the area codes in the data table, as shown in Figure 7-20.

This ensures that the area codes are displayed as the menu items in the List Box component.

Figure 7-20:
You want the area codes displayed as menu items in your List Box component.

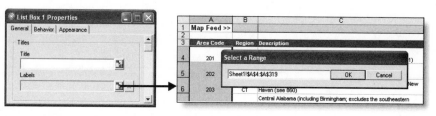

6. Adjust the Insert Option property to Rows, as shown in Figure 7-21.

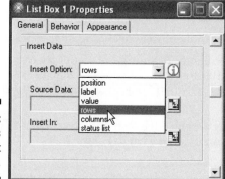

Figure 7-21:
Select Rows as the insert option.

7. Click the Source Data Cell Reference icon and then select the source data for the List Box component, as shown in Figure 7-22.

Figure 7-22:
Select the source data.

> **8. Click the Insert In Cell Reference icon and select the destination range (cells B1:C1), as shown in Figure 7-23.**

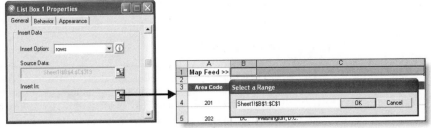

Figure 7-23:
Select the destination range for the List Box component's output.

At this point, you successfully configured your List Box component. This List Box now displays area codes as menu items and delivers data for the selected area code to the range B1:C1.

The next step is to add a Map component and point it to this range. Here's how:

1. **Activate the Components window, drill into the Maps Library, and then drag the United States by State component onto the canvas.**

2. **Double-click the Map component to activate the Properties window.**

   In this example, the state names in your Excel model are represented as two-digit abbreviations. Because the United States map uses the two-digit abbreviations as the default Region Codes, you don't have to adjust the Region Names property.

3. **Click the Source Data Cell Reference icon and then select the source data for the Map component, as shown in Figure 7-24.**

Figure 7-24:
Select the source data.

If the source data for a Map component doesn't contain all the defined Region codes, the Map component simply applies data to the regions that are present and leaves the other regions inactive. This effectively leaves disabled regions in the map — regions that don't react to user interaction. This default behavior comes in handy when you plot data that doesn't necessarily use all regions in your map.

Your Map component is ready to go.

The last thing to add is a Label component to display the area code description.

1. **Activate the Components window, drill into the Text category, and then drag a Label component onto the canvas.**

2. **In the Properties window, adjust the Link To Cell property to link to cell C1, as shown in Figure 7-25.**

Figure 7-25:
Select the cell that delivers the area code description.

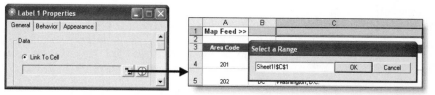

3. **On the Appearance tab, enable the Wrap Text property, as shown in Figure 7-26.**

Figure 7-26:
Make sure the Wrap Text property is active.

From here, you're ready to preview your visual component. Figure 7-27 demonstrates the final result.

4. Click the Preview button on the taskbar to switch to Preview mode.

The visual model shown in Figure 7-27 appears.

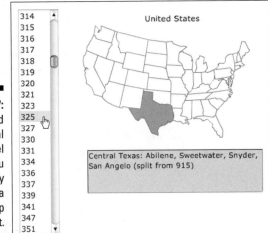

Figure 7-27: You created a visual model where you dynamically feed data to a Map component.

Chapter 8

Focusing in on Dynamic Visibility

*H*ow many times have you been forced to look at four years of data crammed onto one 8½" x 11" sheet of paper? If you're really lucky, you might get a sheet of legal paper with 8 point font. The best, though (yes, that was sarcasm), is when you get a pseudo-dashboard that contains 12 charts the size of quarters.

Crystal Xcelsius helps you avoid these problems by offering *dynamic visibility*, which allows you to control the visibility of a component, making the component appear or disappear based on certain predefined triggers. How does this help? Suppose you have three charts on your dashboard. With dynamic visibility, you can dynamically make two of the charts disappear, leaving one chart on which to focus and analyze. This functionality empowers you to control what your audience sees — and when they see it.

In this chapter, I walk you through the basics of dynamic visibility and look at some examples of how dynamic visibility can help achieve focus on the parts of your dashboard that are important.

Seeing the Basics of Dynamic Visibility

The notion of dynamic visibility tends to be confusing for new users of Crystal Xcelsius, primarily because no function exists in Excel that is directly similar to dynamic visibility. However, if you relate it to the Excel IF function, dynamic visibility is a fairly easy concept to grasp. That's right, dynamic visibility is essentially an IF...Then statement. In that light, if you're familiar with Excel's IF function, you should have no trouble understanding dynamic visibility.

Dynamic visibility in a nutshell

The Dynamic Visibility function is found on the Behavior tab of the Properties window, as shown in Figure 8-1. To get to the properties window, simply double-click on the component with which you are working.

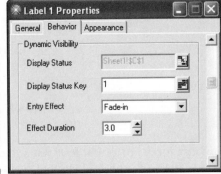

Figure 8-1:
Four
properties
make up the
Dynamic
Visibility
function.

You can think of the four properties in the Dynamic Visibility section as steps that Crystal Xcelsius takes to determine the correct course of action:

- ✔ **Display Status:** Crystal Xcelsius first determines whether the Display Status property references a cell. If the Display Status property does reference a cell, the component is automatically rendered not visible. The cell referenced in the Display Status property becomes the trigger cell, controlling visibility based on its value.

- ✔ **Display Status Key:** Crystal Xcelsius then evaluates the Display Status Key property and determines whether the value in that property matches the value in the trigger cell specified in the Display Status property. If it does, the component becomes visible; otherwise, it remains not visible.

- ✔ **Entry Effect:** After Crystal Xcelsius determines that the component should be visible, it checks the Entry Effect property to ascertain how the component will become visible. With this property, you can choose to have the component simply appear, fade into view, or grow into view. Think of this property as being similar to the animation options found in PowerPoint.

- ✔ **Effect Duration:** The Effect Duration property governs how long it takes the Entry Effect animation to complete.

In the example illustrated in Figure 8-1, Crystal Xcelsius evaluates the value of cell C1. If that value is equal to the Display Status Key, which is 1, the component becomes visible. Otherwise, the component remains not visible. When the component does become visible, the component fades in, based on the Entry Effect property; the fade animation takes three seconds to complete.

Applying basic dynamic visibility

Apply the basics in the preceding section to a simple example. In the `C:\Xcelsius Sample Files\Chapter 8\` directory, find and open the file named `BasicDynamicVisibilty.xlf`. As you can see in Figure 8-2, this is a very simple visual model that contains a Chart component and a Label component. The Label component simply describes the contents of the chart.

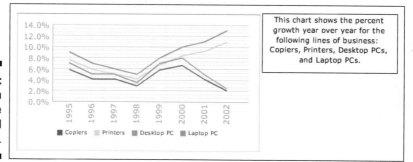

Figure 8-2:
Start with
a simple
visual
model.

The problem is that the Label component distracts focus from the chart. To remedy this, apply dynamic visibility to the Label component.

1. **Double-click the Label component to get to the Properties window.**

2. **Click the Behavior tab.**

3. **Click the Display Status Cell Reference icon, shown in Figure 8-3, to select the cell that is to be the trigger cell.**

   In this case, select cell A9.

   When choosing your trigger cell, make sure the cell you use is a blank cell that is not being used for any other purpose. Choosing a non-blank cell results in that cell being overwritten, which may cause errors in your dashboard.

Figure 8-3:
Use the
Display
Status
property to
choose the
cell that
triggers
visibility.

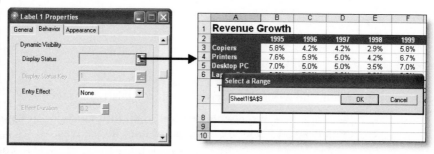

4. In the Display Status Key property highlighted in Figure 8-4, enter the value that triggers visibility.

In this case, leave the default value of 1.

Figure 8-4:
Enter the
value that
triggers
visibility.

The default Display Status Key is 1, but you can change this value to any combination of characters that meets your needs. Keep in mind two things when choosing a Display Status Key:

• The value you use can't exceed 255 characters in length.

• The Display Status Key is case-sensitive, so decide on a case state when using text.

Because the Entry Effect and Entry Duration properties are optional, skip these for now.

5. Click the Preview button on the taskbar to switch Preview mode.

When the visual model loads, Crystal Xcelsius renders the Label component not visible. The only way the Label component becomes visible is if you enter a 1 in cell A9, which you accomplish with a toggle selector.

6. Click the Preview button again to switch back to design mode.

In the category of Selector components are a group of components that I call *toggle selectors.* Included in this group are these components:

• Check Box

• Icon

• Toggle Button components

These components return one of two answers: a 1 or a 0. With that in mind, add a Check Box component to your visual model.

7. Activate the Components window, drill into the Selector category, and then drag a Check Box component onto the canvas.

8. **Double-click the Check Box component to activate the Properties window.**

9. **Type a title in the Title property.**

I named mine Show Chart Description, as shown in Figure 8-5.

Figure 8-5:
Give your
newly added
Check Box
component
a title.

Although you can change the Check Box component's Source Data property, it comes with default configurations that seldom need changing. This is true for all the toggle selectors.

To understand what I mean by this, click the ellipsis button, shown in Figure 8-6, to open the Source Data dialog box. As you can see, the default behavior for this Check Box component is to return a 0 if the check box is left unchecked and to return a 1 if the check box is checked. This is perfect for this running example because (refer to Step 4) you specified that the Display Status Key is 1.

Figure 8-6:
The default
behavior
for a Check
Box com-
ponent is to
return a 0 if
unchecked.

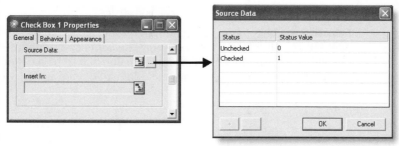

The only thing left to do is to make sure that the output for the Check Box component is delivered to the correct destination cell. By this, I mean the cell that you define as the trigger cell in Step 3 of the preceding steps (cell A9).

10. **Click the Insert In Cell Reference icon and select the destination range (A9), as shown in Figure 8-7.**

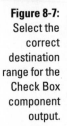

Figure 8-7:
Select the
correct
destination
range for the
Check Box
component
output.

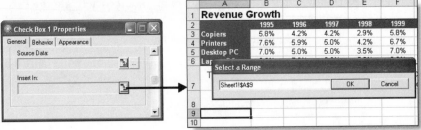

You're ready to go!

11. Click the Preview button on the taskbar to switch to Preview mode.

If all went well, your visual model should look similar to Figure 8-8 when it loads.

Figure 8-8:
Upon
loading
the visual
model, you
should see
a check
box next to
the chart.

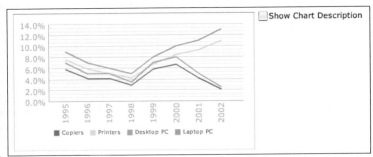

Selecting the check box, as demonstrated in Figure 8-9, forces the value of 1 to be written to cell A9, triggering the Label component to become visible. Removing the check forces the value of 0 to be written to the cell in A9, rendering the Label component invisible once again.

Figure 8-9:
Enabling the
check box
triggers
the Label
component
to become
visible.

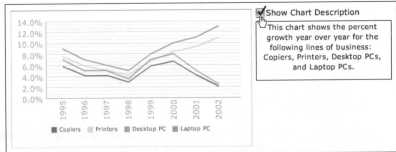

Implementing Menu-Based Visibility

Sometimes you may have so much information to present on your dashboards that you find yourself cramming and shrinking components just to make them fit on one page. Ugh; there are a few issues with doing this. Take a look at Figure 8-10 to see what I mean. First, it's very *busy* (crowded and crammed), making it difficult to know what to focus on first. Second, some of the charts are shrunk down so small that some users will likely find them difficult to read. Finally, so much real estate is taken by these charts that little room is available for any additional components that you may need to add.

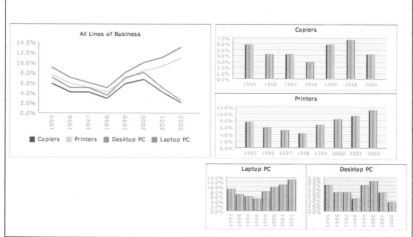

Figure 8-10: Cramming too much on one page creates a busy dashboard that's hard to read.

The quandary is how to give this dashboard a cleaner look and feel. You might have guessed: Dynamic visibility is the answer. Dynamic visibility not only allows you to control the number of components that are seen at once but also to stack components, which enables you to size the components appropriately without worrying about space issues.

What's the best way to implement dynamic visibility in this example? Well, one thing is for sure: Adding one check box for every chart won't look very clean. A more elegant solution is to use a Selector component to implement menu-based visibility. Work with the dashboard in the following example to walk through the process of implementing menu-based visibility.

1. **In the `C:\Xcelsius Sample Files\Chapter 8\` directory, find and open the file named `BasicDynamicVisibilty.xlf`.**

2. **Activate the Components window, drill into the Selector category, and then drag a Label Based Menu component onto the canvas.**

Label Based Menu components are ideal for implementing menu-based visibility. They are easy to configure, easy to customize, and have a clean, professional look.

3. Double-click the Label Based Menu component to activate the Properties window.

4. Click the ellipsis button next to the Labels property, as shown in Figure 8-11.

This activates the Labels dialog box.

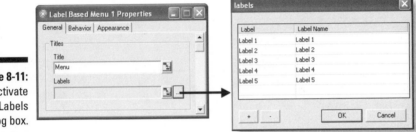

Figure 8-11:
Activate
the Labels
dialog box.

The idea here is that each label is dedicated to one chart. In this example, you have five charts that represent five different views of revenue growth by line of business:

- All Lines of Business

- Copiers

- Printers

- Laptops

- Desktops

To add or remove labels in the Labels dialog box, simply click the buttons that have the plus (+) or minus (–) signs, respectively.

5. Give each label a descriptive name, just as you see in Figure 8-12, and then click OK.

If all went well, you have a nice-looking menu strip that looks similar to the one shown in Figure 8-13.

After you create your menu of choices, configure the menu to return the desired values. For this scenario, you want the position number of the selected label to be returned. As you can see in Figure 8-14, each label has a position number. The position number of each label ultimately becomes the Display Status Key for the components they represent.

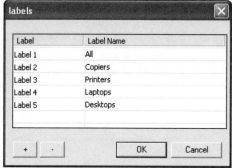

Figure 8-12:
Edit the
Label Name
column to
give your
menu labels
the appropri-
ate names.

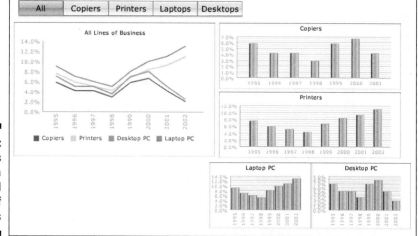

Figure 8-13:
Your edits
result in a
customized
menu of
choices

Given that you're using the position number as the output, the default selection of Position in the Insert Option property is perfect. You don't need to change this property.

Figure 8-14:
Each label
in your menu
has a posi-
tion number.

Position:	1	2	3	4	5
	All	Copiers	Printers	Laptops	Desktops

 6. **Click the Insert In Cell Reference icon and select a destination range (cell A9 is a fine choice), as shown in Figure 8-15.**

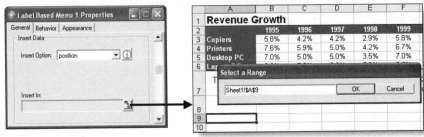

Figure 8-15:
Select a
destination
range for
the Label
Based Menu
component's
output.

At this point, your Label Based Menu component is ready to go. Take a moment to recap what this menu will do. When you make a selection, your component delivers the position number of the label you selected to cell A9. For example, if you select Copiers, the number 2 is delivered to cell A9 because it's the second label.

Time to apply dynamic visibility to each chart on your dashboard. Here's how:

1. **Double-click the Line chart titled All Lines of Business to activate the Properties window; then scroll to the Dynamic Visibility section of the Behavior tab.**

2. **Adjust the Display Status and Display Status Key properties, as shown in Figure 8-16.**

   Because the label for this chart is in position 1 of the menu, the Display Status Key is set to 1.

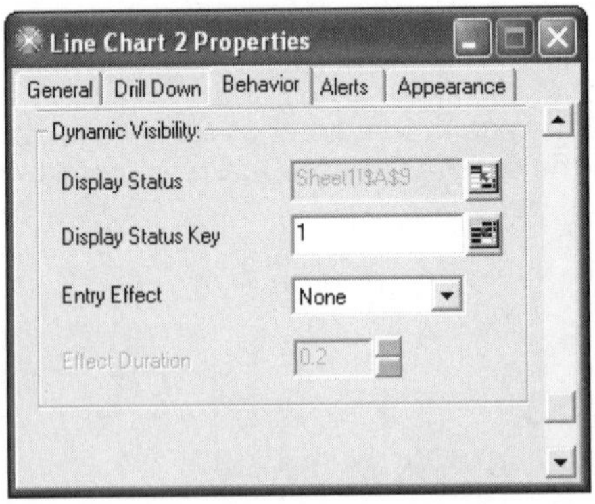

Figure 8-16:
Adjust the
Display
Status and
Display
Status Key
properties.

3. **Double-click the Line chart titled Copiers to activate the Properties window; then scroll to the Dynamic Visibility section of the Behavior tab.**

4. **Adjust the Display Status and Display Status Key properties, as shown in Figure 8-17.**

Because the label for this chart is in position 2 of the menu, the Display Status Key is set to 2.

Figure 8-17:
Adjust the Display Status and Display Status Key properties.

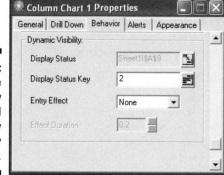

5. **Double-click the Line chart titled Printers to activate the Properties window; then scroll to the Dynamic Visibility section in the Behavior tab.**

6. **Adjust the Display Status and Display Status Key properties, as shown in Figure 8-18.**

Because the label for this chart is in position 3 of the menu, the Display Status Key is set to 3.

See a pattern? Each chart's Display Status Key is set to the position number of its corresponding label on the menu component.

Figure 8-18:
Adjust the Display Status and Display Status Key properties.

7. **Adjust the Display Status and Display Status Key properties for the remaining two charts.**

   Almost done! Finish with a little formatting to make all the charts the same size.

8. **Select all the charts at once and then choose Format➪Make Same Size➪ Both from the application menu.**

9. **Move all the charts to the center of the canvas, right on top of each other.**

   The fact that you can't see them all doesn't matter.

   After the formatting changes, your visual model should look similar to the one shown in Figure 8-19.

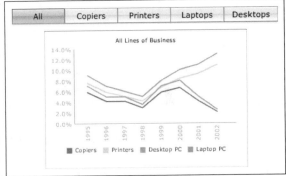

Figure 8-19: Format your charts to be the same size and centered in the middle of the canvas.

10. **Click the Preview button on the taskbar to switch to Preview mode.**

    Your dashboard has a slick, professional feel to it, allowing you to focus on the metrics you choose. Figure 8-20 demonstrates how clicking on a menu item causes the associated component to become visible.

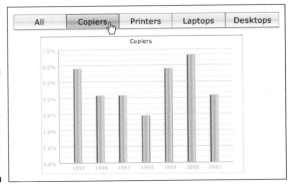

Figure 8-20: You successfully implemented menu-based visibility!

Chapter 9

Working with Crystal Xcelsius Professional

Those of you working with Crystal Xcelsius Professional get the benefit of additional components and functions that are not included in Crystal Xcelsius Standard. This chapter focuses on a few of these components in detail and also discusses how each of these can be used to enhance your visual models.

If you work with the standard version of Crystal Xcelsius, I suppose you could skip this chapter. However, let me suggest that you take a moment to look through the components highlighted here. Who knows? You might find a component in the professional version that does exactly what you need.

Creating Drill-Down Charts

The drill-down functionality found in Crystal Xcelsius Professional enables you to turn a chart into a Selector component. That is, your chart is still a graphical representation of data, but when you click a series in the chart, it delivers a predefined set of data to a destination range just like a Selector component would. This ability allows you to display summarized data by using a chart that drills into more detailed data based on selections made by the user. So the term *drill down* refers to the ability to analyze the detailed data that makes up an aggregate data point. To see what I mean, walk through an example.

In the `C:\Xcelsius Sample Files\Chapter 9\` directory, find the file named `DrillDownChart.xlf`. Open this visual model, which you can see in Figure 9-1: a very simple visual model that contains a Pie Chart component that is linked to a column containing the four-year average population for each age group in the U.S.

Figure 9-1:
Create a
drill-down
chart from
this visual
model.

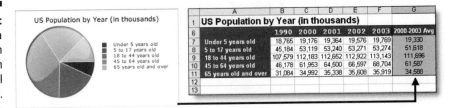

	A	B	C	D	E	F	G
1	**US Population by Year (in thousands)**						
6		1990	2000	2001	2002	2003	2000-2003 Avg
7	Under 5 years old	18,765	19,176	19,364	19,576	19,769	19,330
8	5 to 17 years old	45,184	53,119	53,240	53,271	53,274	51,618
9	18 to 44 years old	107,579	112,183	112,652	112,922	113,143	111,896
10	45 to 64 years old	46,178	61,953	64,500	66,597	68,704	61,587
11	65 years old and over	31,084	34,992	35,338	35,608	35,919	34,588
12							
13							

As you can see, the Excel model feeding this chart actually contains two distinct sets of data:

✔ A four-year average (2000–2003) as plotted in the Pie Chart component (left side)

✔ Detailed year information (right side) for 1990, 2000, 2001, 2002, and 2003

The question is how to represent the detailed year information. Sure, you could use a simple line chart and be done with it, but that would give you a dashboard that looks similar to the one shown in Figure 9-2.

Figure 9-2:
This
dashboard
inundates
the user
with sum-
mary and
detailed
data at
one time.

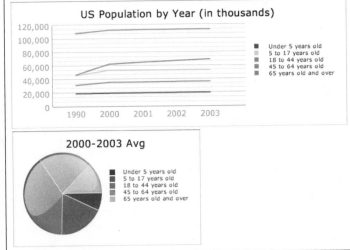

Displaying summary and detail information for the same data points at the same time can be confusing.

A better option is to activate the drill-down functionality in the pie chart, allowing the user to selectively see the detail for the desired age group.

1. **With the `DrillDownChart.xlf` visual model open, double-click the Pie Chart component to activate the Properties window.**

2. **Click the Drill Down tab.**

   The drill-down functionality is available with all chart types except for Radar charts and Area charts.

3. **Select the Enable Drill Down check box, as shown in Figure 9-3.**

   This enables the drill-down properties.

   As I mention earlier in this chapter, enabling the drill-down functionality basically turns your chart into a Selector component. If you've read earlier chapters in this book, the properties in the Chart Drill-Down Options section will likely look familiar.

4. **Select Rows as the Insert Value property.**

   This delivers a row of data to the destination range.

5. **Click the Insert Value In Cell Reference icon to select the destination range, as shown in Figure 9-3.**

   The destination range is the range where you want the selected value to be delivered.

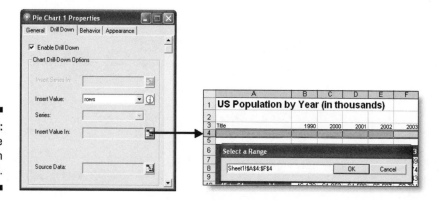

Figure 9-3:
Select the
destination
range.

6. Click the Source Data Cell Reference icon, shown in Figure 9-4, and select the cells that contain the data values you want delivered to the destination range.

At this point, you are ready to tie an Area chart to the range where the Pie Chart component delivers its data.

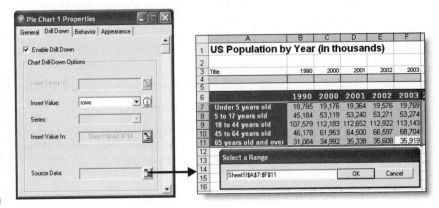

Figure 9-4:
Select the range of cells that contain the data values in your table.

7. Activate the Components window and then add an Area Chart component to the canvas.

Check out Chapter 5 for a refresher on how to add and configure a Chart component.

8. Double-click the Area Chart component to activate the Properties window.

9. In the Titles section of the Properties window, link the Chart Title property to cell A4, as shown in Figure 9-5.

This ensures that the chart title changes with each selected state.

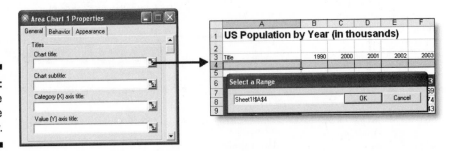

Figure 9-5:
Link the Chart Title property.

10. **Click the Data Range Cell Reference icon, shown in Figure 9-6, and select the source data for the Map component.**

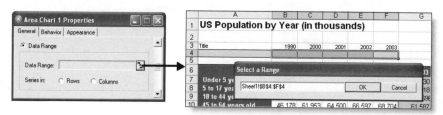

11. **In the Series section, click the Category Axis Labels Cell Reference icon, shown in Figure 9-7, and select the labels that will display in your chart's x axis.**

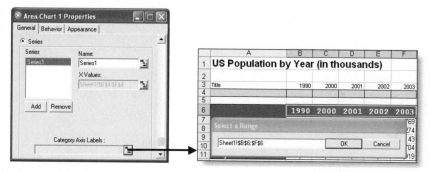

That's it! You successfully tied an Area chart to your drill-down pie chart.

Take a moment to examine what you set up in the preceding steps. When you click a slice of data in the Pie Chart component, the pie chart determines which slice was selected. It then matches the index position of that slice's linked cell to the source data range (cells A7:F11, in this example) in order to find the row of data that has the same index number. After the correct row is identified, that row of data is delivered to the destination range (cells A4:F11), which feeds your Area Chart component.

The net effect of all this activity is that you have a drill-down pie chart that allows you to select the summary data for an age group to see its more detailed yearly data in the Area chart. Switch to Preview mode (click the Preview button on the taskbar) to see your newly created drill-down chart in action; see Figure 9-8.

Figure 9-8:
A drill-down
pie chart
allows you
to selec-
tively see
detailed
data.

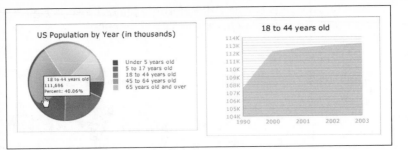

Using Accordion Menu Components

The *Accordion Menu component* is a special kind of selector that allows you to use two-level hierarchies in a slick menu that has fluid drilling capabilities. If you're working with two-level hierarchies, an Accordion Menu component is an ideal alternative to Filter components.

Check out Chapter 6 to get the skinny on Filter components. Some examples of two-level hierarchies that work well in Accordion Menu components are

- States and cities
- Regions and branches
- Managers and employees
- Lines of business and products

For example, the Excel model shown in Figure 9-9 is a perfect candidate for an accordion menu. Here, you have three datasets that represent revenue by state for their respective region.

Figure 9-9:
Accordion
Menu
components
are ideal
for Excel
models
structured
like this.

	A	B	C	D	E
1	**Region**				
2	**State**	$0	$0	$0	$0
3					
4		2000	2001	2002	2003
5	**New England**				
6	Connecticut	$30,086	$34,163	$61,762	$38,786
7	Maine	$59,120	$54,793	$52,752	$53,820
8	Massachusetts	$160,736	$89,708	$131,565	$139,795
9	New Hampshire	$207,623	$148,032	$233,050	$158,855
10	Rhode Island	$48,313	$49,190	$55,562	$34,432
11	Vermont	$34,743	$26,228	$29,632	$26,802
12					
13	**Mideast**				
14	Delaware	$70,914	$60,631	$83,037	$72,278
15	District of Columbia	$62,337	$77,214	$73,361	$76,789
16	Maryland	$33,542	$38,312	$41,595	$35,089
17	New Jersey	$50,443	$54,529	$37,002	$68,454
18	New York	$41,150	$26,215	$52,256	$27,090
19	Pennsylvania	$11,595	$14,502	$18,576	$13,406
20					
21	**Great Lakes**				
22	Illinois	$95,077	$137,889	$87,228	$145,384
23	Indiana	$181,675	$196,771	$207,505	$150,514
24	Michigan	$66,815	$35,347	$49,154	$51,090
25	Ohio	$20,569	$38,158	$25,408	$18,978
26	Wisconsin	$58,797	$61,708	$58,839	$56,622
27					

To get a better understanding of what an accordion menu does, build one based on this model. In the `C:\Xcelsius Sample Files\Chapter 9\` directory, find the file named `AccordionMenu.xlf` and open it. Note that this model contains a Line Chart component that is already configured. The goal here is to add an Accordion Menu component to feed the Line Chart component.

1. **Activate the Components window, drill into the Selectors category, and drag an Accordion Menu component onto the canvas.**

2. **Double-click the Accordion Menu component to activate the Properties window.**

   The main section you want to focus on is the Data section, as shown in Figure 9-10.

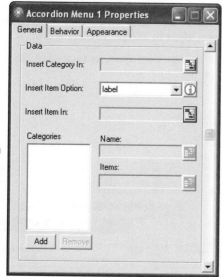

Figure 9-10: Define the basic functionality of the accordion menu.

Note the Categories property and the Add button below it. You add each category, or section of data, to your accordion menu one item at a time. In essence, you make multiple menus that are contained in a larger menu. Get started by adding your first category.

3. **Click the Add button below the Categories property.**

   Upon clicking the Add button, Category1 appears in the Name property.

4. **Rename the category by linking it to the first category name located in the Excel model.**

   As you can see in Figure 9-11, the first category is New England, so you would link to cell A5.

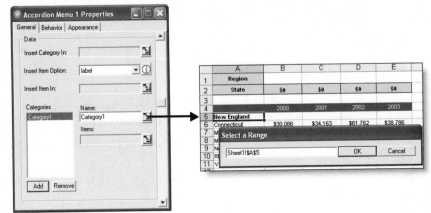

Figure 9-11:
Define the
name for
your newly
added
category.

5. **Click the Items Cell Reference icon and link to the range of cells that contain the data labels you want in the accordion menu.**

   Use the item's property to specify the items, or menu selections, under the category. This is shown in Figure 9-12.

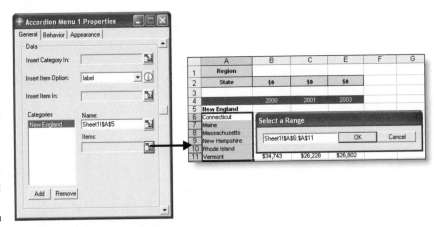

Figure 9-12:
Define the
items to
appear
under
the first
category.

6. **Adjust the Insert Item In property to Rows.**

   Because you're feeding a line chart in this scenario, you want an entire row of data delivered to the range that feeds the line chart.

7. **Click the Source Data Cell Reference icon, shown in Figure 9-13, and select the cells that contain the data values you want delivered to the destination range.**

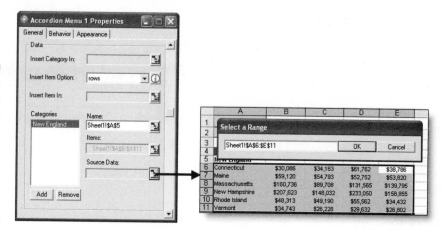

Figure 9-13:
Select the range of cells that contain the values to display in the line chart.

8. **Click the Insert Item In Cell Reference icon to select the destination range, as shown in Figure 9-14.**

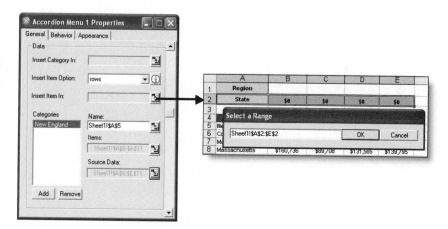

Figure 9-14:
Select the range or location where you want the selected value delivered.

9. **Click the Insert Category In Cell Reference icon, shown in Figure 9-15, to select the destination range of the category name.**

   This is used by the chart as a label.

   You successfully added and configured one category in your Accordion menu.

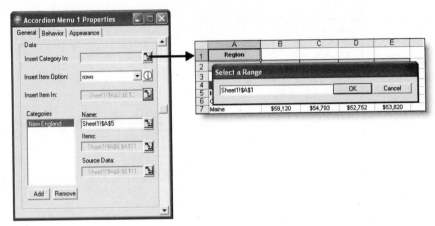

Figure 9-15:
Select the
destination
range for
the category
name.

Next, add the second category (Mideast, in this example).

10. **Click the Add button below the Categories property.**

11. **Repeat Steps 4– 9 for the Mideast category.**

When you're done, the Data section should look similar to Figure 9-16.

Finally, add the last category (Great Lakes).

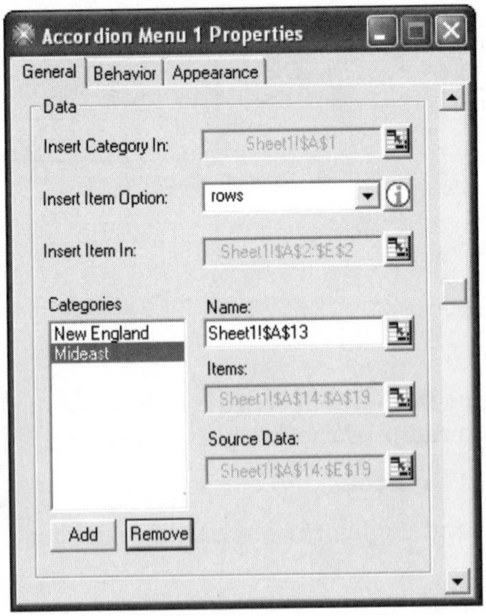

Figure 9-16:
Add and
configure
the second
category.

12. **Click the Add button below the Categories property.**

13. **Repeat Steps 4–9 for the Great Lakes category.**

    When you are done, the Data section should look similar to Figure 9-17.

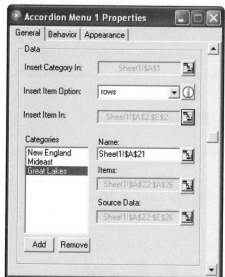

Figure 9-17:
Add and
configure
the second
category.

Believe it or not, that's it. Remember to configure a kind of mini-menu for each category you want included in the accordion menu. To see the end result, shown in Figure 9-18, click the Preview button on the taskbar to switch to Preview mode.

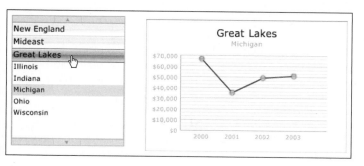

Figure 9-18:
Click the
category
name to drill
into the
available
menu items.

Persistent properties

When you add a category to an accordion menu, some of the properties in the Data section persist, although others do not. More precisely, the first three properties in the data section (Insert Category In, Insert Item Option, and Insert Item In) are component-specific. That is, these properties are set at the component level and persist; in fact, these properties cannot be different from category to category. Moreover, the last three properties in the Data section (Name, Items, and Source Data) are category specific: These properties are set independently at the category level.

Working with Picture Menus

Crystal Xcelsius Professional comes with two types of picture menus:

- ✔ **Fish-Eye Picture Menu:** A menu that allows users to choose from a set or group of icons or images. When one of the images is scrolled over, it is magnified for emphasis. This magnification looks kind of like that of a fish-eye lens, hence the name.

- ✔ **Sliding Picture Menu:** A menu that allows users to scroll through the available choices through the use of arrows. (The menu can also be configured to scroll as you move the mouse over it.)

These components are unique in that they allow you to make selections from a set of pictures instead of data labels. This stunning visualization gives your dashboard an extremely professional look and feel. In fact, these components are so stunning that you might be fooled into thinking they're more complicated than other menu components. However, they're just as easy to use as standard Selector components.

To get an idea of how picture menus work, open the `PictureMenus.xlf` visual model found in the `C:\Xcelsius Sample Files\Chapter 9\` directory. Upon opening this file, see the two components waiting to be fed by a Selector component. However, instead of using a standard Selector component, add a professional touch to your visual model by using the Fish-Eye Picture Menu.

The steps and techniques used to configure a Fish-Eye Picture Menu are the same for a Sliding Picture Menu. So what is the difference between the two? The difference is that with the Sliding Picture Menu, you can format the component to display only a few pictures (menu items) at a time. Then at run-time, you can use arrows to scroll through the pictures. This is not true with the Fish-Eye Menu, however. By default, the Fish-Eye Menu displays all the pictures it contains. This means that if you have more than eight or so menu items, you'll have a hard time trying to fit them all onto your visual model with a Fish-Eye Menu because of its default behavior. Play it safe: If you have more than eight menu items, you should consider using a Sliding Picture Menu component.

1. **Activate the Components window, drill into the Selectors category, and then drag a Fish-Eye Picture Menu component onto the canvas.**

2. **Double-click the Fish-Eye Picture Menu to activate the Properties window.**

On the General tab of the Properties window are three main sections:

- *Titles:* The properties in this section manage the names and labels in the picture menu.

- *Image Files:* The properties in this section define the images that are to be used in the picture menu.

- *Insert Data:* The properties in this section link the images in the picture menu to the data in the Excel model.

Start with the Image Files section.

Embedded vs URL

How do you decide whether to embed your images or to link them to a URL? To answer that, consider the differences between the two methods.

Embed: When an image is embedded, Crystal Xcelsius literally imports its own local copy of the file into the XLF file. After the file is imported, the original file is no longer accessed or used in the model. This has two major advantages:

✔ Because the image files are stored within the XLF file, your visual model can be distributed as a single file.

✔ Your visual model isn't dependent on the availability of external files that might change or become unavailable unexpectedly.

URL: When using URLs to feed images to your visual model, the visual model goes out at run-time and loads the image files as needed. Keep in mind that the URL you use doesn't necessarily have to be on the Internet; it can point to a particular path on your hard drive. Using the URL option also has its advantages.

Because external files are loaded only when necessary, you don't experience the performance slowdown you would when embedding many large image files into the visual model. Also, because the image files are not part of the visual model, there is no need to re-distribute the .xlf file when the image files change.

The bottom line is this. Embedding your image files is typically a great choice if you are working with a small number of image files that won't need to be updated regularly. Using URL links is ideal when you are working with lots of image files that will change frequently.

Crystal Xcelsius gives you two methods of feeding images to a picture menu:

- ✔ Embed the images into the visual model.
- ✔ Point the picture menu to specific URLs where the images reside.

In this example, embed your images by importing them directly into your visual model.

1. **In the Image Files section, enable the Embedded radio button and then click the Import button.**

   This activates the Import Thumbnail dialog box, as shown in Figure 9-19.

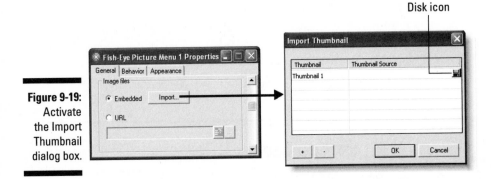

Figure 9-19:
Activate
the Import
Thumbnail
dialog box.

2. **Click the disk icon to import the first image, find the image in the Open dialog box that opens (shown in Figure 9-20), and then click the Open button.**

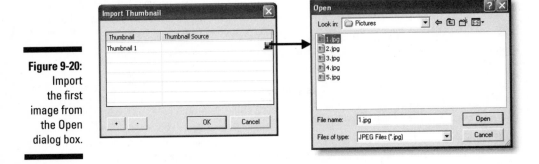

Figure 9-20:
Import
the first
image from
the Open
dialog box.

The order in which you import the image files matters. The first image file you import is the first image in your picture menu. The second image file you import is the second image file in the picture menu; and so on. Given this pattern, give some thought on how you want to present your images and how they will link to the data in your visual model. I generally like to number my image files after I determine their order but before I import them. This way, I can easily import them in the correct order without confusion. In this example, all the image files you will use are found in the `C:\Xcelsius Sample Files\Chapter 9\Pictures` directory.

3. **In the Import Thumbnail dialog box, click the button with the plus (+) symbol to add another thumbnail entry, and then select your second image, as shown in Figure 9-21.**

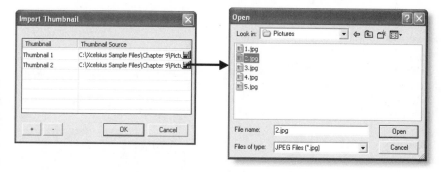

Figure 9-21:
Import your
second
image.

4. **Continue this process until you add all the image files in order.**

   This example uses five files. When you finish importing, click the OK button to finalize.

   You should now be able to see the imported images in the Fish-Eye Picture Menu. Next, define the labels for these images so that when clicked, each image activates its own label.

5. **Click the Cell Reference icon for the Labels property, shown in Figure 9-22, and select the range of cells that contain the labels for the picture menu.**

   The order of the labels you assign corresponds to the position of the images. This means that the first label is assigned to the first image, the second label to the second image, and so on.

   The pictures are set up and ready to be given some functionality. This functionality comes from the Insert Data section. *Hint:* This section should look very familiar to you if you've read earlier chapters about Selector components.

Figure 9-22:
Assign
labels to
the newly
imported
images.

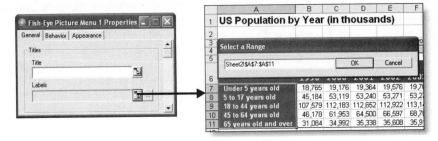

6. **Adjust the Insert Option property to Rows.**

7. **Click the Source Data Cell Reference icon, shown in Figure 9-23, and select the valid dataset.**

Figure 9-23:
Select the
range of
cells con-
taining the
values to be
delivered to
the destina-
tion range.

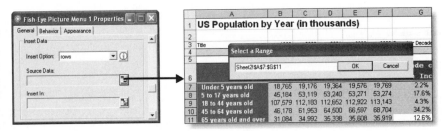

8. **Click the Insert In Cell Reference icon to select the destination range, as shown in Figure 9-24.**

In this scenario, you feed cells A4:G4.

Figure 9-24:
Select
where you
want the
selected
values
delivered.

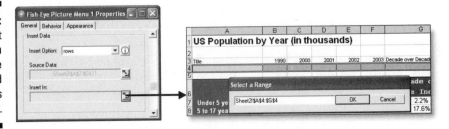

9. **Click the Preview button on the taskbar to switch to Preview mode.**

The result shown in Figure 9-25 doesn't do the live action visual model justice. Here's what you can't see: When you move the mouse over each item in the menu, the picture is magnified for emphasis. Clicking the picture then tells the component to deliver data to the cells that feed the two other components. This gives you an extremely slick presentation.

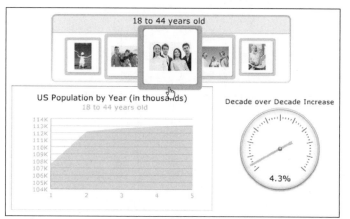

Figure 9-25: The Fish-Eye Picture Menu in action.

Using Interactive Calendar Components

The *Interactive Calendar component* is a unique component that gives you the ability to incorporate data selection into your visual model. When using this tool, a user can select a date, and the calendar outputs the selected date into a single cell.

This ability might not sound very useful, but combining this functionality with Excel functions such as VLOOKUP can lead to some very powerful visual models that are ideal for reporting and presenting daily information. VLOOKUP is a function in Excel that allows you to search and find data based on a value comparison between two tables.

If you're not familiar with advanced Excel formulas such as VLOOKUP, pick up a copy of *Excel Formulas and Functions For Dummies* (Ken Bluttman and Peter Aitken, Wiley). This book offers a solid understanding of all the functions in Excel.

Before you dive deeper into the Interactive Calendar component, take a look at the typical Excel model, which is ideal for use with the Interactive Calendar component. Go to the `C:\Xcelsius Sample Files\Chapter 9` directory and open the Excel model named `CalendarComponent.xls`.

As you can see in Figure 9-26, this particular model is designed to show the number of units sold per day by each sales rep. The data table starts on row 5 and contains data for each day, starting 8/1/2005 and ending 9/30/2005.

	A	B	C	D	E	F	G
1	**Units Sold Per Day**						
2	8/1/2005	66	34	72	96	4	74
4							
5	Day	Mike	Danny	Mark	Kathy	Matt	Robert
6	8/1/2005	66	34	72	96	4	74
7	8/2/2005	62	95	55	8	97	60
8	8/3/2005	92	99	64	6	96	96
9	8/4/2005	61	54	96	33	84	72
10	8/5/2005	75	85	69	72	0	95
11	8/6/2005	18	34	69	12	1	7
12	8/7/2005	45	88	63	95	96	46
13	8/8/2005	19	5	94	74	98	99
14	8/9/2005	54	23	23	75	4	3
15	8/10/2005	47	64	33	46	56	24
16	8/11/2005	30	10	31	4	37	68
17	8/12/2005	84	3	54	57	79	3
18	8/13/2005	15	11	83	55	66	73
19	8/14/2005	15	78	57	92	28	22
20	8/15/2005	40	3	16	21	19	90
21	8/16/2005	35	54	42	19	78	56

Figure 9-26: This Excel model contains daily sales data for each rep.

Place your cursor in cell B2, as shown in Figure 9-27, and look at the formula bar to see the VLOOKUP formula in cell B2. This particular formula looks up the date found in cell A2 and retrieves that date's second data point. Cell C2 has a VLOOKUP formula that looks up the data found in cell A2 and retrieves the *third* data point. This continues for cells D2, E2, F2, and G2.

B2		f_x	=VLOOKUP($A$2,$A$6:$G$66,2,FALSE)				
	A	B	C	D	E	F	G
1	**Units Sold Per Day**						
2	8/1/2005	66	34	72	96	4	74
4							
5	Day	Mike	Danny	Mark	Kathy	Matt	Robert
6	8/1/2005	66	34	72	96	4	74
7	8/2/2005	62	95	55	8	97	60
8	8/3/2005	92	99	64	6	96	96
9	8/4/2005	61	54	96	33	84	72
10	8/5/2005	75	85	69	72	0	95
11	8/6/2005	18	34	69	12	1	7
12	8/7/2005	45	88	63	95	96	46
13	8/8/2005	19	5	94	74	98	99
14	8/9/2005	54	23	23	75	4	3
15	8/10/2005	47	64	33	46	56	24
16	8/11/2005	30	10	31	4	37	68
17	8/12/2005	84	3	54	57	79	3
18	8/13/2005	15	11	83	55	66	73
19	8/14/2005	15	78	57	92	28	22
20	8/15/2005	40	3	16	21	19	90
21	8/16/2005	35	54	42	19	78	56

Figure 9-27: Use VLOOKUP formulas to retrieve the daily information for the dates.

The source for the date in cell A2 is where the Interactive Calendar component comes in. Each time a user selects a date in the Calendar component, the component inputs that date in cell A2. The data in cells B2:G2 change as a result of the VLOOKUP formulas.

Time to build your first Interactive Calendar component.

1. **Open the `PictureMenus.xlf` visual model found in the `C:\Xcelsius Sample Files\Chapter 9\` directory.**

   A Column Chart component is set up and ready to go. The idea here is to add an Interactive Calendar component that interacts with the chart, allowing you to use the calendar to select the data that is displayed.

2. **Activate the Components window, drill into the Other category, and then drag an Interactive Calendar component onto the canvas.**

3. **Double-click the Interactive Calendar component to activate the Properties window.**

   On the General tab, note the Insert Data section, as shown in Figure 9-28. As with other Selector components, this section defines the destination range where data values are to be delivered. The difference is that the Calendar component outputs only those values related to the date that was selected: for example, Year, Month, Date, and Day. You can use any or all of these properties to deliver various types of data to different cells in your Excel model.

   In this example, you need to enter a date only into cell A1 of your Excel model.

4. **Adjust the Insert Option property to Date.**

5. **Click the Insert Source Data In Cell Reference icon to select the destination range, as shown in Figure 9-28.**

   In this scenario, you feed cell A1.

Figure 9-28:
Deliver the
selected
date to
cell A1.

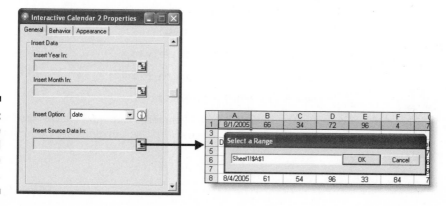

Each property in the Insert Data section must be the only one dedicated to a particular cell; otherwise, the component will fail to deliver data. For example, if you set the Insert Month In property to cell A1 and then set the Insert Source Data In property to the same cell, no data is delivered.

Move to the Behavior tab of the Properties window and configure the behavior of the Calendar component.

6. Click the Behavior tab.

Besides setting up dynamic visibility, this tab is dedicated to ensuring that only valid dates are available in the Calendar control. The two sections to focus on in this example are

- *Default Date:* The properties found in the Default Date section define the date that is initially activated in the Calendar component when the visual model is loaded.

- *Calendar Limits:* The properties found in the Calendar Limits section allow you to specify how far into the future or past a user can select data.

7. In the Default Date section, choose to use the current date or a custom date.

- *Use Current Date:* Using this option causes the calendar to load with the current system date as the selected starting date. This means that the starting date for the calendar will change from day to day to reflect the current day's date.

- *Use Custom Date:* Using this option allows you to specify the exact date on which the calendar should start. This means that the calendar will load with the same starting date no matter what.

In this example, the data in the Excel model spans from 8/1/2005 to 9/30/2005. Therefore, you will want the Calendar component to automatically open to August 1, 2005, when the visual model loads. So, click the Use Custom Date radio button to enable the Default Month, Default Year, and Default Day properties.

8. Set the Default Date parameters.

For this example, set the following.

- *Default Month:* Set this property to 8.

- *Default Year:* Set this property to 2005.

- *Default Day:* Set this property to 1.

To enable the Default Date parameters, you must choose the Use Custom Date radio button. If you choose the Use Current Date radio button, these properties remain disabled.

Figure 9-29 demonstrates these changes.

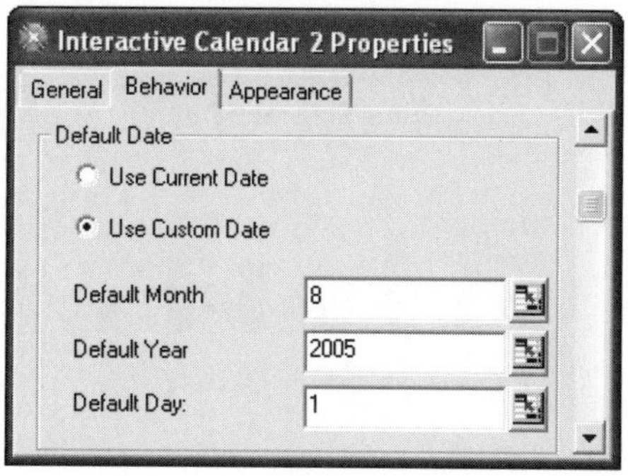

Figure 9-29: Define the starting date for the Calendar component.

Set the Calendar Limits properties in order to keep your users from clicking a date that does not exist in your source data. Remember that the data in this Excel model spans from 8/1/2005 to 9/30/2005. That means that your calendar should make only August and September available to the user.

9. **In the Calendar Limits section, enable (select) the Use Calendar Limits check box to activate its properties.**

10. **Set the Start Month and Start Year dates.**

    In this example, set the Start Month to 8 and the Start Year to 2005.

11. **Set the End Month and End Year dates.**

    In this example, set the End Month to 9 and the End Year to 2005.

    When you're done, the Calendar Limits section should look like Figure 9-30.

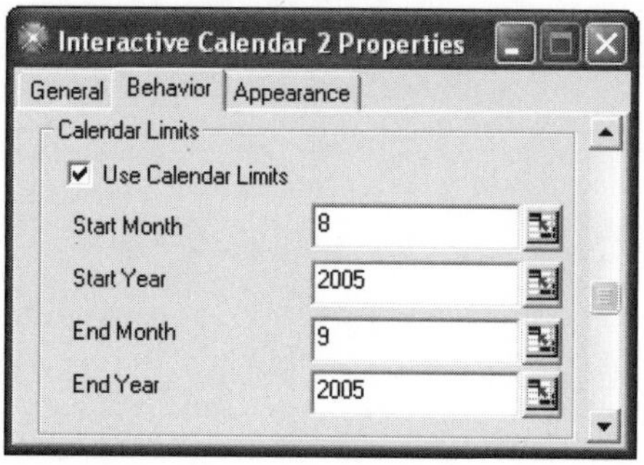

Figure 9-30: Calendar limits ensure that only certain dates are available.

Switch to Preview mode (click the Preview button on the taskbar) to see your Interactive Calendar in action. See Figure 9-31.

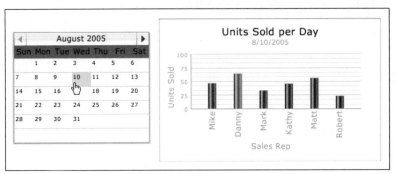

Figure 9-31:
You built
your first
interactive
calendar!

Part IV

Wrapping Things Up

In this part . . .

This section focuses on the last two actions a user would take when wrapping up the production of a dashboard: formatting and distribution. Chapter 10 focuses on the functions and utilities that enable you to show off your artistic side and add your own style to your visual models. In Chapter 11, I show you just how easy it is to take your dashboards to market, and I share a few other tricks on how to share the data in a visual model.

Chapter 10

Adding Style and Personality to Your Dashboards

....

In This Chapter

▶ Using the formatting functions

▶ Aligning and grouping components

▶ Using the Art & Backgrounds components

▶ Working with the Object Browser

▶ Employing templates

▶ Applying styles and skins

....

Crystal Xcelsius has made business intelligence sexy again. The dazzling visualizations and Flash-based components alone are enough to create dashboards that are both visually appealing and informative. But as you can read here, Crystal Xcelsius also comes with a whole host of additional functions and utilities that enable you to show off your artistic side and add flair to your visual models. In this chapter, I take a closer look at some of the tools that allow you to add your own style to your visual models. I also provide you with several techniques that will help you format your dashboards with ease.

Employing the Five Formatting Must-Haves

When building basic visual models that use just a few components, the Crystal Xcelsius formatting functions are rarely needed; you simply drag the components where you need them. However, more elaborate visual models

that use many overlapping components can be a nightmare to deal with —
that is, unless you know about the five formatting must-haves:

- ✔ Copy and Paste
- ✔ The Properties window
- ✔ Alignment and positioning
- ✔ Grouping
- ✔ The Object Browser

As I describe in the following sections, you can use these tools and functions
to help you conquer the more frustrating aspects of positioning, configuring,
and formatting multiple components. Knowing these tools and functions
saves you lots of time and heartache when trying to format your dashboard.

Before exploring the five must-haves of formatting, open the `Formatting`
`Example.xlf` visual model in the `C:\Xcelsius Sample Files\Chapter`
`10\` directory. (See Figure 10-1.) Use this file in the examples in the next few
sections.

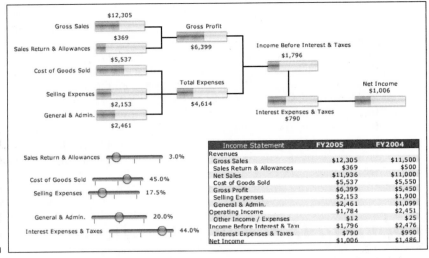

Figure 10-1:
The For-
matting
Example.
xlf visual
model.

Using Copy and Paste

That's right, your stalwart friends Copy and Paste are available at your
command. Trust me: The easiest way to format new components is to avoid
starting from scratch. That is to say, leverage the work you already did on
previous components. To see what I mean, check out the Gross Sales Progress
Bar component from the example file, which has already been configured and
formatted. Here's how easy it is to copy and paste:

1. **Right-click the Gross Sales Progress Bar component and choose Copy.**

2. **Right-click the canvas and choose Paste.**

   You see a Progress Bar component that is identical to the one you copied; down to the last property. This means that every aspect of the component persists, including the formatting. You can imagine how this would come in handy when the need arises for many of the same type of component.

Using the Properties window

You can use the Properties window to simultaneously edit multiple components. This allows you to apply formatting changes such as color schemes, font size, and alerts to more than one component at a time, saving you tons of time and effort. Here's how:

1. **Select all five of the Horizontal Slider components at the bottom of the visual model.**

2. **Activate the Properties window by double-clicking the selection.**

   (Optional) You can also right-click the selection and then choose Properties.

   The Properties window activates just as though you were working with only one Horizontal Slider component. Any changes you make are applied to all five components.

Keep in mind a few things when using this technique:

✔ If you're working with components of the same type, you can edit any property that is specific to that component type. For example, suppose you are working with five Column Chart components. You can set the Appearance properties of all five of your Column Chart components at one time.

✔ If you're working with a selection of components of mixed types or groups, the editable properties are limited to the properties that control dynamic visibility.

Using the alignment and position functions

In Crystal Xcelsius, you can easily get sucked into spending hours lining up the edges of the components in a visual model. *Hint:* Avoid the meticulous adjusting of components by using the built-in alignment and position functions found under Format in the main menu. These functions are Align, Make Same Size, Space Evenly, and Center in Document.

The Align functions

Use the Align functions to automatically align the boundaries of a selected group of components, helping you achieve symmetry and flushness without burning out your eyes doing this manually. You can get to these functions by choosing Format⇨Align from the main menu. The six Align functions are

- **Left:** Aligns the horizontal position of the selected objects, putting the left edges in line with the first selected object

- **Right:** Aligns the horizontal position of the selected objects, putting the right edges in line with the first selected object

- **Top:** Aligns the vertical position of the selected objects, putting the top edges in line with the first selected object

- **Bottom:** Aligns the vertical position of the selected objects, putting the bottom edges in line with the first selected object

- **Center Horizontal:** Aligns the horizontal position of the selected objects, putting the horizontal center in line with the first selected object

- **Center Vertical:** Aligns the vertical position of the selected objects, putting the vertical center in line with the first selected object

The Make Same Size functions

Use the Make Same Size functions to make the components in a selected group the same size based on a specified dimension. The Make Same Size functions are found under Format⇨Make Same Size in the main menu.

- **Width:** Makes the width of selected objects the same as the first selected object

- **Height:** Makes the height of selected objects the same as the first selected object

- **Both:** Makes both the width and the height of selected objects the same as the first selected object

---

First selected objects

The *first selected object* refers to the component in the selected group that is listed first in the Object Browser. (Read more about the Object Browser in the upcoming section.) Components, by default, are listed in the Object Browser in the order of placement onto the canvas. Therefore, the component in the selected group that's placed onto the canvas first is typically considered the first selected object. This is the component that is used as the standard for any alignment and sizing.

The Space Evenly functions

The Space Evenly functions enable you to easily distribute the selected group of components across or down in an evenly spaced fashion. These functions can be found under Format⇨Space Evenly in the main menu.

- ✔ **Across:** Spaces objects evenly between the leftmost and rightmost objects
- ✔ **Down:** Spaces objects evenly between the topmost and bottommost objects

The Center in Document functions

The Center in Document functions allow you to center a selected group of components to the middle of the canvas. These functions can be found under Format⇨Center in Document in the main menu.

- ✔ **Vertical:** Aligns the middle of the selected objects to an invisible vertical line in the middle of the canvas
- ✔ **Horizontal:** Aligns the middle of the selected objects to an invisible horizontal line in the middle of the canvas
- ✔ **Both:** Aligns the middle of the selected objects to both the imaginary vertical and imaginary horizontal lines in the middle of the canvas

Try aligning a few of the components in your visual model.

1. **Select the components you want to align.**

   In the sample file example (`FormattingExample.xlf`), the horizontal sliders are a mess, so select all five of the Horizontal Slider components at the bottom of the visual model.

2. **From the main menu, choose your first alignment goal.**

   For this example, I start with a left alignment by choosing Format⇨ Align⇨Left.

3. **From the main menu, choose your next alignment goal.**

   For this example, I use a spacing alignment adjustment by choosing Format⇨Space Evenly⇨Down.

4. **From the main menu, choose your next alignment goal.**

   For this example, I use a sizing alignment adjustment by choosing Format⇨Make Same Size⇨Both.

   As you can see in the before-and-after illustration in Figure 10-2, it took four easy actions to get these sliders as aligned as can be.

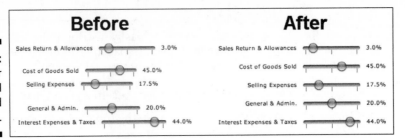

Figure 10-2:
Give your
visual model
a polished
look.

Using the Grouping function

Grouping is exactly what it sounds like: a way for you to join selected components into one group. After components are grouped, you can move them, align them, and adjust them, just as though they were one component. In fact, you can take any action you would normally take on a single component with the exception of changing individual component properties.

To demonstrate the benefits of grouping, take a look at the metric tree in your visual model. Every object you see in this tree is a separate component, right down to the horizontal and vertical lines that make up the branches. Here's the sweet stuff: If you need to move the entire tree, using the built-in Grouping function means that you don't have to move each component separately. Here's how to group components:

1. **Select all the components that you want to group.**

   In this example, select all the components that make up the metric tree, as shown in Figure 10-3.You can do this by holding down the control (Ctrl) key on your keyboard as you select each component.

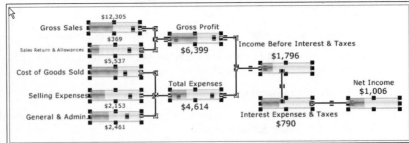

Figure 10-3:
Select the
components
you want
to group.

2. From the main menu, choose Format➪Group.

At this point, you can move your newly created group as needed without fear of leaving rogue components behind. In addition, you can double-click the newly created group and set up dynamic visibility, allowing you to control the visibility of all the components in the metric tree as one group.

Feel free to review Chapter 8 for a refresher on dynamic visibility.

To ungroup components, simply select the group and then choose Format➪ Ungroup from the main menu. You can also group and ungroup components by right-clicking the selected components or by using the Group components and Ungroup components buttons on the application toolbar, respectively.

Using the Object Browser

Use the Object Browser to manage the components in your visual model from a central location. This tool is extremely handy when you work with a visual model that contains many components. You can easily select and work with the components in your visual model without the need to move, ungroup, or risk accidentally damaging components.

Open the Object Browser window, shown in Figure 10-4, by choosing View➪ Object Browser Window from the main menu.

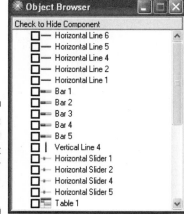

Figure 10-4:
Use the Object Browser to manage components.

The Object Browser is opened by default each time you start Crystal Xcelsius.

Here are the basics of the Object Browser:

- **Each component is assigned a default browsing name when placed on the canvas.** This is the name that appears in the title bar of the Properties window as well as the entry in the Object Browser. For an example, find the Horizontal Slider 1 entry in the Object Browser and click it, as shown in Figure 10-5. The component named Horizontal Slider 1 is now selected.

- **Double-clicking an entry activates the Properties window for that component.** This functionality might sound a little mundane, but believe me, this comes in very handy when you're trying to find a component that's buried underneath dozens of other components.

- **Holding down the Ctrl key on your keyboard allows you to make a multiple selection.**

- **Right-clicking selected entries in the Object Browser and then clicking Group allows you to group the selected components.**

   A cool thing about the Object Browser is that it represents grouped components with a folder that contains all the components in that group. Figure 10-6 demonstrates that you can click a group's folder to see its contents.

   Grouping in the Object Browser allows you to pinpoint and group multiple components without having to rummage through your visual model.

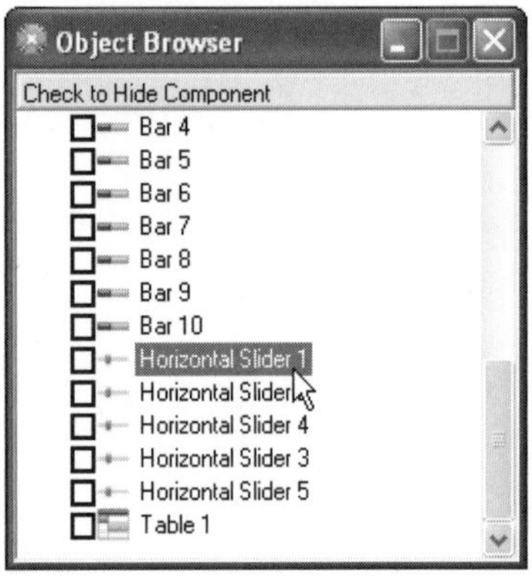

Figure 10-5:
Select components directly from the Object Browser.

Object Browser

Check to Hide Component
- Bar 4
- Bar 5
- Bar 6
- Bar 7
- Bar 8
- Bar 9
- Bar 10
- Horizontal Slider 1
- Horizontal Slider
- Horizontal Slider 4
- Horizontal Slider 3
- Horizontal Slider 5
- Table 1

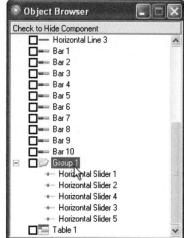

Figure 10-6:
Grouped
components
are clus-
tered in
a folder.

Click a named group, wait two seconds, and then click it again. This allows you to edit the name of the group by simply typing the new name. Rename the group as you wish; see Figure 10-7.

✔ **To delete a component, right-click the entry in the Object Browser and then choose Delete.** This functionality gives you an easy way to pinpoint and delete unneeded components via the Object Browser.

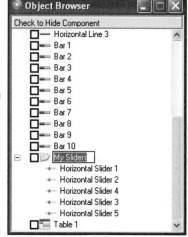

Figure 10-7:
Rename any
entry in the
Object
Browser
by slowly
clicking
the entry.

✔ **Hide a component by using the check boxes made available in the Object Browser.** This allows you to see and work with components that may be buried beneath other components. For example, place a check in the check box next to the My Sliders group, shown in Figure 10-8, to hide the top layers — sliders in the example.

This is not the same as dynamic visibility. If you switch to Preview mode, the sliders are indeed visible. Rather, enabling this component's check box makes the sliders invisible only in design mode. Why would you want to do that? It all goes back to being able to manage components in complex visual models. When you work with a visual model that contains many layers of components, you can temporarily hide the top layers by using the check boxes made available in the Object Browser, allowing you to see and work with the bottom layers.

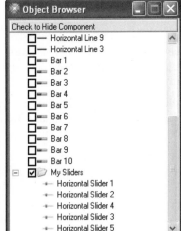

Figure 10-8: Hide components via the Object Browser.

Adding Style and Personality

In this section, I show you how tools such as the Art & Background components and Global Styles can make it easy to add style and personality to your dashboards.

To see what I mean, open the `NationalPark.xlf` visual model from the `C:\Xcelsius Sample Files\Chapter 10\` directory. When it opens, switch to Preview mode to see the dashboard shown in Figure 10-9. This dashboard allows you to select a state and then select a national park in that state. Then the visitor stats for that park can be seen in the chart on the right. This presentation is rather bland. When you open a visual model, the design and layout should suggest the nature of the information it contains, and this visual model doesn't do that.

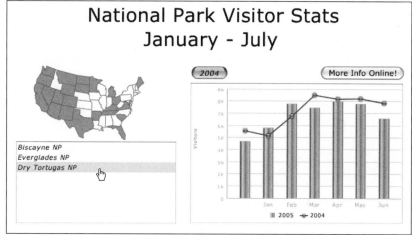

Figure 10-9: This dashboard needs a little personality.

To add some personality to a dashboard, start by switching to design mode.

Using Art & Backgrounds components

As you can see in Figure 10-10, the Art & Backgrounds category consists of a mix of backgrounds and formatting objects that can be used to improve the layout and design of your visual models. With these components, you can give each of your visual models a look that is professional looking and unique.

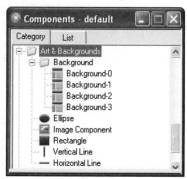

Figure 10-10: Use these components to help design your visual models.

Follow along with the `NationalPark.xlf` visual model as I show you how to change the look and feel of a dashboard's background:

1. **Activate the Components window, drill into the Art & Backgrounds category, and then drill into the Backgrounds folder.**

2. **Drag a Background component onto the canvas.**

   For this example, use the Background-3 component.

3. **Right-click the Background component you want and then choose Send To Back, as shown in Figure 10-11.**

Cut	Ctrl+X
Copy	Ctrl+C
Paste	Ctrl+V
Delete	Del
Properties...	Alt+Enter
Bring To Front	Ctrl+Plus
Send To Back	Ctrl+Minus
Bring Forward	+
Send Back	-
Group	
Ungroup	

Figure 10-11: Place the background behind the other components.

Because this component is meant to be a background, make sure to set it to fall behind all the other components on the canvas by using the Send To Back function.

(Optional) You can also call the Send To Back function by choosing Format⇨Send to Back from the main menu.

4. **Adjust the size and position of the background to encapsulate the components you want to show. You can do this by clicking on the bounding box handles and dragging them until the background is the appropriate size.**

   In this example, you want the Map and List Box components to appear on top of the new background, as shown in Figure 10-12. Encapsulating the selectors on the left calls attention to these components and designates them as a group.

5. **Drag another Background component onto the canvas.**

   Try using Background-0. This background will encapsulate the Chart component, separating it from the other parts of the dashboard.

   For this example, drag the Background-0 component onto the canvas.

6. **Right-click the newly added second Background component and choose Send To Back.**

   Try using Background-0.

7. **Adjust the size and position of the background to encapsulate the components you want to show.**

   In this example, you want to adjust the size and position of the background to encapsulate the Chart and Toggle components, as shown in Figure 10-12, to designate them as a group.

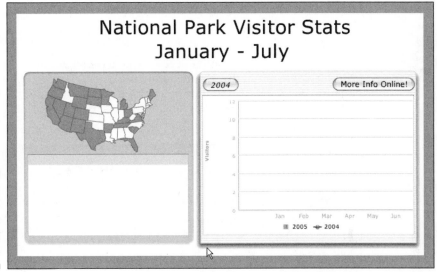

Figure 10-12:
Use backgrounds to highlight groups.

You can also add an image to your visual model to help identify the nature of the data displayed. You can add an image to your dashboard by using the Image component (found in the Art & Backgrounds category). With an Image component, you can add a picture or a logo that portrays the nature of the data being presented. Continuing with the sample file, follow along to see how to add a logo.

1. **Drag an Art element onto the canvas and double-click it to open its Properties window.**

   For this example, I use an Image Component element.

2. **On the General tab of the Properties window, click the Import button.**

3. **From the Open dialog box that opens, browse to and choose the image you want; then click OK.**

   I select the NPSLogo.jpg image. See Figure 10-13. You can find this image in the C:\Xcelsius Sample Files\Chapter 10\ directory.

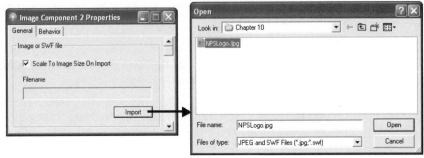

Figure 10-13:
Import the
desired
image from
the Open
dialog box.

The Image component can import only JPEG images or SWF files.

4. **Adjust the size and position of the imported image file so that it sits where you want in the visual model; see the added logo (upper left in Figure 10-14. You can do this by clicking on the bounding box handles and dragging them until the background is the appropriate size.**

Figure 10-14:
Use images
to enhance
the data
presented.

Another way to enhance your visual model with an art element is to add an accent border to bring out the components a bit. Here's how:

1. **Activate the Components window, drill into the Art & Backgrounds category, and drag a Rectangle component onto the canvas.**

2. **Expand the Rectangle component to the size you want by clicking and dragging.**

In Figure 10-15, I added a border and enlarged it to surround all the elements on the canvas.

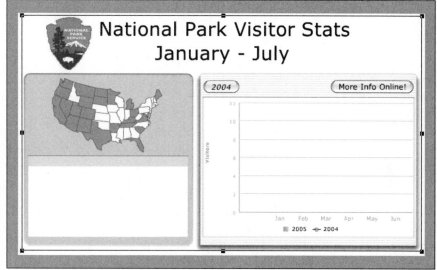

Figure 10-15:
Use the
Rectangle
component
to add a
border to
your visual
model.

3. **Double-click the Rectangle component and adjust the border properties you want to change.**

   I use a Border Weight of 4, as seen in Figure 10-16. Thickening a border gives it a more robust feel.

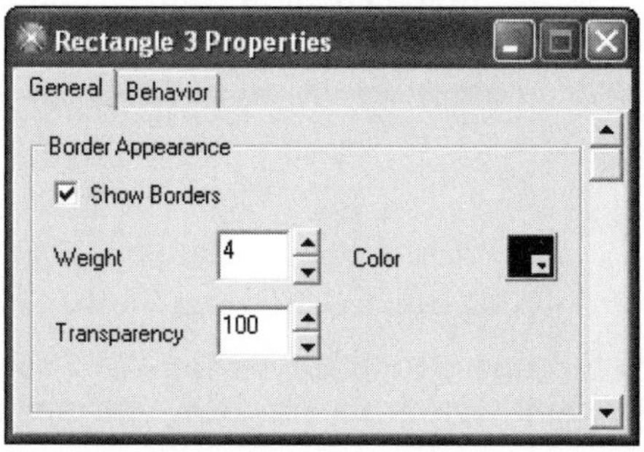

Figure 10-16:
Change
border
formatting
here.

4. **Right-click the Rectangle component and choose Send To Back.**

   I should probably mention that there is no need to change the border weight or any other property before sending the rectangle to the back.

Figure 10-17 shows how adding a few Art & Backgrounds components dramatically improves the look and feel of a visual model.

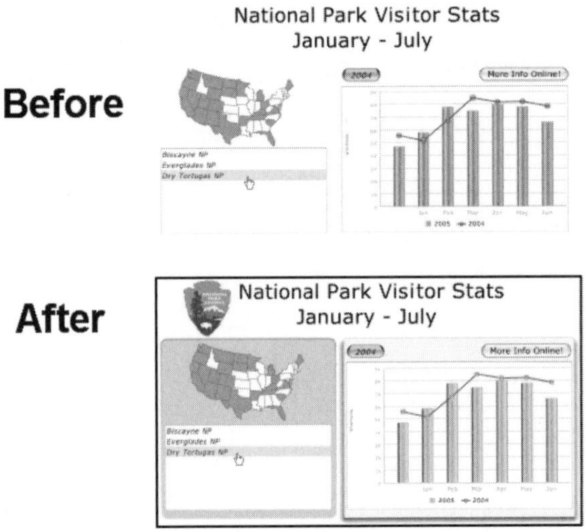

Before

National Park Visitor Stats
January - July

After

National Park Visitor Stats
January - July

Figure 10-17:
A visual
model
before
and after
adding a
few basic
Art & Back-
grounds
components.

Applying color schemes with global style

Another way to improve the design of a visual model is to add color. Although you can configure the properties of each component to achieve a desired color scheme, that takes time and effort. Stick with me here to see an easier way: Change the default colors and appearance of components by specifying a global style. This means that if you want a green color scheme, you would simply set the global style to a scheme that most closely matches what you are looking for — instead of setting the properties of each component manually to green.

Here's how to set a global style:

1. **Activate the Global Styles dialog box by choosing View⇨Change Style.**

    The Global Styles dialog box opens to the Styles tab. Also, as you can see in Figure 10-18, the Default style is active, giving you components that are formatted in the old familiar Crystal Xcelsius style.

2. **Choose a style from the Current Style drop-down list box (see the preview of that style to the right), and then click the Apply button to set that style as the default.**

    Select a style conducive to the type of data you're working with. In this scenario, working with National Park Service data, the Earthy style is a good fit. See Figure 10-19.

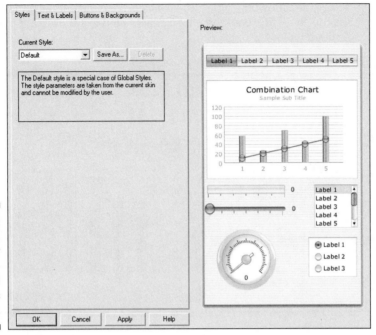

Figure 10-18:
Change the default color and appearance of all components here.

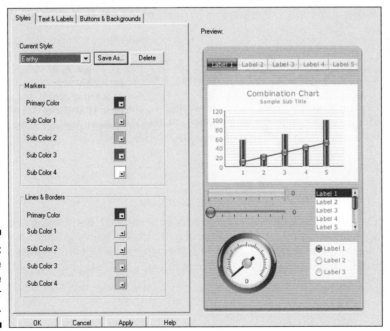

Figure 10-19:
Change the default style to fit your data.

The result, shown in Figure 10-20, is a professional-looking dashboard that not only presents the data but also conveys the nature of the data through its formatting.

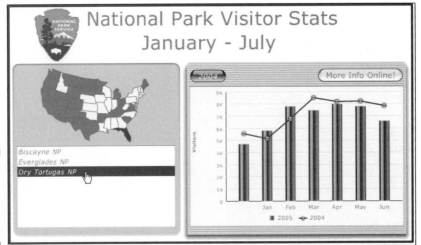

Figure 10-20:
Use a color
scheme to
enhance
data.

The Text & Labels tab and the Buttons and Backgrounds tab allow you to assign and apply color scheme changes to the individual default properties.

Discovering Skins and Templates

Crystal Xcelsius comes with a few built-in *skins* — preformatted shells that give an application its look and feel — and templates that can help in your formatting efforts. Discover here how to best use these formatting options.

Changing skins

The skin of an application gives it its look and feel. More and more software applications offer peripheral features that allow savvy users to customize their application to fit their needs; these peripheral features are typically cosmetic, such as the ability to change the look and feel of the application via the skin.

In Crystal Xcelsius, you can choose from one of three skins:

- ✔ **Aqua** (The default skin)
- ✔ **Aero**
- ✔ **élan**

The differences in the skins are demonstrated in Figure 10-21.

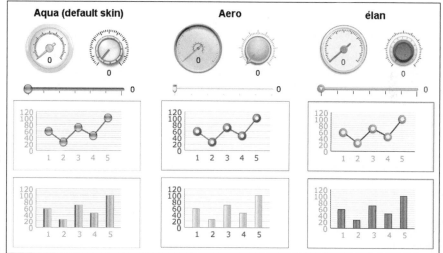

Figure 10-21:
Each skin
has its own
unique look
and feel.

To change skins, simply choose View⇨Change Skin from the main menu. Then choose the skin you want from the Skins dialog box, shown in Figure 10-22, and click OK.

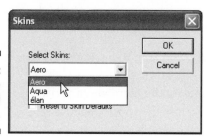

Figure 10-22:
Choose
the desired
skin here.

Using templates to save time

Like any good application, Crystal Xcelsius comes with a few *templates* — preset layouts with a set of font sizes, colors, elements, and general layout — for users who just don't have the time to craft their own. These templates offer a broad spectrum of scenarios so that you can choose the one that best fits your needs. Trust me: You'll save time by not having to design the layout and structure of your visual model.

To choose a template

1. **Choose File⇨New From Template from the main menu.**

2. **From the New From Template dialog box that opens (see Figure 10-23), peruse the samples to find one that fits your needs, and then click OK. This will open the selected template.**

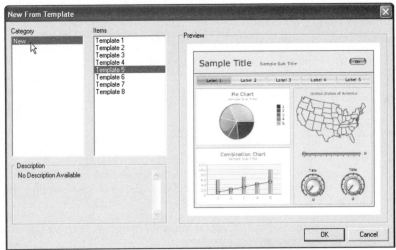

Figure 10-23: Starting from a template can help you get up and running in no time.

3. **Import your Excel model by choosing Data⇨Import Model from the main menu.**

4. **Start linking the components on the template to your Excel model as appropriate.**

   Once you finish configuring the template, you can save it just as you would any other visual model you have created from scratch.

Chapter 11

Taking Your Dashboards to Market

*F*ace it: You're not making dashboards for your health. At some point, you'll want to share your handiwork with others. Luckily, the developers of Crystal Xcelsius made exporting and sharing your visual models just as easy as creating them. In this chapter, I show you just how easy it is to take your dashboards to market. I'll also share a few tricks on how to export or import just the data in a visual model.

Exporting a Visual Model

Exporting your visual model is a fairly straightforward concept. When you're happy with the look and functionality of your visual model, you have the option of exporting it to one of several formats:

✔ **Macromedia Flash:** Crystal Xcelsius compiles your visual model to a SWF file. The SWF (often pronounced *swiff*) file is the vector-based graphics format designed to run in Macromedia Flash Player. This file is then saved to a location of your choice and can be used and distributed as needed.

✔ **HTML:** After Crystal Xcelsius compiles your visual model to a SWF file, it then creates an HTML file that references the SWF file automatically. This option enables your clients to view your dashboard by opening one HTML file, thus allowing you to publish to the Web.

✔ **PowerPoint:** After Crystal Xcelsius compiles your visual model to a SWF file, it then generates a PowerPoint file with your model embedded on the first slide of the presentation. When the PowerPoint presentation is run, your model has all its interactivity and functionality.

- ✔ **Adobe PDF:** After Crystal Xcelsius compiles your visual model to a SWF file, it then generates an Adobe PDF file with your model embedded on the first page of the document. When the PDF document is opened, your model has all its interactivity and functionality. Keep in mind that this option is not available in Crystal Xcelsius Standard.

- ✔ **Outlook:** After Crystal Xcelsius compiles your visual model to a SWF file, it then launches Outlook. From there, Crystal Xcelsius attaches your SWF file to a new mail message from which you can type your text, select the recipients, and send the e-mail.

- ✔ **Plumtree:** After Crystal Xcelsius compiles your visual model to a SWF file, it then creates an HTML file that references the SWF file automatically. Crystal Xcelsius then publishes both files to a specified URL in an existing Plumtree Portal (a Web portal used in some enterprise solutions).

To export your visual model, simply choose File➪Export from the main menu and then select your desired format.

If you're exporting to PowerPoint, Outlook, or Adobe PDF, you can use their respective toolbar icons, as shown in Figure 11-1.

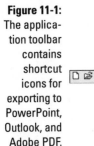

Figure 11-1:
The application toolbar contains shortcut icons for exporting to PowerPoint, Outlook, and Adobe PDF.

Export shortcuts

Paying Attention to Distribution Matters

Exporting your visual models to a certain format is one thing, but distributing them is yet another. Issues come with distributing any dashboarding tool to a large number of users. Anything from missing software to bad file paths can cause a client to have problems viewing your dashboard. Take a moment to go over some of the precautions you can take to avoid these issues.

Macromedia Flash considerations

Macromedia Flash Player ensures that any SWF or HTML file you export will work perfectly on your system; conversely, without Flash Player, dashboards will fail to open. Therefore, make sure that your clients have Flash Player installed. Any client that doesn't have Macromedia Flash Player installed can download it for free at www.macromedia.com.

Because of today's extremely Flash-oriented Internet, more and more users use Flash Player on a daily basis (whether they know it or not). This, of course, means that chances are good that your clients have Flash Player installed already.

Naming considerations

When you export your visual model to an HTML format, Crystal Xcelsius exports both a SWF file and an HTML file. Each file bears the same name.

You can change the name of the HTML file if needed, but you *cannot* change the name of the SWF file because the source code in the HTML file is hard-coded to open a specific SWF file with a specific name. Changing the name causes the HTML file to fail.

Directory considerations

Sometimes when you export a visual model, Crystal Xcelsius outputs several files in a directory. These combinations of files are necessary to make your final dashboards work. For example, Crystal Xcelsius might output an HTML file and a SWF file. These two files work in conjunction and must be kept together in order for the final dashboard to function. This means that no matter what directory you place them in, they must be kept together.

This goes for external files, too. Oftentimes, you use external files (such as images) and other Flash files in your visual model as nonembedded components. When you export these models, any external files used are automatically placed in a directory with the same name and location as the exported model. These files must be kept with the final dashboard in order for the dashboard to work properly. If you move the dashboard, you must move all accompanying files with it.

Canvas size considerations

When you export your visual model to PowerPoint or Adobe PDF, remember that Crystal Xcelsius embeds the entire canvas. This is important because canvas size affects your ability to size and position your embedded model within your PowerPoint slide or PDF document. Conduct a small test to see what I mean.

1. **Start a new visual model.**

2. **Activate the Components window and drag a Pie Chart component directly into the middle of the canvas, just as you see in Figure 11-2.**

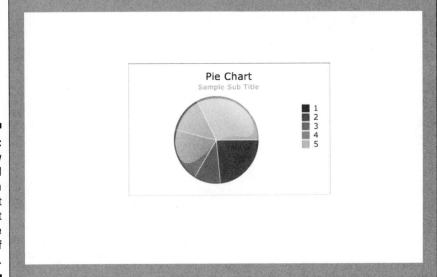

Figure 11-2: Start a new visual model and add a Pie Chart component in the middle of the canvas.

3. **Export the visual model to PowerPoint by choosing File⇨Export⇨ PowerPoint from the main menu.**

   This export is for demonstration purposes only, so you don't need to import an Excel model.

4. **After the PowerPoint presentation is created, click the embedded model.**

   As Figure 11-3 illustrates, the edges of the embedded model — represented by the small circles — are not around the Pie Chart component. Instead, they are around the entire canvas area, making the embedded model bigger than it has to be.

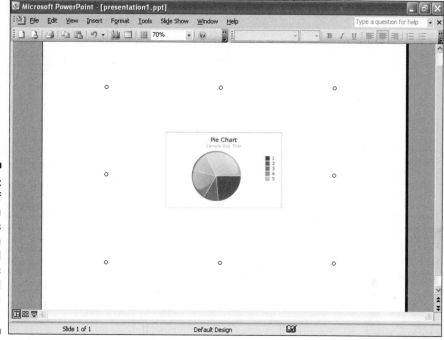

Figure 11-3:
Because of
the extra
canvas
space, the
embedded
model takes
up more real
estate than
it has to.

This is a problem, as you can see when you try to enlarge the Pie Chart component to fill the slide. Because the empty canvas makes up so much of the embedded model, the Pie Chart component is limited as to how big it can grow. You can solve this problem by cutting out any unused canvas area before you export the visual model. Here's how, continuing from the preceding steps:

5. **Close the PowerPoint presentation without saving it.**

6. **Go back to the visual model with one Pie Chart component.**

7. **Click the Fit Canvas to Components icon on the toolbar, as shown in Figure 11-4.**

The Fit Canvas to Components toolbar function resizes the canvas to match the width and height of the composite size of all components on the canvas. The end result is that all the unused canvas space is cut from the model.

8. **Export the visual model to PowerPoint by choosing File⇨Export⇨ PowerPoint from the main menu.**

The small circles that represent the edges of the embedded model are now tight around the Pie Chart component. As Figure 11-5 illustrates, you can now enlarge the Pie Chart component to fill the slide.

Fit Canvas to Components function

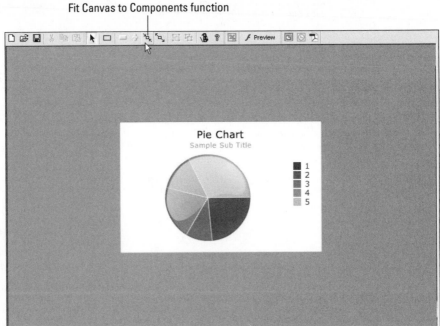

Figure 11-4:
Click the Fit
Canvas to
Components
toolbar
function.

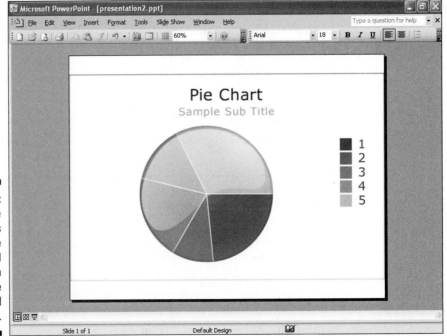

Figure 11-5:
Without the
extra canvas
space, the
embedded
model can
easily be
sized to fill
the slide.

Sending Data Back to Excel

One of the most useful features in Crystal Xcelsius is the Snapshot Back to Excel functionality, which allows you to make changes to your model in Preview mode and then save the changes to a separate Excel file. This functionality is ideal in situations when you are using Crystal Xcelsius as a what-if analysis tool, and you want to save the results of your analysis back to Excel. Look at one scenario where this functionality would come in handy.

Imagine that you've been given a budget of $12,256,895, and you've been asked to allocate that budget across months accounting for seasonality. In response to the task, you build a what-if analysis based on the Excel model shown in Figure 11-6.

Figure 11-6:
This Excel model is the basis for your what-if analysis.

	A	B	C	D	E	F	G	H	I	J	K	L	M
1	**2006 Budget**												
2	$ 12,256,895												
3													
4	**Seasonality Allocation**												
5		Jan	Feb	Mar	Apr	May	Jun	Jul	Aug	Sep	Oct	Nov	Dec
6		1,021,408	1,021,408	1,021,408	1,021,408	1,021,408	1,021,408	1,021,408	1,021,408	1,021,408	1,021,408	1,021,408	1,021,408
7													
8	Seasonality	8.33%	8.33%	8.33%	8.33%	8.33%	8.33%	8.33%	8.33%	8.33%	8.33%	8.33%	

Both the Excel model and the XLF visual model featured in this example can be found in the `C:\Xcelsius Sample Files\Chapter 11\` directory.

The idea behind the what-if analysis shown in Figure 11-7 is to be able to visualize the seasonality trends as you allocate the budgets across months.

Figure 11-7:
This what-if analysis allows you to visualize the seasonality trends as you build them.

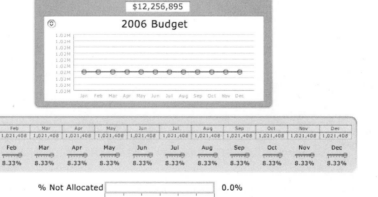

Using the sliders in Preview mode, you adjust each month's percent allocation until you reach the most appropriate seasonality trend, as shown in Figure 11-8.

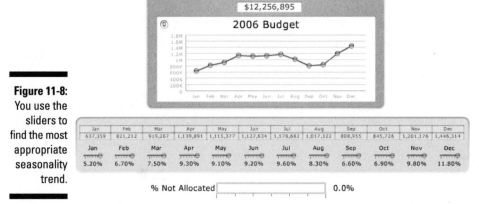

Figure 11-8:
You use the sliders to find the most appropriate seasonality trend.

After you find your answer, the easiest way to get your final budget allocations back to your manager is to use the Snapshot Back to Excel function.

In order to enable the snapshot feature, you must be in Preview mode. After you're in Preview mode, the Snapshot submenu is enabled on the File menu.

While still in Preview mode, choose File⇨Snapshot⇨Back To Excel. This creates a new Excel file that contains the contents of the imported Excel model plus the changes that were made in Preview mode. After you save the Excel file, you can open it, adjust it, or send it off to your manager. Figure 11-9 shows the saved snapshot.

Figure 11-9:
The saved snapshot file contains the imported Excel model plus the changes made in Preview mode.

	A	B	C	D	E	F	G	H	I	J	K	L	M
1	2006 Budget												
2	$ 12,256,895												
3													
4	**Seasonality Allocation**												
5		Jan	Feb	Mar	Apr	May	Jun	Jul	Aug	Sep	Oct	Nov	Dec
6		637,359	821,212	919,267	1,139,891	1,115,377	1,127,634	1,176,662	1,017,322	808,955	845,726	1,201,176	1,446,314
7													
8	Seasonality	5.20%	6.70%	7.50%	9.30%	9.10%	9.20%	9.60%	8.30%	6.60%	6.90%	9.80%	11.80%

The Snapshot Back to Excel functionality can also come in handy if you need to re-create the Excel model originally used to generate the visual model, or if someone sends you an XLF file and you need to see the spreadsheet used to create it.

Incorporating Input from Others

A little known feature in Crystal Xcelsius is Replace Data Selection, which enables Crystal Xcelsius to replace internal data with data from an external Excel file before generating the export for your visual model. This means that each time you export your visual model, Crystal Xcelsius grabs the latest data from a predefined external Excel file and uses it in your final dashboard. You can imagine how, with this feature, a kind of collaboration tool can be developed, allowing different users to provide their input on what goes into your dashboard via a shared Excel file.

In this section, I show you how to build your own little collaboration tool by using the Replace Data Selection dialog box. In the process, you will gain an understanding of how this function works and how it can be used to incorporate input from others.

To begin, open the `ProjectionDashboard.xlf` visual model found in the `C:\Xcelsius Sample Files\Chapter 11\` directory.

As you can see in Figure 11-10, this visual model is designed to display 2006 revenue projections (on the left) based on projected growth rates (on the right).

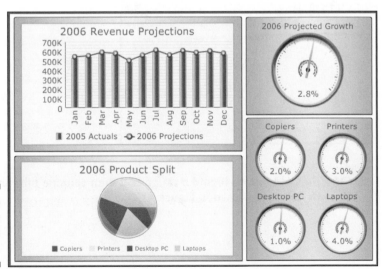

Figure 11-10:
Open this
visual
model.

The driving data points that dictate the final revenue projections are the growth rate percentages for each of the four lines of businesses (cells A3:A6), as shown in Figure 11-11.

Figure 11-11:
The growth
rate per-
centages in
cells A3:A6
determine
the 2006
revenue
projections.

	A	B	C	D	E
1	2006 Projected Growth				
2			Jan	Feb	Mar
3	2.0%	Copiers	54,743	69,369	52,111
4	3.0%	Printers	103,527	101,257	139,640
5	1.0%	Desktop PC	121,344	126,513	132,375
6	4.0%	Laptops	263,851	255,716	265,571
7	2.8%	Total	543,466	552,855	589,697
8					

The idea is to let the product managers update these numbers themselves, and then you incorporate their inputs the next time you export your visual model. The first step is to determine exactly which data points in the visual model will be replaced by an external data source. In this case, the four growth rate percentages in cells A3:A6 will be adjusted by the product managers.

1. **From the main menu, choose Data➪Replace Data Selection to activate the Replace Data Selection dialog box, as shown in Figure 11-12.**

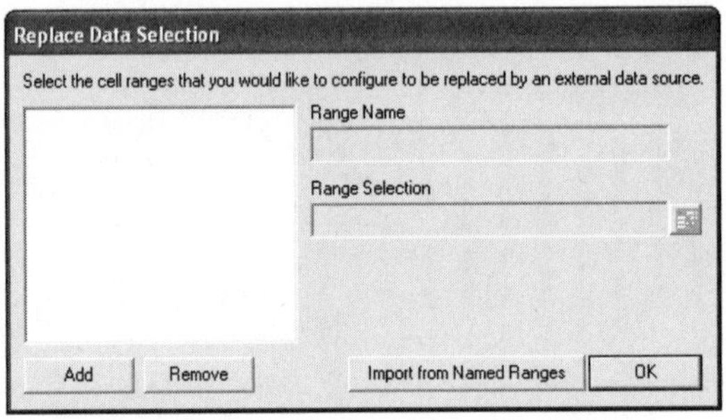

Figure 11-12:
Activate the
Replace
Data
Selection
dialog box.

Replace Data Selection

Select the cell ranges that you would like to configure to be replaced by an external data source.

Range Name

Range Selection

Add   Remove   Import from Named Ranges   OK

2. **Click the Add button to add a range and then rename the range to Growth Rates, as shown in Figure 11-13.**

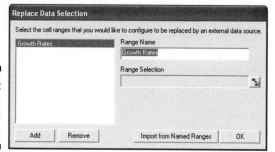

Figure 11-13:
Add a
range and
rename it.

3. Click the Cell Reference icon, shown in Figure 11-14, and select the range that will be replaced.

In this example, cells A3:A6 are replaced.

Figure 11-14:
Select the
range of
data to be
replaced
each time
the visual
model is
exported.

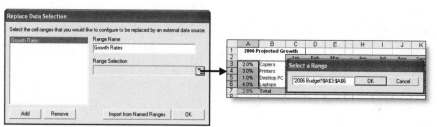

4. Click OK to apply the changes.

Next, specify which Excel file you want Crystal Xcelsius to search out for the replacement data. Do this by adjusting the Export Settings for the visual model.

5. Choose File⇨Export Settings from the main menu.

This activates the Export Settings dialog box, as shown in Figure 11-15.

6. Select the Use Another Excel File radio button in order to enable the input box.

7. Browse to and select the Excel file that contains the replacement data, as shown in Figure 11-16.

Figure 11-15:
Activate
the Export
Settings
dialog box.

In this example, you can use the `2006Projections.xls` Excel file found in the `C:\Xcelsius Sample Files\Chapter 11\` directory.

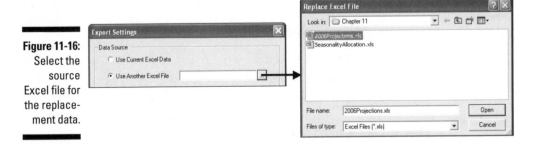

Figure 11-16:
Select the
source
Excel file for
the replace-
ment data.

Ideally, the selected file would be in a shared location (that is, a shared directory or a network drive) where the appropriate users are able to use the same Excel file to edit their portion of the data.

8. **Click OK to apply the changes.**

You successfully created a collaboration tool.

Each time the product managers update the growth percentages for their lines of business, those updates will be captured in the next visual model export. To see this, do the following:

1. **Open the `2006Projections.xls` Excel file found in the `C:\Xcelsius Sample Files\Chapter 11\` directory.**

2. **Adjust the growth percentages, shown in Figure 11-17, and then save and close the Excel file.**

Figure 11-17: Update the growth percentages and save your changes.

	A	B	C	D
1	2006 Projected Growth			
2			Jan	Fe
3	1.0%	Copiers	54,207	68,6
4	-6.0%	Printers	94,481	92,4
5	-9.0%	Desktop PC	109,330	113,
6	12.0%	Laptops	284,147	275,
7	2.0%	Total	542,165	550,

3. **Go back to the `ProjectionDashboard.xlf` visual model and export to PowerPoint.**

As Figure 11-18 shows, the changes made in the Excel spreadsheet are reflected in the export even though you didn't reimport the data.

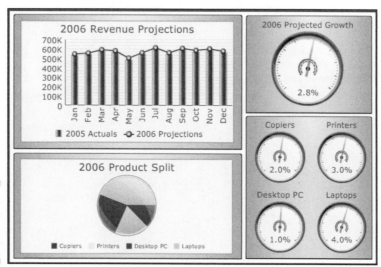

Figure 11-18: All the edits are reflected in the export.

Part V
The Part of Tens

The 5th Wave   By Rich Tennant

"I think the cursor's not moving, Mr. Dundt, because you're using the chalk board eraser instead of a mouse."

In this part . . .

*E*ach of the chapters found in this part offer ten or more pearls of wisdom, delivered in bite-sized pieces. In Chapter 12, I share with you ten best practices that help you design Excel models that allow you to go beyond simple dashboards. In Chapter 13, I share ten of my best Crystal Xcelsius tricks, making ordinary components do extraordinary things. And finally, Chapter 14 focuses on answering some of the questions that I hear most often.

Chapter 12

Designing Effective Excel Models: Ten Best Practices

• •

I have to admit that when I started using Crystal Xcelsius, I was eager to jump right in and create a dashboard from every spreadsheet I could find. I soon realized, however, that my ability to create effective Crystal Xcelsius dashboards depended heavily on how effective my Excel models were. I wanted to create more elaborate and complex visual models, but I was limited by my poorly designed Excel models. Through a process of trial and error, I learned that the right data structure, the right formatting, and a few key Excel formulas can dramatically enhance the effectiveness of my Excel models, allowing me to create more robust dashboards.

In this chapter, I share with you a few best practices that will help you create more effective Excel models that allow you to go beyond creating simple dashboards.

Best Practice #1

Build your Excel model to fit the dashboard; don't build your dashboard to fit the Excel model.

One of the most common mistakes that new users make is that they try to slap a dashboard right on top of their existing spreadsheets. Oftentimes, this yields a very basic dashboard at best, primarily because the spreadsheet doesn't have the correct data structure for anything more complicated.

Consider the spreadsheet in Figure 12-1. Try to think about what component you would use with this data — a Filter component, a list box, a chart? How would you distinguish the data from region to region? Could you do any region comparison analyses?

Figure 12-1:
Creating a
visual model
around
this data
structure
would be a
nightmare.

	A	B	C	D	E	F
1	Line of Business	Lob Manager	Jan	Feb	Mar	Apr
2	**North**					
3	Copier Sale	Jim Graham	$1,670,642	$1,908,785	$2,185,037	$2,239,37
4	Parts	Mike Alexander	$2,378,240	$2,372,974	$2,537,793	$2,429,56
5	Printer Sale	Allan Howe	$1,443,106	$1,628,517	$1,745,271	$1,545,07
6	Service Plan	Kelly Richardson	$17,098,331	$17,045,471	$17,497,027	$16,903,4
7		Totals	$22,590,319	$22,955,747	$23,965,128	$23,117,4
8	**SOUTH**					
9	Copier Sale	Jim Graham	$2,703,264	$2,923,311	$2,869,761	$2,892,76
10	Parts	Mike Alexander	$2,457,824	$2,658,591	$2,736,089	$2,493,45
11	Printer Sale	Allan Howe	$2,016,462	$2,378,109	$2,467,409	$2,089,98
12	Service Plan	Kelly Richardson	$18,922,385	$19,240,187	$19,100,783	$19,072,7
13		Totals	$26,099,935	$27,200,198	$27,174,042	$26,548,9
14	**WEST**					
15	Copier Sale	Jim Graham	$1,672,342	$1,913,201	$2,000,897	$2,073,04
16	Parts	Mike Alexander	$1,840,374	$2,041,408	$1,899,784	$2,028,64
17	Printer Sale	Allan Howe	$1,383,284	$1,630,537	$1,676,003	$1,495,75
18	Service Plan	Kelly Richardson	$12,840,822	$12,878,362	$12,728,642	$12,405,4
19		Totals	$17,736,822	$18,463,508	$18,305,326	$18,002,8

As you think about the logistics of dashboarding your spreadsheet data, you'll find that you start compromising on dashboard functionality to make the dashboard fit the structure of the spreadsheet. The truth is that although this data can logically be reported in a table format, some structural changes would have to be made in order for this spreadsheet to become an effective Excel model for a Crystal Xcelsius dashboard. Slapping a dashboard on this spreadsheet, as is, would just leave you with a bad dashboard.

Figure 12-2 presents the same data, but you'll notice the data is structured differently. When I created this spreadsheet, I had a kind of mental blueprint of what the dashboard that holds this data should look like: a Filter component, a few charts, and maybe a few gauges. I then structured and positioned the data to both support these components and provide empty cells for input and output fields.

Figure 12-2:
Structure
data to be
more con-
ducive to
building a
visual model.

	A	B	C	D	E	F
1						
2						
3						
4	Region	Line of Business	Lob Manager	Jan	Feb	Mar
5	North	Copier Sale	Jim Graham	$1,670,642	$1,908,785	$2,185,0
6	North	Parts	Mike Alexander	$2,378,240	$2,372,974	$2,537,7
7	North	Printer Sale	Allan Howe	$1,443,106	$1,628,517	$1,745,2
8	North	Service Plan	Kelly Richardson	$17,098,331	$17,045,471	$17,497,0
9	South	Copier Sale	Jim Graham	$2,703,264	$2,923,311	$2,869,7
10	South	Parts	Mike Alexander	$2,457,824	$2,658,591	$2,736,0
11	South	Printer Sale	Allan Howe	$2,016,462	$2,378,109	$2,467,4
12	South	Service Plan	Kelly Richardson	$18,922,385	$19,240,187	$19,100,7
13	West	Copier Sale	Jim Graham	$1,672,342	$1,913,201	$2,000,89
14	West	Parts	Mike Alexander	$1,840,374	$2,041,408	$1,899,7
15	West	Printer Sale	Allan Howe	$1,383,284	$1,630,537	$1,676,0
16	West	Service Plan	Kelly Richardson	$12,840,822	$12,878,362	$12,728,6

I'm not saying that your Excel model should be perfect before you get started. Making changes to your Excel model as you build your dashboard is okay. The point is that you should start with an Excel model that provides you with the appropriate structure and flexibility to make your visual model as robust as you would like it to be.

Best Practice #2

Leverage tabs to enhance, document, and organize your Excel model.

Trying to keep your Excel model limited to one worksheet tab is natural. After all, keeping track of one tab is much simpler than using different tabs. However, limiting your Excel model to one tab has its drawbacks.

When Crystal Xcelsius imports an Excel model, it imports all tabs. Furthermore, when you link components to a range of cells in your imported model, you're not limited to only the tab that is showing. You can select a range in any of the worksheet tabs that were imported.

- ✔ **Using one tab typically places limits on your analysis.** Because only so many datasets can fit on a tab, using one tab limits the number of analyses that can be represented in your Excel model. In turn, this limits the analysis that your dashboard can offer. Consider adding tabs to your Excel model to provide additional data and analysis that might not fit on just one tab. This makes for a much more robust dashboard.

- ✔ **Too much information on one tab makes for a confusing Excel model.** Large datasets typically take up a lot of cells on a tab, often leaving little room for dashboard elements such as formulas, input ranges, and output ranges. Nevertheless, most people simply position these dashboard elements below or to the right of their datasets. Although this might provide all the elements needed for the visual model, a good deal of scrolling is necessary to view these elements that are positioned in a wide range of areas. This makes the Excel model difficult to understand and maintain. Consider using separate tabs to hold dashboard elements, particularly in Excel models that contain large datasets that take a lot of real estate.

Best Practice #3

Dedicate the first tab of your Excel model to summarizing the model.

I have found that Crystal Xcelsius is so versatile and flexible that it's extremely easy to create a complex system of intertwining links between components, input ranges, output ranges, and formulas. Oftentimes, when I open an Excel model that I haven't seen for a while, I'm afraid to touch it because I forgot how each range interacted with the visual model. To avoid this problem, I use the first tab in my Excel model as a *model map*, which essentially summarizes the key ranges in my Excel model and allows me to see how each range interacts with the components in my visual model.

As you can see in Figure 12-3, a model map is nothing fancy — just a table that lists some key information about each range in the model.

You can include any information you think appropriate in your model map. The idea is to give yourself a handy reference to guide you through the elements in your Excel model.

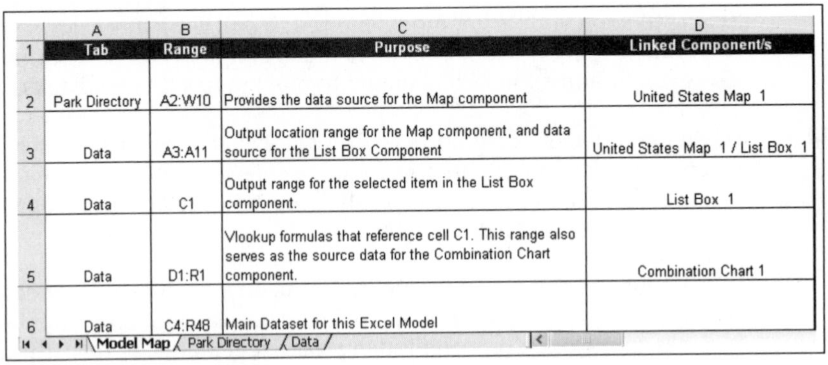

	A	B	C	D
1	**Tab**	**Range**	**Purpose**	**Linked Component/s**
2	Park Directory	A2:W10	Provides the data source for the Map component	United States Map 1
3	Data	A3:A11	Output location range for the Map component, and data source for the List Box Component	United States Map 1 / List Box 1
4	Data	C1	Output range for the selected item in the List Box component.	List Box 1
5	Data	D1:R1	Vlookup formulas that reference cell C1. This range also serves as the source data for the Combination Chart component.	Combination Chart 1
6	Data	C4:R48	Main Dataset for this Excel Model	

H ◄ ► H \ **Model Map** / Park Directory / Data /

Figure 12-3: A model map allows you to see how each range interacts with your visual model.

Best Practice #4

Use comments and labels to document your work.

Another way to document the logic in your Excel model is to use comments and labels liberally. It's amazing how a few explanatory comments and labels can help clarify your spreadsheets. Again, documentation doesn't have to be all that fancy; it can be as simple as the comments and labels that you see in Figure 12-4. The logic in your model should be clear to you even after you've been away from your Excel model for a long period of time.

Figure 12-4: Simple comments and labels can help clarify the logic in your Excel models.

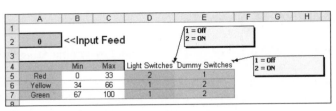

Best Practice #5

Use colors to identify the purpose of the ranges in your Excel model.

Using colors in your Excel model enables you to quickly look at a range of cells and get a basic indication of what that range does. The general concept behind this best practice is that each color represents an element type. For example, yellow could represent the source data for a chart, blue could represent a Selector component's display range, gray could represent a formula used for a Single Value component, and purple could represent a dynamic visibility trigger.

You can use any color you want; it's up to you to give these colors meaning. The important thing is that you'll have a visual distinction between a normal range and a range being used as a dashboard element.

Best Practice #6

Keep frequently used dashboard elements readily visible.

In every Excel model are a handful of ranges, such as formulas, input ranges, and output ranges, that serve as dashboard elements. Very often, these ranges become the primary drivers in your visual model. You want to relegate these important ranges to the far ends of your spreadsheet because keeping your dashboard elements readily visible helps make your Excel model easy to understand and easy to edit. I personally like to keep the first three to six rows of an Excel model reserved for dashboard elements such as formulas, input ranges, and output ranges.

Best Practice #7

Avoid adding rows and columns to your Excel model by leaving yourself room for improvements.

Imagine that you have an Excel model in which you use a row of cells as the source data for a Line Chart component. Crystal Xcelsius will use that range's cell address to make the association. Now imagine adding a row before row 1 of your Excel model, moving everything down one row. The range that you linked to the Line Chart component will have moved down also, effectively changing its cell address. When you reimport your newly changed Excel model, Crystal Xcelsius has no way of knowing that the range that you linked to the Line Chart component has a different address. Therefore, you have to manually relink the line chart to ensure that it captures the data for the correct cell address. Now imagine that you have to relink dozens of components just because you added a single row to your Excel model. I'm sure it won't take you long to conclude that making any post-import row or column additions to your Excel model is a bad thing.

To avoid the need to add rows and columns to your Excel models, leave some space between data groupings. In Figure 12-5, for example, notice that not only is there ample spacing between the groups of data, but the first three rows have been left blank. This way, if I ever need to add new data or an additional data element, I can use these cells instead of changing the structure of the Excel model by adding rows or columns.

Figure 12-5:
Be sure to leave space between groups of data in anticipation of additional data elements.

	A	B	C	D	E	F	G	H	I	J
1										
2										
3										
4		q1	q2	q3	q4	total	q1	q2	q3	q4
5	North America	654	678	678	567	654	2,577	2,577	4,476	6,375
6	Latin America	270	260	321	322	218	1,173	1,121	2,034	2,834
7	Europe	125	178	187	156	178	646	699	1,167	1,679
8	Asia	529	500	491	411	476	1,931	1,878	3,309	4,696
9	Australia & Pacific	260	308	348	317	287	1,233	1,260	2,184	3,096
10	Insert in Row >>									
11										
12										
13										
14										
15	XY Chart	Sales	Expenses				Bubble Chart	Sales	Expenses	Headcount
16	North America	$ 14.22	$ 20.12				North America	$ 444	$ 322	123
17	Latin America	$ 21.05	$ 19.54				Latin America	$ 321	$ 300	45
18	Europe	$ 21.06	$ 20.45				Europe	$ 234	$ 234	234
19	Asia	$ 12.25	$ 17.12				Asia	$ 210	$ 88	123
20	Australia & Pacific	$ 15.36	$ 25.74				Australia & Pacific	$ 395	$ 384	87

Best Practice #8

Apply formatting in your Excel model, not in your visual model.

Keep in mind that when you link a Crystal Xcelsius component to cells in an Excel model, you don't just bring over the values of those cells. You also bring over their formatting. In fact, the default behavior for all components is to use the formatting in the Excel model.

For example, imagine that you link a Column Chart component to cells that have the Numeric format. Because the format in the Excel model is Numeric, the Column Chart component displays its data in the Numeric format by default. Now imagine that you change the component's Numeric Format property to Currency. This obviously tells the component to display its data in the Currency format. All is well until you reimport the Excel model. When you reimport the model, the Column Chart component reverts to displaying its data in the Numeric format because Crystal Xcelsius essentially concludes that the Excel model knows best. I mean, why would you feed it one format, only to change it to another? The bottom line is that you should take time to format the data in your Excel model appropriately before importing it into Crystal Xcelsius. This saves you time and frustration in that you won't have to alter the Numeric format of your components.

Best Practice #9

Leverage the supported Excel functions to enhance your model.

It doesn't take most users long to realize that their proficiency in Crystal Xcelsius is largely dependent on how proficient they are at Excel. In fact, I find that the more proficient users are with Excel, the more sophisticated and complex their dashboards are. This interesting observation is in large part because Excel power users are more likely to employ Excel functions in their models.

Crystal Xcelsius supports over 130 Excel functions. The support of these functions has two major benefits. First — and most importantly — a large majority of your formula-based processes and operations remain functional in your visual model. Second, you can add functionality to your visual models that can only be achieved through formulas. For example, you can test for conditions by using the IF function, you can quickly search out and extract data from large datasets by using the VLOOKUP function, you can use the INDEX and MATCH functions to work with complex data matrices, and the list goes on.

Table 12-1 is an index of the Excel functions supported in Crystal Xcelsius. Use this table to pick out functions that can help you enhance the functionality of your visual models.

You should also review this index to identify those functions that aren't supported by Crystal Xcelsius. This will help you avoid incorporating unsupported functions in your Excel model. If you run a visual model that contains unsupported functions, you will get an error message stating that the generated model might not display properly.

Table 12-1	Index of Supported Excel Functions	
Function	*Purpose*	*Support Restrictions*
ABS	Returns the absolute value of a number	None
ACOS	Returns the arccosine of a number	None
ACOSH	Returns the inverse hyperbolic cosine of a number	None
AND	Returns TRUE if all its arguments are TRUE	None
ASIN	Returns the arcsine of a number	None
ASINH	Returns the inverse hyperbolic sine of a number	None

(continued)

Table 12-1 *(continued)*

Function	Purpose	Support Restrictions
ATAN	Returns the arctangent of a number	None
ATAN2	Returns the arctangent from x- and y-coordinates	None
ATANH	Returns the inverse hyperbolic tangent of a number	None
AVEDEV	Returns the average of the absolute deviations of data points from their mean	None
AVERAGE	Returns the average of its arguments	None
AVERAGEA	Returns the average of its arguments, including numbers, text, and logical values	None
BETADIST	Returns the beta cumulative distribution function	Supported only in the Professional and Workgroup versions of Crystal Xcelsius.
CEILING	Rounds a number to the nearest integer or to the nearest multiple of significance	None
CHOOSE	Chooses a value from a list of values	None
COMBIN	Returns the number of combinations for a given number of objects	None
CONCATENATE	Joins several text items into one text item	None
COS	Returns the cosine of a number	None
COSH	Returns the hyperbolic cosine of a number	None
COUNT	Counts how many numbers are in the list of arguments	None
COUNTA	Counts how many values are in the list of arguments	None
COUNTIF	Counts the number of nonblank cells within a range that meet the given criteria	None

Function	Purpose	Support Restrictions
DATE	Returns the serial number of a particular date	Dates and times passed to this function as text must be U.S. dates or times. The 1904 date system is not supported.
DATEVALUE	Converts a date in the form of text to a serial number	Dates and times passed to this function as text must be U.S. dates or times. The 1904 date system is not supported.
DAVERAGE	Returns the average of selected database entries	None
DAY	Converts a serial number to a day of the month	Dates and times passed to this function as text must be U.S. dates or times. The 1904 date system is not supported.
DAYS360	Calculates the number of days between two dates based on a 360-day year	Dates and times passed to this function as text must be U.S. dates or times. The 1904 date system is not supported.
DB	Returns the depreciation of an asset for a specified period using the fixed-declining balance method	None
DCOUNT	Counts the cells that contain numbers in a database	None
DCOUNTA	Counts nonblank cells in a database	None
DDB	Returns the depreciation of an asset for a specified period using the double-declining balance method or some other method you specify	None
DEGREES	Converts radians to degrees	None
DEVSQ	Returns the sum of squares of deviations	None
DGET	Extracts from a database a single record that matches the specified criteria	None

(continued)

Table 12-1 *(continued)*

Function	Purpose	Support Restrictions
DMAX	Returns the maximum value from selected database entries	None
DMIN	Returns the minimum value from selected database entries	None
DOLLAR	Converts a number to text, using the $(dollar) Currency format	None
DPRODUCT	Multiplies the values in a particular field of records that match the criteria in a database	None
DSTDEV	Estimates the standard deviation based on a sample of selected database entries	None
DSTDEVP	Calculates the standard deviation based on the entire population of selected database entries	None
DSUM	Adds the numbers in the field column of records in the database that match the criteria	None
DVAR	Estimates variance based on a sample from selected database entries	None
DVARP	Calculates variance based on the entire population of selected database entries	None
EDATE	Returns the serial number of the date that is the indicated number of months before or after the start date	Dates and times passed to this function as text must be U.S. dates or times. The 1904 date system is not supported.
EOMONTH	Returns the serial number of the last day of the month before or after a specifiednumber of months	Dates and times passed to this function as text must be U.S. dates or times. The 1904 date system is not supported.
EQUALS	Tests whether two values are equal	None
EVEN	Rounds a number up to the nearest even integer	None

Function	Purpose	Support Restrictions
EXACT	Checks to see whether two text values are identical	Supported only in the Professional and Workgroup versions of Crystal Xcelsius.
EXP	Returns e raised to the power of a given number	None
EXPONDIST	Returns the exponential distribution	None
FACT	Returns the factorial of a number	None
FALSE	Returns the logical value FALSE	None
FIND	Finds one text value within another (case-sensitive)	Supported only in the Professional and Workgroup versions of Crystal Xcelsius.
FISHER	Returns the Fisher transformation	None
FISHERINV	Returns the inverse of the Fisher transformation	None
FIXED	Formats a number as text with a fixed number of decimals	None
FLOOR	Rounds a number down, toward zero	None
FORECAST	Returns a value along a linear trend	None
FV	Returns the future value of an investment	None
GEOMEAN	Returns the geometric mean	None
HARMEAN	Returns the harmonic mean	None
HLOOKUP	Looks in the top row of an array and returns the value of the indicated cell	None
HOUR	Converts a serial number to an hour	Dates and times passed to this function as text must be U.S. dates or times. The 1904 date system is not supported.
IF	Specifies a logical test to perform	None

(continued)

Table 12-1 *(continued)*

Function	Purpose	Support Restrictions
INDEX	Uses an index to choose a value from a reference or array	Crystal Xcelsius supports only the Array syntax of the INDEX function. Also, Crystal Xcelsius requires all three arguments for the INDEX function to evaluate properly.
INT	Rounds a number down to the nearest integer	None
INTERCEPT	Returns the intercept of the linear regression line	None
IPMT	Returns the interest payment for an investment for a given period	None
IRR	Returns the internal rate of return for a series of cash flows	None
KURT	Returns the kurtosis of a dataset	None
LARGE	Returns the k-th largest value in a dataset	None
LEFT	Returns the leftmost characters from a text value	Supported only in the Professional and Workgroup versions of Crystal Xcelsius.
LEN	Returns the number of characters in a text string	Supported only in the Professional and Workgroup versions of Crystal Xcelsius.
LN	Returns the natural logarithm of a number	None
LOG	Returns the logarithm of a number to a specified base	None
LOG10	Returns the base 10 logarithm of a number	None
LOOKUP	Looks up values in a vector or array	Supported only in the Professional and Workgroup versions of Crystal Xcelsius.

Function	Purpose	Support Restrictions
LOWER	Converts text to lowercase	Supported only in the Professional and Workgroup versions of Crystal Xcelsius.
MATCH	Looks up values in a reference or array	None
MAX	Returns the maximum value in a list of arguments	None
MEDIAN	Returns the median of the given numbers	None
MID	Returns a specific number of characters from a text string starting at the position you specify	Supported only in the Professional and Workgroup versions of Crystal Xcelsius.
MIN	Returns the minimum value in a list of arguments	None
MINUTE	Converts a serial number to a minute	Dates and times passed to this function as text must be U.S. dates or times. The 1904 date system is not supported.
MIRR	Returns the internal rate of return where positive and negative cash flows are financed at different rates	None
MOD	Returns the remainder from division	None
MODE	Returns the most common value in a dataset	None
MONTH	Converts a serial number to a month	Dates and times passed to this function as text must be U.S. dates or times. The 1904 date system is not supported.
N	Returns a value converted to a number	Supported only in the Professional and Workgroup versions of Crystal Xcelsius.

(continued)

Table 12-1 *(continued)*

Function	Purpose	Support Restrictions
NETWORKDAYS	Returns the number of whole workdays between two dates	Dates and times passed to this function as text must be U.S. dates or times. The 1904 date system is not supported.
NORMDIST	Returns the normal cumulative distribution	None
NORMINV	Returns the inverse of the normal cumulative distribution	None
NORMSDIST	Returns the standard normal cumulative distribution	None
NORMSINV	Returns the inverse of the standard normal cumulative distribution	None
NOT	Reverses the logic of its argument	None
NOW	Returns the serial number of the current date and time	Dates and times passed to this function as text must be U.S. dates or times. The 1904 date system is not supported.
NPER	Returns the number of periods for an investment	None
NPV	Returns the net present value of an investment based on a series of periodic cash flows and a discount rate	None
ODD	Rounds a number up to the nearest odd integer	None
OR	Returns TRUE if any argument is TRUE	None
PI	Returns the value of pi	None
PMT	Returns the periodic payment for an annuity	None
POWER	Returns the result of a number raised to a power	None
PPMT	Returns the payment on the principal for an investment for a given period	None

Function	Purpose	Support Restrictions
PRODUCT	Multiplies its arguments	None
PV	Returns the present value of an investment	None
RADIANS	Converts degrees to radians	None
RAND	Returns a random number between 0 and 1	None
RANK	Returns the rank of a number in a list of numbers	None
RATE	Returns the interest rate per period of an annuity	None
REPLACE	Replaces characters within text	Supported only in the Professional and Workgroup versions of Crystal Xcelsius.
REPT	Repeats text a given number of times	Supported only in the Professional and Workgroup versions of Crystal Xcelsius.
RIGHT	Returns the rightmost characters from a text value	Supported only in the Professional and Workgroup versions of Crystal Xcelsius.
ROUND	Rounds a number to a specified number of digits	None
ROUNDDOWN	Rounds a number down, toward zero	None
ROUNDUP	Rounds a number up, away from zero	None
SECOND	Converts a serial number to a second	Dates and times passed to this function as text must be U.S. dates or times. The 1904 date system is not supported.
SIGN	Returns the sign of a number	None
SIN	Returns the sine of the given angle	None

(continued)

Table 12-1 *(continued)*

Function	Purpose	Support Restrictions
SINH	Returns the hyperbolic sine of a number	None
SLN	Returns the straight-line depreciation of an asset for one period	None
SMALL	Returns the k-th smallest value in a dataset	None
SQRT	Returns a positive square root	None
STANDARDIZE	Returns a normalized value	None
STDEV	Estimates standard deviation based on a sample	None
SUM	Adds its arguments	None
SUMIF	Adds the cells specified by a given criteria	None
SUMPRODUCT	Returns the sum of the products of corresponding array components	None
SUMSQ	Returns the sum of the squares of the arguments	None
SUMX2MY2	Returns the sum of the difference of squares of corresponding values in two arrays	None
SUMX2PY2	Returns the sum of the sum of squares of corresponding values in two arrays	None
SUMXMY2	Returns the sum of squares of differences of corresponding values in two arrays	None
SYD	Returns the sum-of-years' digits depreciation of an asset for a specified period	None
TAN	Returns the tangent of a number	None
TANH	Returns the hyperbolic tangent of a number	None
TEXT	Formats a number and converts it to text	Supported only in the Professional and Workgroup versions of Crystal Xcelsius.

Function	Purpose	Support Restrictions
TIME	Returns the serial number of a particular time	Dates and times passed to this function as text must be U.S. dates or times. The 1904 date system is not supported.
TIMEVALUE	Converts a time in the form of text to a serial number	Dates and times passed to this function as text must be U.S. dates or times. The 1904 date system is not supported.
TODAY	Returns the serial number of today's date	Dates and times passed to this function as text must be U.S. dates or times. The 1904 date system is not supported.
TRUE	Returns the logical value TRUE	None
TRUNC	Truncates a number to an integer	None
VALUE	Converts a text argument to a number	Supported only in the Professional and Workgroup versions of Crystal Xcelsius. Numbers with comma and/or $ signs are known to not work.
VAR	Estimates variance based on a sample	None
VDB	Returns the depreciation of an asset for a specified or partial period using a declining balance method	Fractional periods are not supported.
VLOOKUP	Looks in the first column of an array and moves across the row to return the value of a cell	If the index column of the lookup array is a formula, the cell will always contain the initial value. This means that run-time changes to the value of that cell will not be reflected in the lookup array.
WEEKDAY	Converts a serial number to a day of the week	Dates and times passed to this function as text must be U.S. dates or times. The 1904 date system is not supported.

(continued)

Table 12-1 *(continued)*

Function	Purpose	Support Restrictions
WEEKNUM	Converts a serial number to a number representing where the week falls numerically within a year	Dates and times passed to this function as text must be U.S. dates or times. The 1904 date system is not supported.
WORKDAY	Returns the serial number of the date before or after a specified number of workdays	Dates and times passed to this function as text must be U.S. dates or times. The 1904 date system is not supported.
YEAR	Converts a serial number to a year	Dates and times passed to this function as text must be U.S. dates or times. The 1904 date system is not supported.
YEARFRAC	Returns the year fraction representing the number of whole days between start_date and end_date	Dates and times passed to this function as text must be U.S. dates or times. The 1904 date system is not supported.

Best Practice #10

Test your Excel model before importing it into Crystal Xcelsius.

This best practice is simple. Make sure that your model does what it's supposed to do before importing it to Crystal Xcelsius. In that vein, here are a few things to watch for:

- ✓ Test your formulas to ensure that they work properly.
- ✓ Double-check your main dataset to ensure that it's complete.
- ✓ Make sure all numeric formatting is appropriate.
- ✓ Ensure column widths aren't set too narrowly, causing number symbols to display in your dashboard labels.

Your goal is not to make your Excel model perfect before importing it. The goal is to eliminate easily avoidable errors and reimports.

Chapter 13

Ten Cool Crystal Xcelsius Tricks

- -

*I*n this chapter, I want to share a few tricks with you to get you thinking about the components in Crystal Xcelsius as tools that can be used to create your own utilities. At the end of this chapter, you will realize that the components included in Crystal Xcelsius are not the end-all-be-all. With a little imagination and ingenuity, you can create you own effects that go beyond the basics.

The example files for the tips in this chapter can be found in the `C:\Xcelsius Sample Files\Chapter 13\` directory.

Creating a Waterfall Chart

Like a stacked column chart, a *waterfall chart* allows you to compare items in a specific range of values as well as show the relationship of the individual sub-items to the whole. However, as you can see in Figure 13-1, the difference is that in a waterfall chart, a floating bar effect highlights the distribution of the values.

Figure 13-1:
Waterfall
charts more
dramatically
show
relationships
between
data items.

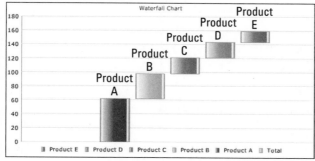

Creating these types of charts in Crystal Xcelsius is surprisingly simple. You start with a data table similar to the one shown in Figure 13-2, and then create a Stacked Column chart from that data.

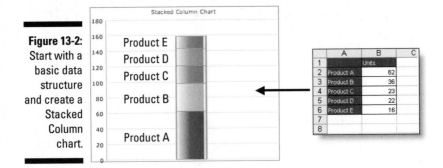

Figure 13-2:
Start with a
basic data
structure
and create a
Stacked
Column
chart.

Double-click the Stacked Column chart and go to the Appearance tab of the Properties window that appears. On the Series sub-tab, you will find a property in Bar Overlap. Adjust this property to 0, as shown in Figure 13-3, and that is it. You created a waterfall chart.

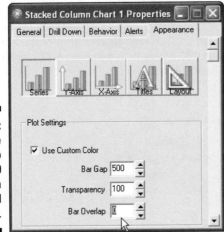

Figure 13-3:
Adjust the
Bar Overlap
property to 0
to create a
waterfall
chart.

You can get really fancy and add a Total column to your waterfall chart, as shown in Figure 13-4. A *Total column* allows you to visualize the sum of the data items in your chart as well as the breakdown of each item.

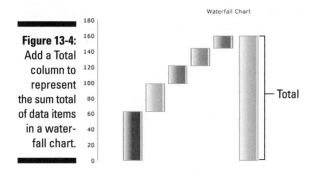

Figure 13-4:
Add a Total column to represent the sum total of data items in a water-fall chart.

To do this, you need only to add a Total series to the dataset that you're using to create the Stacked Column chart. As you can see in Figure 13-5, this series should consist only of the sum total of the data items. After you make this addition to your dataset, simply create a Stacked Column chart and change its Bar Overlap property to 0, just as in the previous example.

Figure 13-5:
The Total series is added by appending a Total column to the data-set you use to create the Stacked Column chart.

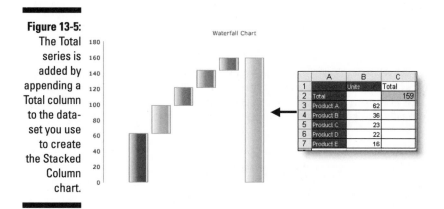

Password-Protecting Your Dashboard with Dynamic Visibility

In Chapter 8, I talk about using dynamic visibility to control what a user sees. It stands to reason that if you can control what a user sees, you can lock users out of a dashboard with a password requirement. Password protection can come in handy when your dashboard contains sensitive data that should be limited to an authorized set of users.

The idea behind this trick is simple: You first group a set of components, and then you set the Display Status and Display Status Key for that group. As you can see in Figure 13-6, the Display Status Key can be anything you want it to be; in this example, the Display Status Key is *winter05*. This will eventually become the password that your clients have to know to make this group visible.

Although your chosen password does not necessarily have to have letters in it, if you do use letters, bear in mind that the Display Status Key is case–sensitive. In that light, you want to consciously decide whether you use an uppercase, lowercase, or a mixed-case password.

Figure 13-6: Set a group password by setting the Display Status and Display Status Key.

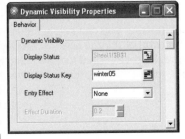

After you have dynamic visibility set, you need to give your users a way to enter the password. You do this by using the Input Text component. Simply add the Input Text component and set the Insert In property, shown in Figure 13-7, to the same cell that's used as the trigger cell for the dynamic visibility.

Figure 13-7: Give your clients a place to feed the trigger cell for the dynamic visibility.

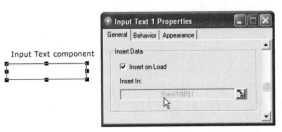

If you want to get really fancy, you can set some Behavior Options properties, shown in Figure 13-8, to give the Input Text component the look and feel of a standard password input.

In this example, I enabled the Password Input property to ensure that as the user enters the password, only asterisks are displayed. This is a standard security feature that prevents onlookers from seeing the password as it is being typed. I also set the Maximum Characters property to match the length of the password I'm using. This property allows you to limit the number of characters a user can type.

Figure 13-8:
Set options
to make your
Input Text
component
look and
feel like a
standard
password.

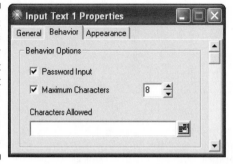

After you configure your Input Text component, you can add some basic formatting around it to give it a professional dialog box feel. The final result can look something like Figure 13-9. With this setup, your clients enter a password and then press Enter to make the dashboard visible.

If you can still see your password dialog box even after your dashboard becomes visible, right-click the password dialog box and choose Send To Back.

Figure 13-9:
A little
formatting
gives your
password
entry a pro-
fessional
feel.

Highlighting the Below-Average Data Points in a Chart

Crystal Xcelsius makes conditional formatting in a chart as easy as referencing cells. The following trick is just one example of how you can leverage conditional formatting to highlight particular data points. As you can see in Figure 13-10, the idea is to get an instant visual indication on which months' performance fell below the average.

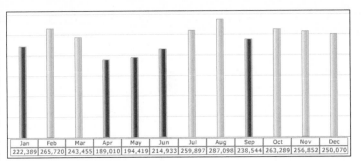

Figure 13-10: Use conditional formatting to see which data points fall below the average.

The Excel model for this setup is shown in Figure 13-11. As you can see in the figure, you must create a row that sets the target performance for each month to the Average of all data points. The key to this trick is to provide both an actual performance and a target performance. By using the Excel AVERAGE function, you set the target for each month to the average of all the data points.

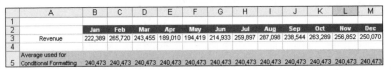

Figure 13-11: The Excel model for conditional formatting.

When you import this model into Crystal Xcelsius, you can create a basic Column chart with the data that represents actual performance.

From there, you can use the Alerts tab to compare each data point with its respective target. As you can see in Figure 13-12, you do this by linking the Target property of the Alerts tab to the target performance row that you created in your Excel model.

Figure 13-12: Giving your chart the desired conditional formatting.

Making a Data Series Disappear and Reappear

This trick involves using a toggle button to make a data series in a chart disappear and reappear. Figure 13-13 demonstrates how this works.

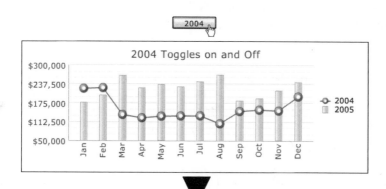

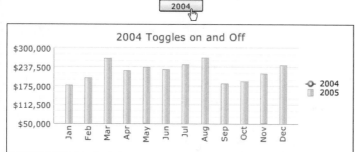

Figure 13-13:
Clicking the toggle button allows you to make the data series appear and disappear.

The magic behind this trick is in the Excel model. If you open the Excel model, you can see that cells C3:N3 feed the 2004 series for the chart. As you can see in Figure 13-14, these cells are made up of IF formulas. These formulas essentially say that if there is a 1 in cell A3, use the 2004 data for that data point; otherwise, make the data point blank.

Figure 13-14:
Use the
Excel IF
function to
test for
certain
conditions
to create
an effect.

		C3	▼		*fx*	=IF($A3=1,C9,"")	
		A	B	C	D	E	
	1						
	2	**Toggle for 2004 Data**		Jan	Feb	Mar	
	3	1	2004	$222,389	$224,524	$136,104	
	4		2005	$176,648	$201,000	$265,720	
	5						
	6						
	7			**Raw Data**			
	8			Jan	Feb	Mar	
	9		2004	$222,389	$224,524	$136,104	
	10		2005	$176,648	$201,000	$265,720	

Meanwhile, in the visual model, use the Toggle Button component to output the values 1 and 0, alternating between the two. The toggle button is linked to cell A3 (referenced in the formula) by using the Insert In property, as shown in Figure 13-15.

Figure 13-15:
A Toggle
Button
component
outputs the
values 1
and 0, in an
alternating
fashion,
to the cells
you want.

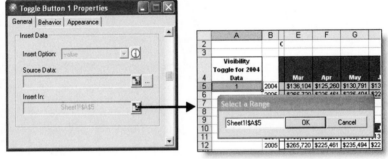

The end result is that when the toggle button outputs a 1 to cell A3, the data points are filled with 2004 data. When the Toggle Button component outputs a 0, the data points are kept empty.

Creating a Scrolling Chart

The scrolling chart is one of my favorite things to build in Crystal Xcelsius. This tool not only allows me to show tons of data in a compact package, but it also allows me to add animation that shows trending in motion.

This trick involves only two components: Play Selector and Line Chart. Simply click the Play button, and the line chart starts scrolling through four years of revenue data, six months at a time. Figure 13-16 shows the scrolling chart in motion.

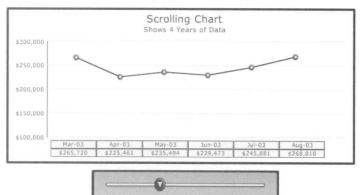

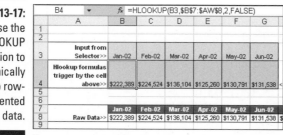

Figure 13-16: Use scrolling charts to display lots of data in an animated fashion.

So instead of showing all four years of data in one chart, I set up a situation where six months of data is showing at one time.

The primary driver behind this trick is Excel's HLOOKUP function, which is the row-oriented cousin of the VLOOKUP function. With the HLOOKUP function, you can look up data in a specified row based on column names. Figure 13-17 shows the Excel model that feeds the scrolling chart. Notice that cells B4:G4 are HLOOKUP formulas that look up data from cells B7:AW8 based on the column names B3:G3.

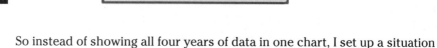

Figure 13-17: Use the HLOOKUP function to dynamically look up row-oriented data.

As the column names in cells B3:G3 change, the values that feed the line chart change. To dynamically change these column names at run-time, use a Play Selector component.

The *Play Selector component* sequentially inserts data from a defined dataset by using playback controls. In this example, the Play Selector component is linked to a dataset that contains the column names you use to feed the HLOOKUP formulas. Figure 13-18 demonstrates this.

Figure 13-18: The Play Selector component is linked to a table of column names used to feed the HLOOKUP formulas.

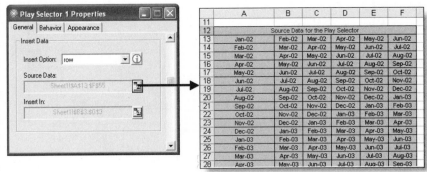

Double-click on the Play Selector component to get to the Properties dialog box. As you can see in Figure 13-19, the Insert In property is set to feed cells B3:G3.

The end result is a dashboard that can be animated by pressing the Play button, or as Figure 13-20 demonstrates, analyzed by moving the slider to a desired point in time.

The scaling on this chart is fixed; it does not change as you interact with the dashboard. I achieve this effect by setting the Scale behavior of the chart to Manual Scale. Refer to Chapter 5 for a refresher on setting the Scale Behavior of charts.

Figure 13-19: The Play Selector component is set to output the column names to the needed cells.

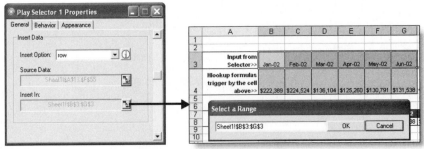

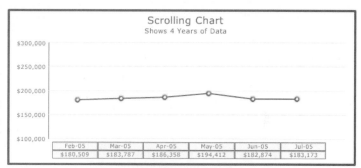

Figure 13-20:
Press Play
to animate
the chart or
use a slider
to pinpoint a
time period.

Using Conditional Formatting to Create Regions on a Map

Many organizations like to split their branches or locations into organizational regions such as North, South, and West. I sometimes use conditional formatting to color-code states based on the organizational region that they're in. For example, in Figure 13-21, I color-coded each state based the organizational region to which it belongs.

Figure 13-21:
Use
conditional
formatting
to color-
code states
to represent
regions.

Here's how to accomplish this:

1. **Create a dataset in your Excel model to be used specifically to apply conditional formatting.**

   As you can see in Figure 13-22, I assigned each state a numerical region code, which represents the organizational region. These region codes are used as the alert targets.

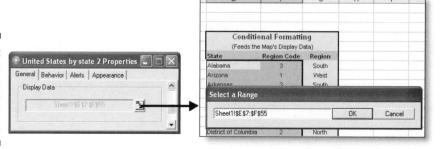

2. **Set the Display Data property to include the state and region code, as shown in Figure 13-23.**

   This property defines the actual value of each state in the Map component.

3. **Configure the Alerts tab, as shown in Figure 13-24, to apply value-based alerts, using the region codes as the alert triggers.**

   After the alerts take effect, the Map component is color-coded based on organizational region.

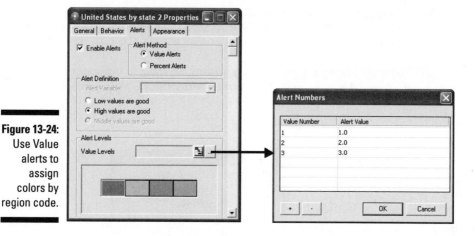

Figure 13-24:
Use Value
alerts to
assign
colors by
region code.

Making Your Own Map Component

Although the Map components in Crystal Xcelsius are cool, your choice of maps is severely limited. This might leave you wondering how you can create your own Map components in Crystal Xcelsius. Although there is no way to technically make a Map component, you do have a workaround that you can use to create interactivity based on your own maps.

As an example, I created the dashboard in Figure 13-25 to report on population data for the five counties in Rhode Island. In this dashboard, moving your mouse from county to county changes the data that displays.

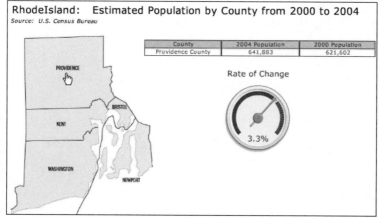

Figure 13-25:
You can
create your
own inter-
active maps.

Take a closer look at this dashboard to see that the map is nothing more than an Image component that has a few Icon Selector components on top. Here's how it works:

1. **Import an image of the map by adding an Image component onto your dashboard and selecting the image using the Filename property, as shown in Figure 13-26.**

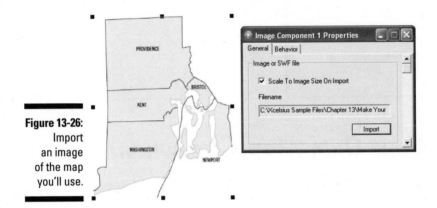

Figure 13-26:
Import
an image
of the map
you'll use.

2. **Add Icon Selectors on each point in the map where you want interactivity.**

   These icon selectors provide the *hot spot* areas on your map (see Figure 13-27): that is, the areas that give you interactivity at run-time.

Figure 13-27:
Create hot
spots to
provide
interactivity.

3. **Expand the selectors to ensure that you optimize the hot spots on your map. (See Figure 13-28.)**

You can expand the Icon selectors by clicking on the bounding box handles and dragging them until the selector is the appropriate size and shape. Expanding the size of the selectors reduces the chance of hitting dead spots that don't have interactivity at run-time.

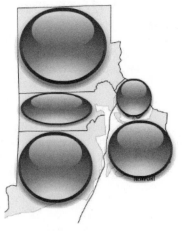

Figure 13-28:
Expand icon
selectors to
optimize hot
spot areas.

At this point, the icon selectors can be given some functionality based on some scenario, but that's not your focus here. The point is that after you configure the icon selectors with some functionality, you have essentially added interactivity to your map.

Time for smoke and mirrors.

4. **Make the icon selectors invisible so that only the map is showing by going to the Appearance tab and adjusting the Transparency property to 0, as shown in Figure 13-29.**

The final effect is a custom map that has interactivity.

Figure 13-29:
Setting the
Trans-
parency
property to
0 makes an
icon selec-
tor invisible.

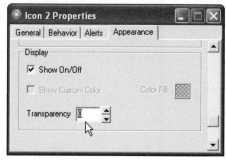

Keep in mind that you can use this technique with any image; it doesn't have to be a map per se. For instance, you can use this technique with organizational charts, floor plans, park maps, and various types of diagrams. Incorporating pictures into your dashboards in this way can help you add something extra to your dashboards.

Adding an Export to PowerPoint Button

Every time I created a dashboard and put it on my company's intranet site, I would get calls from users asking whether they could save it to their computer. I finally got into the habit of adding an Export to PowerPoint button on every dashboard I created so that each user could save a PowerPoint version of the dashboard locally.

This is a fairly easy trick that involves a pre-exported PowerPoint dashboard and a URL component. The idea here is to export your visual model to PowerPoint beforehand and then place the PowerPoint presentation on your Web server along with the HTML dashboard and SWF file. After the PowerPoint presentation is on the Web server, you can use a URL component to open the file.

The saved PowerPoint file will open in the user's Web browser. From there, the user can choose File➪Save As in their Web browser to save the dashboard as a PowerPoint file.

The URL component is quite simple to use. As you can see in Figure 13-30, all you have to do is enter the URL or file path of the PowerPoint presentation.

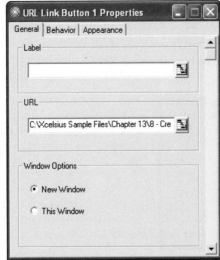

Figure 13-30:
Use the URL component to open a pre-exported PowerPoint dashboard.

At this point, your URL component is ready to use. However, if you want to get really fancy, you can make the component invisible and then overlay it onto a simple image. This allows your users to simply click an image to open the URL.

To make the URL component invisible, just remove the check from the Show Background property on the Behavior tab. Then you can place the URL component over an imported image. For example, the visual model in Figure 13-31, which contains an image of the PowerPoint logo, highlights the steps you take to overlay a URL component on top of an Image component.

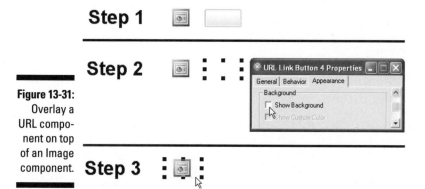

Figure 13-31:
Overlay a URL component on top of an Image component.

Nesting a Dashboard within Another Dashboard

Some dashboards are so complex and require so many components that not even dynamic visibility can help you manage and maintain them. In these situations, the best thing to do is to split your dashboard into multiple dashboards, each containing a specific function. Then you can combine them all into a master dashboard.

This is made possible by using the Image component. In addition to JPEG files, you can also import SWF flash files for use in your dashboards. This allows you to nest existing Crystal Xcelsius SWF files into your visual model. For instance, the dashboard shown in Figure 13-32 contains nothing more than three Image components that consist of nested SWF files. All the work is being done by the nested Flash files.

Nesting dashboards is as simple as adding an Image component. All you need to do is simply add the Image component to the visual model and then import the SWF file by using the File Name property.

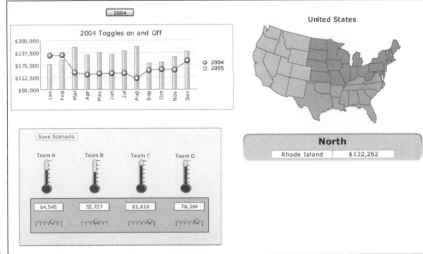

Figure 13-32:
This visual model contains only three Image components.

When you import a SWF file by using an Image component, the SWF file becomes attached to the visual model but only as an external file with references. When you export the final dashboard, Crystal Xcelsius outputs the nested SWF file into a directory with the final dashboard. These files must be kept with the final dashboard in order for the dashboard to work properly. If you move the dashboard, you must move all accompanying files with it.

Using Crystal Xcelsius to Build Your Web Site

The more I work with Crystal Xcelsius, the more I try to do with it. I recently took a crack at building a small Web site using only Crystal Xcelsius. You can see the results at

```
http://www.datapigtechnologies.com/xcelsiusexamples/mywebpage.html
```

Figures 13-33 and 13-34 show screenshots from the site.

Keep in mind that I built this site in 45 minutes! I simply built the site as if I was building a dashboard using the techniques highlighted in this book.

What this demonstrates is that with enough imagination, creativity, and time, you can create a fully functional Web site with no FrontPage or HTML experience. This won't appeal to everybody, but I know somebody out there is intrigued by this idea.

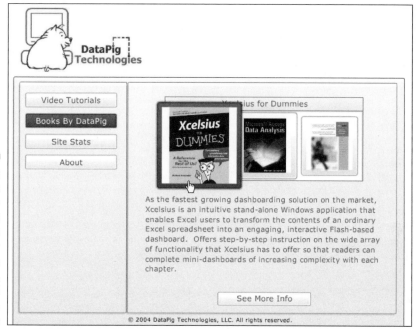

Figure 13-33:
Components
like the Fish-
Eye Picture
menu can
give your
Web site
a slick,
professional
feel.

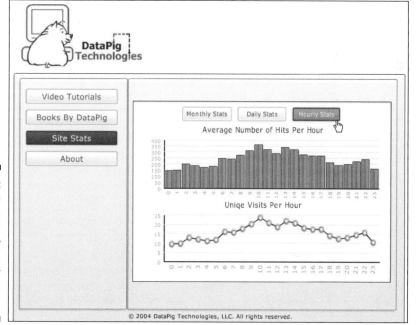

Figure 13-34:
Add
stunning
charts and
functionality
with no pro-
gramming or
Web design
experience.

Chapter 14

Frequently Asked Questions (Two Sets of Ten)

· ·

*I*n this chapter, I answer a few of the questions that I frequently get asked by users who are just starting to use Crystal Xcelsius. Hopefully, some of these topics will answer some of your pending questions.

Basic Questions about Crystal Xcelsius and Excel

What is the maximum limit of rows for a single spreadsheet selection?

There is no limit to the number of rows for a selection. Just keep in mind that the size of your selection can affect the performance of your visual model.

Crystal Xcelsius has a default limit of 512 rows that can be referenced in a single selection. You can increase the number of rows allowed by adjusting the Maximum Number of Rows setting. To do this, choose Data⇨Maximum Rows from the main menu to get to the Set Maximum Rows dialog box.

How large can my Excel file be?

There is no limit to the size of an Excel spreadsheet that can be used in Crystal Xcelsius. However, the amount of data being moved and changed during the simulation can affect the performance of your dashboard.

Can I import a password-protected model?

Crystal Xcelsius can properly change or move data in a password-protected model. You do, though, need to unprotect the Excel model before importing it. You can unprotect your Excel model by choosing Tools⇨Protection⇨ Unprotect Sheet from Excel's main menu.

Are any Excel functionalities not supported by Crystal Xcelsius?

✔ Crystal Xcelsius doesn't support links to other Excel files.

✔ Crystal Xcelsius doesn't support macros. If you import an Excel model that contains macros, you must disable the macros. To disable macros, simply click the Disable Macros button when presented with Excel's security notice.

✔ Crystal Xcelsius doesn't support named ranges.

✔ Crystal Xcelsius can't control or use pivot tables in an Excel model.

✔ Crystal Xcelsius can't control or use AutoFilters in an Excel model.

✔ Crystal Xcelsius can't use the Form or ActiveX controls in an Excel model.

Why doesn't Crystal Xcelsius work after I upgrade or reinstall Excel?

Crystal Xcelsius runs a script to configure itself to work with the version of Microsoft Office that you're running at the time of installation. If you upgrade or change the version of Microsoft Office on your machine, Crystal Xcelsius must be reinstalled to reconfigure itself to work properly with the new version.

My dashboard takes a long time to load, and it's slow to respond to my actions. What's going on?

A few factors can affect how your dashboard loads and performs. These include the number of components you have on your canvas, the number of external files that need to load, the amount of data that is being changed during the simulation, the complexity of the calculations being performed, and the speed of the computer on which the dashboard is running. For complex dashboards, you might want to create several smaller dashboards and then embed them into a central visual model that serves as a shell for these dashboards. This technique is one of the cool tricks highlighted in Chapter 13.

Common Error Messages and What They Mean

```
Server Busy
```

This error is typically triggered when you try to open Crystal Xcelsius. If you get this error, Excel has a process pending or is busy performing some other operation. You can either click the Retry button on the error dialog box or manually close all instances of Excel that are running.

A script in this movie is causing Flash Player to run
slowly . . .

This error is a Macromedia Flash Player error that is triggered when a
script has taken more than 60 seconds. You will most likely see this error
when trying to run a large visual model on a slow machine. You bypass
this error by simply clicking No to continue loading model.

Truncation Occurred . . . (when trying to preview a model)

You receive this error message if your model references an array of cells
that exceeds the default Maximum Number of Rows setting. This setting
specifies the maximum number of rows that can be referenced in either
a formula or a component's source data. To bypass this error, you must
increase the number of rows allowed by adjusting the Maximum Number
of Rows setting; choose Data⇨Maximum Rows from the main menu to get
to the Set Maximum Rows dialog box.

Generated Model May Not Display Properly (when trying to
preview a model)

You get this error if your Excel model contains an unsupported Excel
function. Although your visual model might work fine, you will continue
to get this error until you remove the unsupported function. The name of
the invalid function precedes the error message, pointing you directly to
the problem. You can find a list of supported Excel functions in Chapter 12.

To help protect your security, Internet Explorer has
restricted this file from showing active content that
could access your computer. Click here for options.

This is an Internet Explorer error that is thrown when you try to view
a dashboard via Internet Explorer. This is actually less of an error and
more of a security setting that's designed to protect your computer
by disabling ActiveX content. Unfortunately, this safeguard can also
prevent you from viewing your dashboard. You can permanently enable
Internet Explorer to view active content on local files by following these
steps:

1. **In Internet Explorer, choose Tools⇨Internet Options.**

2. **Click the Advanced tab of the Internet Options dialog box and
then scroll down to the Security section.**

3. **Check Allow Active Content To Run In Files On My Computer.**

Although this change enables only files that are local, you should do this only
if you feel confident in your computer's other security measures.

Commonly Asked Component Questions

I reimported my Excel model, and now none of my components work properly. What happened?

You either renamed the tabs in your Excel model, or you changed the structure of your Excel model. Remember that Crystal Xcelsius components use static references to link to your Excel models. This means that if you rename the tabs in your Excel model or if you change the structure of your Excel model, you might compromise the links that you created. After you build your visual model based on an imported Excel model, avoid the following actions: renaming tabs; inserting or deleting rows; and inserting or deleting columns.

Why can't I adjust the sliders and dials in my dashboards at run-time?

If you can't adjust the sliders and dials in your dashboard at run-time, this may mean that they are linked to cells with formulas. The values of a Single Value component can't be adjusted if they are linked to formula-based cells.

Why do my dials respond only to up and down mouse movements?

All Dial components have a property called the Mouse Tracking property. This property can be found in the Behavior tab under the Interaction Options, as shown in Figure 14-1.

Figure 14-1:
Set the
Mouse
Tracking
property to
Radial to
allow cir-
cular mouse
movement.

By default, all dials have the Mouse Tracking property set to Vertical, meaning that the dial will turn only when you move the mouse up or down. If you want the dial to respond to circular mouse movements, simply set this property to Radial.

How do I remove dynamic visibility?

To remove dynamic visibility from a component, click the Display Status Cell Reference icon, shown in Figure 14-2, clear the selection in the Select a Range dialog box, and then click OK.

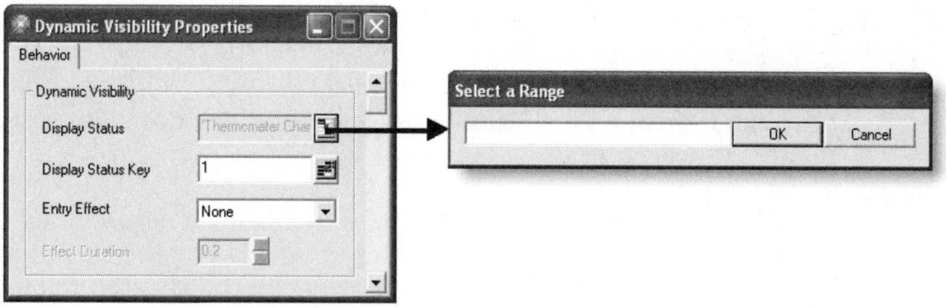

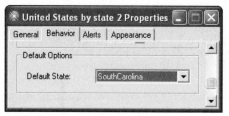

Figure 14-2: Remove dynamic visibility here.

How can I make my Map component start on a specific state?

By default, the U.S. Map component starts with Alabama selected because it's the first state alphabetically. To change this behavior, set the Default State property to the desired state. For example, the setting in Figure 14-3 ensures that my Map component starts with SouthCarolina selected.

Figure 14-3: Set the Default State property here.

Can I use my own maps in Crystal Xcelsius?

The short answer is yes. Using your own maps involves embedding an image of your map into your visual model and then applying Icon components to give your map functionality. This technique is one of the cool tricks highlighted in Chapter 13.

How do I embed a Crystal Xcelsius model into an existing PowerPoint presentation?

To embed a model into an existing PowerPoint presentation, simply export your visual model to PowerPoint, copy the model from the generated PowerPoint presentation, and paste it into your existing presentation. Keep in mind that if your model requires any external files to function, you also need to copy these into the same directory as your PowerPoint presentation.

Why can't I expand my visual models to fill the entire slide when I send them to PowerPoint?

The reason why you can't expand the embedded model to the optimal size is that empty canvas space makes up so much of the embedded model. You can solve this problem by resizing the canvas to match the width and height of the composite size of all the components on the canvas. To do this, click the Fit Canvas to Components icon on the toolbar, as shown in Figure 14-4.

Figure 14-4:
Use this to expand an embedded model.

The result is that all the unused canvas space is cut from the model, allowing you to expand the embedded model to optimum size.

How do I save different analysis scenarios in my what-if dashboard?

You have two ways to save the different analysis scenarios in your what-if dashboards: the Snapshot feature or the Local Scenario component.

The Snapshot feature allows you to export the changes you make to your model while you're in Preview mode. To use this feature, go into Preview mode, apply your desired analysis, and choose File⇨Snapshot. From here, you can select one of five formats:

- **Back to Excel:** Saves the changes that were made in Preview mode back to an Excel file

- **HTML:** Generates an HTML file and a Macromedia Flash (SWF) file with the changes made in Preview mode

- **PowerPoint:** Generates a Microsoft PowerPoint file with one slide that contains a Macromedia Flash (SWF) file with the changes made in Preview mode

- **Macromedia Flash:** Generates a Macromedia Flash (SWF) file with the changes made in Preview mode

- **Outlook:** Generates a Microsoft Outlook e-mail that contains the Macromedia Flash (SWF) file with the changes made in Preview mode

Because you must be in Preview mode to use this feature, this option is viable only if you have Crystal Xcelsius on your system.

If you want to give your clients a way to save their analyses, you can use the Local Scenario component. This component, found in the Other category of the Components window, can be used to allow your users to save results of their what-if analyses. Simply drag the component onto the visual model, and it's ready to go! Users who use that model can save different scenarios to their local machines by choosing Save from the Local Scenario component. Figure 14-5 demonstrates the saving of a scenario.

Figure 14-5: Use the Local Scenario component to allow clients to save various scenarios to their local machines.

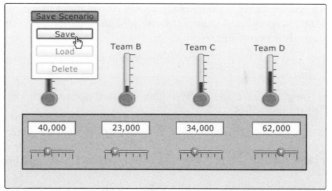

Afterward, these scenarios can quickly be loaded by clicking the Load button from the Local Scenario component. Loading a saved scenario restores the model to the same state as when it was saved.

Figure 14-6 demonstrates how a user chooses from saved scenarios to load a particular one.

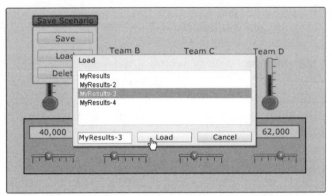

Figure 14-6:
Use the Local Scenario component to save and load an unlimited number of scenarios.

Keep in mind a few limitations when deciding to use the Local Scenario component:

- Your clients can save an unlimited number of scenarios as long as enough local storage is allocated for the Flash Player. If a client attempts to save a scenario and there is not enough local storage, the Player prompts the client to allocate more.

- Because these scenarios are saved to the local machine, the scenarios aren't available if the model has been e-mailed or moved to another computer.

- Scenarios saved in Preview mode will not persist outside the preview session.

- The states of external SWF files are also not restored when a scenario is loaded.

Chapter 15

Ten (or So) Real World Examples

In this chapter, I want to show you a few real-world examples of how Crystal Xcelsius can help people in different industries improve their business processes. As you look through these examples, you will start to realize that the uses for Crystal Xcelsius go beyond simple dashboards. By using a little imagination and industry knowledge, you can create tools that actually solve the practical problems of your day-to-day operations.

The examples highlighted here can be found in the `C:\Xcelsius Sample Files\Chapter 15\` directory.

Load Optimization (Logistics)

The Crystal Xcelsius model that you see in Figure 15-1 is actually a calculator. This calculator leverages the inherent interactivity of Crystal Xcelsius to help perform what-if analyses for shipping a load of boxes.

Suppose you run a small transportation firm that ships units all over the country. In your daily operations, part of your job would most certainly revolve around optimizing the number of units that you ship per load. This Crystal Xcelsius calculator provides an easy-to-use tool to determine the optimal way to load the pallets for the shipment specified. Simply select the size of truck you're using, enter the number of boxes that you need to ship, and then enter the cost per round trip. From there, you can use the sliders to determine the most cost-effective way to load the truck.

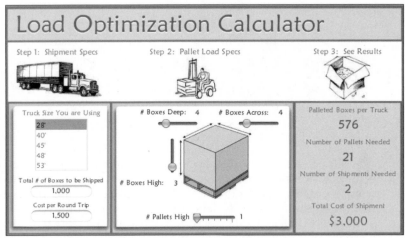

Figure 15-1:
This Crystal
Xcelsius
calculator
can help
you optimize
a shipping
load.

Instructor Staffing (Education)

Here is a simple example of a staffing calculator that you can create with Crystal Xcelsius. Imagine that you're an administrator for a small community college. You've been asked to determine the number of adjunct professors that will be required per academic department based on student population growth and the school's policy on a student/professor ratio. Again, you could do this in a spreadsheet, but the number of variables that need tracking would make this a relatively painful process.

To help solve this problem, you can create a simple Crystal Xcelsius dashboard that allows you to dynamically change any one of the variables in your calculations. The dashboard shown in Figure 15-2 demonstrates how a handful of components can help you build a simple tool that can be used to quickly run through several staffing scenarios.

Again, this is just one example of the many different types of interactive staffing calculators that you can create based on your business requirements.

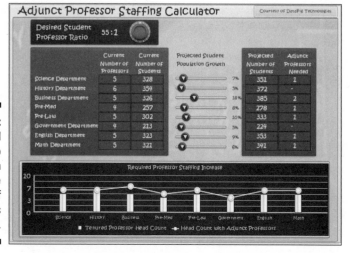

Figure 15-2:
Use Crystal
Xcelsius to
perform
multiple
what-if
scenarios
for staffing.

Basic ROI Calculator (Finance)

Anyone who has been in the Finance arena for any period of time can tell you that Excel is the cornerstone of the finance department. Countless financial models and calculators are built on the power of Excel alone. Crystal Xcelsius can help finance gurus turn complex models into interactive works of art that are not only easy to use but also easy on the eyes.

Here is a simple example of how Crystal Xcelsius can help. Figure 15-3 shows a basic ROI (return on investment) model in Excel. Although you yourself might be able to translate this into English, this Excel model could prove difficult for others to follow.

	F	G	H	I	J	K
1	Costs	Cost Of Goods Sold	28,417	Total Cost		
2		Selling Expense	18,944	52,953		
3		Depreciation	5,000			
4		Other Expense	592	Pretax Margin		
5				10.56%	PreTax ROI	AfterTax ROI
6	Revenues	Revenues	59,202	Asset Turnover	22.74%	22.69%
7				2.15		
8	Benefits	Cash	12,456	Total Assets	Tax Rate	
9		Accounts Receivable	7,689	27,476	25.0%	ROE
10		Inventories	4,567			34.83%
11		Marketable Securities	897			
12		Other Current Assets	265			
13		Land	432			
14		Buildings	816	Equity Multiplier		
15		Equipment	354	1.54		
16						
17	Stockholder's Equity	Stockholders' Equity	17,895			

Figure 15-3:
A basic ROI
model in
Excel can
be hard to
follow.

However, placing this ROI model into a Crystal Xcelsius dashboard not only makes the model interactive but can also help clarify the logic in the calculations. Figure 15-4 shows the new and improved ROI model.

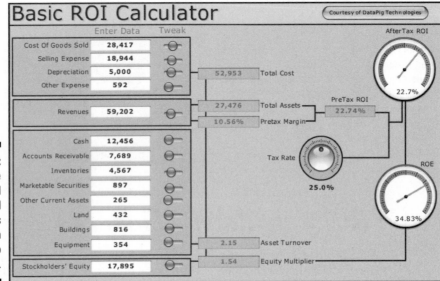

Service Outage Analyzer (IT)

This example demonstrates how Crystal Xcelsius can help an IT manager analyze the effect of service outages.

Imagine that you run an IT operation that services the various lines of business in your organization. Each of these business units contributes to your operating budget. Your annual budget is in the neighborhood of four to six million dollars. You have a Service Level Agreement with the business units in your organization specifying that any outage in the operation beyond a set threshold comes from your discretionary funds — not the business unit. Not only do you have to foot the bill for the outage, but you will undoubtedly require additional resources to restore operations. Depending on the severity of the outage, you will likely have to monitor the recovered operation for some period of time.

Although you can most certainly track this information in a spreadsheet, such as the one shown in Figure 15-5, performing proactive what-if analyses in this environment would be difficult.

Figure 15-5:
A spread-
sheet like
this makes
proactive
what-if
analyses
difficult to
perform.

	A	B	C	D
1		Annual	Daily	
2	XYZ Systems Group Operating Budget	$6,000,000.00	$16,438.00	$/day
3	Outage duration		1	day
4	Service Level Agreement	BCP Guarantee	0.75	days
5	LOB reimbursement (loss of BAU services beyond threshold of 0.75 days)	$4,110.00		
6	Additional incremental effort	50.00%		
7	Recovery Effort Factor	1.5	$24,657.00	
8	monitoring duration	14	days	
9	monitoring factor	12.50%		
10	monitoring costs	$28,766.50		
11	Effective Budget Impact		$57,533.50	

In contrast, Crystal Xcelsius allows you to see the bottom-line effect of a service outage to your department. As you can see in Figure 15-6, you can adjust the various sliders and dials to determine the impact of various scenarios.

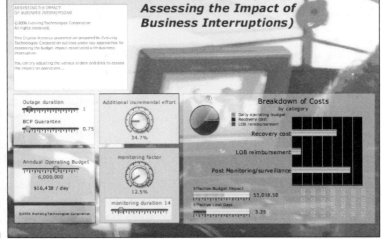

Figure 15-6:
Crystal
Xcelsius
provides for
an easy-to-
use analysis
tool.

Fuel Cost Analysis (Transportation)

This example illustrates how you can build a fuel cost calculator in Crystal Xcelsius to interactively analyze and calculate fuel costs. Although the example in Figure 15-7 deals with airline costs, this type of model can be applied to most transportation scenarios.

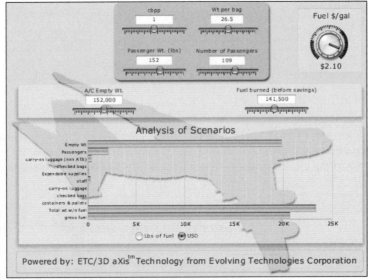

Figure 15-7: This model allows you to adjust a variety of factors that affect the cost of fuel.

Software Development

Understanding and estimating software development costs is never simple because they're based on a variety of factors, including the number of lines of code, how much code turnover you will have, and the expense of personnel. This is further augmented by the degree of sophistication of software development tools and practices as well as the application environment where the software will be deployed.

The dashboard shown in Figure 15-8 is an example of a constructive cost model that allows you to estimate the level of effort, schedule, staffing requirements, and costs associated with your software development project. Click the various tabs to adjust individual parameters. To see the outcome, select the radio buttons for effort, schedule, staffing, and costs.

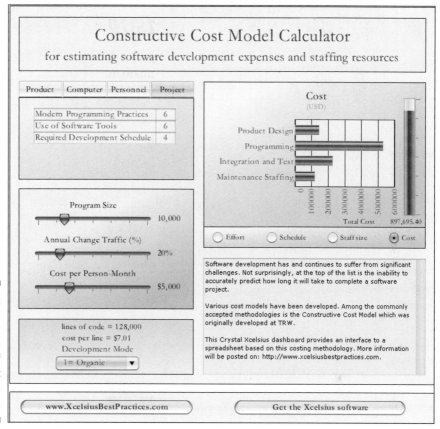

Figure 15-8:
This model allows you to adjust a variety of factors that affect the cost of fuel.

This dashboard is an excellent example of how you can save a lot of screen space by using tabs and radio buttons to accommodate a great deal of information in a single page display.

Site Statistics (Web Site Management)

The example shown in Figure 15-9 illustrates how Crystal Xcelsius can help you make sense of the activity on your Web site.

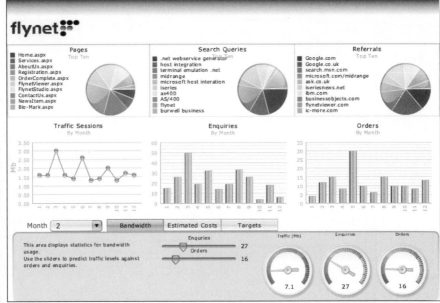

Figure 15-9:
You can use Crystal Xcelsius to track and analyze critical Web site statistics.

This particular dashboard is packed with information on site activity, including

✓ **Top 10 Page Requests:** This graph gives you an exact percentage of which pages on the site are the most popular.

✓ **Top 10 Search Queries:** This gives you an overview of the ten most popular search queries that have generated traffic to your site.

✓ **Top 10 Referrals:** This chart gives you an overview of where your traffic comes from.

✓ **Traffic Sessions:** This line graph gives you a visual representation of the amount of traffic in megabytes from all sessions by month.

✓ **Enquiries:** This is the amount of contact by users. This data can be monitored and used to compare against successful orders.

✓ **Orders:** This allows you to monitor and report order levels and trends. Keeping track of your most popular month for sales allows you to prepare your inventory levels in advance.

✓ **Bandwidth:** This section allows you to visually compare data flow, adjust levels of orders and enquiries, and see what effect they have on bandwidth in megabytes.

✔ **Estimated Costs:** This tool allows you to price bandwidth and calculate your bandwidth bill. This is useful if you use a hosting company that charges for bandwidth per month.

✔ **Targets:** This area allows you to calculate how much income you will generate depending on the amount of orders. This is useful for determining the impact you need to generate before a marketing campaign is started.

Google AdWords Tracker (Marketing)

If you have a site that is registered to a Google AdWords account, you can create reports that visually represent the success of your Google marketing campaign. The example shown in Figure 15-10 illustrates how Crystal Xcelsius allows you to monitor the performance of specified keywords as they relate to cost-per-click and the average position of your site on generated Google searches.

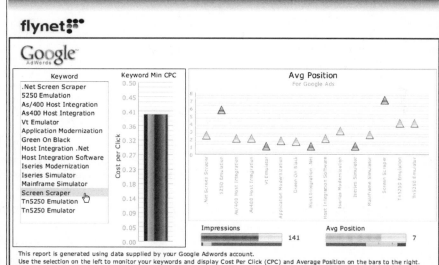

Figure 15-10: Crystal Xcelsius can report on your Google AdWords campaign.

Headcount Visibility Reporting (HR)

Human Resources is another area where Crystal Xcelsius can help. HR departments are often asked to produce several views on employee data. With Crystal Xcelsius, you can consolidate several reports into a brilliant, interactive reporting tool that serves as a central data source for HR reporting. The dashboard highlighted in Figure 15-11 is a simple example of this concept.

Figure 15-11: Crystal Xcelsius is ideal for reporting HR data.

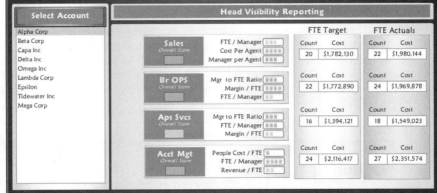

Getting help with your Crystal Xcelsius project

If you find yourself needing help with your Crystal Xcelsius project — or you simply want to leave such projects to the professionals — try one of these resources that specialize in Crystal Xcelsius development:

✔ **Evolving Technologies Corporation:** Provides end-to-end consulting on Crystal Xcelsius development, from identifying key metrics to deployment. www.xcelsiusbest practices.com

✔ **Flynet:** Specializes in developing tools that connect Crystal Xcelsius dashboards to enterprise data, allowing you to connect dashboards via Web Services. www.fly netviewer.com

✔ **DataPig Technologies:** Specializes in converting established Excel models into functional calculators in Crystal Xcelsius. www.datapigtechnologies.com

Appendix

Going Beyond Spreadsheets

I know it's tempting to give an appendix a polite once-over and then move on, but I encourage you to take a moment to think about the concepts here.

This appendix is a reprint of a white paper written by Loren Abdulezer, CEO of Evolving Technologies Corporation, titled "Going beyond Spreadsheets: How visual modeling can enhance decision analysis." In his piece, Loren provides a clear perspective on how Crystal Xcelsius can help you extend your decision analysis beyond the spreadsheet paradigm.

The More Things Change, the More They Remain the Same

Spreadsheets, which have been around since the late 1970s, were an instant sensation. Among other things, they were intuitive, they transformed the way people analyzed data, and they were extremely easy and cost-effective to deploy. Over the years, spreadsheets have evolved and matured, but the basic form and substance of spreadsheets has hardly changed. Although new features and capabilities continue to be added to spreadsheets, for the most part, spreadsheet technology has reached a plateau. This is typical of a highly successful product.

These days, the principal changes that you see to spreadsheets tend to be incremental, like better support for multiple languages, the ability to connect to Web-based resources, and support for greater numbers of rows in PivotTables.

Such enhancements serve only to entrench the spreadsheet paradigm. The technology is, to be sure, terrific. However, new approaches and paradigms are beginning to emerge.

The next Killer App

At some point, the next Killer App will be introduced, and it will entirely usurp Excel and traditional spreadsheets. That Killer App will manifest itself by containing three crucial ingredients. Not surprisingly, these are the same ingredients that allowed the spreadsheet to be labeled a Killer App a few decades ago:

- ✔ It will be intuitive to understand and use.
- ✔ It will totally transform how data analysis is done.
- ✔ It will be extremely easy and cost effective to deploy.

A lot of vendors with non-spreadsheet products would lay claim to these attributes, but these features alone do not qualify an application as a Killer App.

Myriad products that introduce major innovations are signaling a paradigm shift. However, most of these promising technologies and products focus on a tightly defined application or use. This funneling, or narrowing of scope, makes them particularly effective tools, but their applications find use in a restrictive range.

The scope of the evolution of spreadsheets is far more revealing when the use and innovations of products and technologies are being shaped more by the user community than by the original developers.

Spreadsheets and decision analysis

Take a moment to reflect on the different ways that spreadsheets are used in decision analysis. Table A-1 outlines representative examples.

Table A-1	Common Forms of Decision Analysis in Spreadsheets	
Type	*Detailed Description*	*Additional Comments*
Binary and discrete decisions	This often takes the form of a Yes/No question.	This often lends itself to statistics hypothesis testing.
Analog decisions	This often takes the form of, "How much?," such as in a financial projection or forecast.	Uncertainty analysis and sensitivity analysis can be easily incorporated into analog decisions.
Data folding (or digital origami)	This often takes the form of PivotTables, multidimensional analysis, or drilling down.	Drilling down or subsectioning data is important.

Type	Detailed Description	Additional Comments
Search	This can be as simple as using Excel functions like VLOOKUP, or can be a full-blown system connecting to back-end data-bases and servers.	Data exchange using XML
Optimization	This can be as simple as using the Goal Seek facility of Excel, or can entail involved mathematical techniques.	When performing large-scale optimizations, Excel is usually used to shuttle information back and forth to a third-party analysis engine that does all the hard work.
Verification	Spreadsheets can be used in summarizing, analyzing, and reconciling complex data.	Challenges exist with incomplete information, incorrect assumptions and formulas, inconsistent data (relationships that point to conflicting outcomes), and redundant information.

The one thing that might become clear from the information in Table A-1 is that sophisticated decision analysis is often accompanied by a tool or technology that requires sophistication on the part of the user to apply it. The major exception to this rule is the digital dashboard.

Digital Dashboards and Visual Models

The very notion of a digital dashboard is to provide a single point from which all relevant information can be seen, interpreted, and acted upon. Although traditional spreadsheets are capable of providing dashboard-like functionality, some effort is required to progress from a static report to one that is highly interactive.

Sampling of digital dashboards and visual models

The many types of dashboards often display Key Performance Indicators, or *metrics,* as shown in Figure A-1.

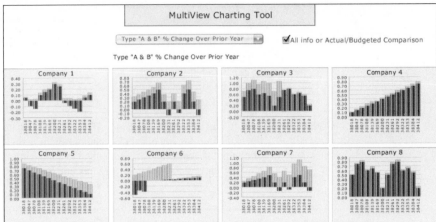

Figure A-1:
Dashboards
allow
simultan-
eous
viewing of
Key
Perform-
ance
Indicators
and metrics.

Although it is nice to have a single panel on which to view everything, the information that a decision maker might need to examine could be complex. Figure A-2 shows a browsing tool based on an Accordion-style organizer. This scenario has a variety of broad-based categories, and each of these categories has subcategories.

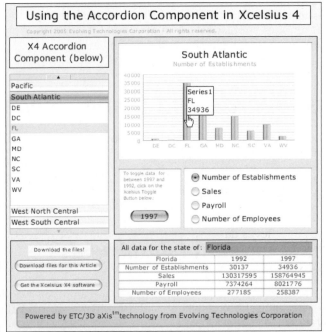

Figure A-2:
Accordion
data viewer.

Notice two key features here:

- ✔ The items selected in the categories and subcategories create a context from which to do further analysis. In the example illustrated in Figure A-2, clicking a specific state (FL) automatically retrieves a swatch of data for that state.

- ✔ The items to be treated as categories and subcategories can be determined at run-time. It becomes possible to turn the subcategory into a category, allowing for further drilling-down, if the data is available.

A dashboard can be connected to the underlying dataset or model. So why not utilize the underlying model to create an interactive visual model? It would allow you to change the underlying data, and see the results immediately on the dashboard. Figure A-3 shows a Fuel Savings Calculator for airlines that does this.

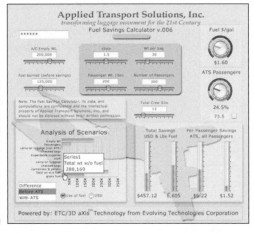

Figure A-3:
This visual modeling dashboard serves as a tool to analyze fuel savings.

In Figure A-3, various knobs and sliders to adjust the underlying assumptions appear in the model. Basically, this visual model connects to an Excel spreadsheet and database to calculate estimates of fuel and cost savings.

This fuel savings tool is both a dashboard and a visual model. Although it assembles and retrieves data for presentation, it also harnesses the computational facilities of an underlying spreadsheet model and allows the user to adjust assumptions by using sliders, dials, and other visual input interfaces.

In this visual model are pick lists, check boxes, and radio buttons that allow for context switching. Context switching is important because it allows views and scenarios to dynamically change during the decision analysis.

Another feature to notice is the automatic alert levels integrated into the visual model components (see Figure A-4).

Figure A-4:
Components
connect to
an
underlying
spreadsheet
model.

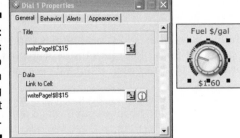

Feel free to review Chapter 4 to get the skinny on integrating alerts into your visual models.

These components routinely allow for the incorporation of colorized alerts (see Figure A-5). In this case, the needle or dial indicator changes color as values are changed.

Figure A-5:
Color
schemes for
alerts need
to be
specified.

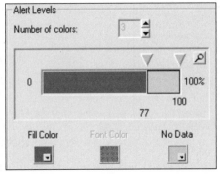

Alert values for each color can also be set, as is shown in Figure A-6.

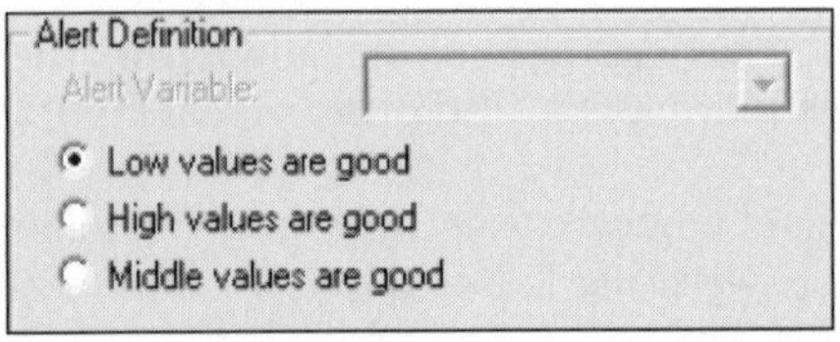

Figure A-6:
Alert levels
need to be
specified.

New approaches to old problems

The concept of visual modeling using the dashboard metaphor opens new avenues for decision analysis.

Consider a forward-looking dashboard in which a number of estimate assumptions can be set as well as the uncertainty for those estimates. If you project expenses based on number of units, as well as price, to produce each unit, you can calculate your aggregate costs pretty easily. In reality, though, there could very well be some variation or uncertainty on the number of units that you will sell as well as the cost per unit. What will be the bottom-line effect of these uncertainties?

This problem is not as simple as it appears. You might be tempted to say, "I'll take the best-case scenario of all my options and the worst-case of all my options and see what they point to." Although it's true that the projection has to lie somewhere between these best- and worst-case scenarios, this might not be exact enough for your purposes. The uncertainties are, after all, unknowns that can't be nailed down until your business operation is actually in progress. Not only are your purchasing costs and number of units produced subject to uncertainty, but so are a whole other host of factors, including operating expenses as well as general and administrative expenses. All these independent uncertainties will unlikely all be beneficial or detrimental at one time. In that case, your absolute best-case or absolute worst-case scenarios provide little aid in decision analysis. Chances are that the value for each item in your model will hover around a value in the middle and not veer to any extreme.

A mathematical technique called *Addition in Quadrature* has been applied to problems of this kind. (You can find out more about this technique by checking out the book *Excel Best Practices for Business* by Loren Abdulezer, Wiley.) Although the technique works well with spreadsheets, it works better in a visual modeling venue — for example, the abacus-style visual model that you see in Figure A-7.

The central "beads" in the bottom panel represent expected values, and the beads to either side represent the spread or deviations from the expected values.

To find a working version of the abacus-style visual model, go to

www.xcelsiusbestpractices.com/landingZone/articles/abacus.html

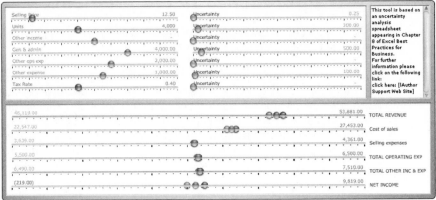

Figure A-7: This abacus-style visual model integrates uncertainty.

How visual models extend spreadsheets

Many software applications have spreadsheet-like qualities. Rather than trying to replicate what a spreadsheet can do, consider utilizing what a spreadsheet already has to offer and extend it. This novel approach turns out to be very sensible.

The basic idea of visual modeling as an extension of a spreadsheet is very simple. It involves having a ready-made spreadsheet, identifying its inputs and outputs, and mapping it to visual components external to the spreadsheet.

A quick way to understand the visual modeling technique is to deconstruct one. A simple and practical example for this purpose is the retirement calculator in Figure A-8.

To find a working version of the visual retirement calculator, go to

`www.xcelsiusbestpractices.com/landingZone/samplefiles.html`

You can easily see the factors that drive this model. They are

✔ Annual rate of return

✔ Years of saving

✔ Annual amount invested

✔ Annual amount of withdrawal from the retirement account

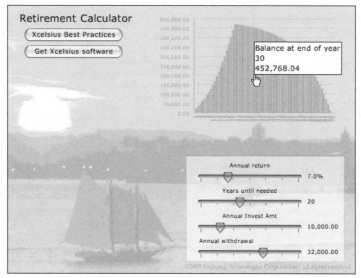

Figure A-8:
A visual
retirement
calculator.

Matching the visual sliders are the assumptions used by an underlying spreadsheet, as shown in Figure A-9. When you move sliders on the visual model, new data values for each of the items are inserted into the underlying spreadsheet model. The model is recalculated, and results are returned to the visual presentation layer (the column chart in the top-right corner of Figure A-8). For completeness of the model, the initial balance is set to 0 (zero).

Figure A-9:
Drivers in
the
spreadsheet
model.

	A	B
1	XCELSIUS VISUAL MODEL	
2	Investment Planning Tool	
3	essential parameters for model	
4		
5	Initial Balance	0.00
6	Annual return	7.0%
7	Annual Invest Amt	10,000.00
8	Years until needed	20
9	Annual withdrawal	32,000.00

⏮ ◀ ▶ ⏭ \Config / Sheet3 /

Deeper inside the model (see Figure A-10) are the calculations that drive the column chart.

	A	B	C	D	E
1	XCELSIUS VISUAL MODEL				
2	Investment Planning Tool				
3	analysis page				
4					
5	Yr	start bal	additions	end bal	Y/E withdr
6					
7	1	0.00	10,000.00	10,700.00	0.00
8	2	10,700.00	10,000.00	22,149.00	0.00
9	3	22,149.00	10,000.00	34,399.43	0.00
10	4	34,399.43	10,000.00	47,507.39	0.00
11	5	47,507.39	10,000.00	61,532.91	0.00
12	6	61,532.91	10,000.00	76,540.21	0.00
13	7	76,540.21	10,000.00	92,598.02	0.00
14	8	92,598.02	10,000.00	109,779.88	0.00
15	9	109,779.88	10,000.00	128,164.47	0.00
16	10	128,164.47	10,000.00	147,835.98	0.00
17	11	147,835.98	10,000.00	168,884.50	0.00
18	12	168,884.50	10,000.00	191,406.42	0.00
19	13	191,406.42	10,000.00	215,504.87	0.00
20	14	215,504.87	10,000.00	241,290.21	0.00

I◄ ◄ ► ►I \ **AnalysisSheet** / Config / Sheet3 /

Figure A-10: Computational analysis.

The formulas in the model are elementary interest calculations, taking into account additions and withdrawals.

Typically, the spreadsheet model should have some safeguards built in at the spreadsheet level. For instance, ending up with negative balances wouldn't make sense.

This is an important point: The spreadsheet model must have a requisite level of integrity, and the inputs and outputs should be obvious enough to make the mapping process of the spreadsheet to the visual interface easy.

The mapping between spreadsheet and visual interface starts out at the interface level. All the components are specified in an Object Browser (see Figure A-11). As components are grouped, compound objects are created, which allows for easier management during the visual model construction process.

Figure A-11: The Object Browser holds all the components that interact with the calculation model.

Refer to Chapter 10 for more information on managing components via the Object Browser.

Deployment Issues

Three factors play a role in the deployment of a Crystal Xcelsius visual model:

- ✔ Preparing a spreadsheet for use within a visual model
- ✔ Visual model design and deployment
- ✔ Economics of preparing and maintaining software

Spreadsheet preparation

The essential idea for a visual model is to build upon a ready-made spreadsheet. *Ready-made* means that nothing further should have to be done with the spreadsheet.

All the calculation formulas that would be utilized within the visual model should already exist in the spreadsheet.

To facilitate the mapping between the visual presentation layer (components displayed on the canvas) and the underlying spreadsheet, identifying all the essential inputs and outputs within the spreadsheet is helpful.

If the spreadsheet uses an Excel function that's not implemented in Crystal Xcelsius, you might need to revise some of the spreadsheet formulas to remove this dependency.

Design and deployment

The basic cycle for preparing a visual model for deployment is

1. Create or use an existing spreadsheet as the basis for your model.

2. Prepare the spreadsheet for use with Crystal Xcelsius.

   Revise formulas as necessary and make the model inputs and outputs easily identifiable.

 3. Create an "image" of the spreadsheet within the Crystal Xcelsius work area.

    This is done by importing the spreadsheet.

 4. Add the desired visual components onto the canvas. Map them to the spreadsheet image and define their attributes, behavior, and appearance.

 5. Test and validate the Crystal Xcelsius visual model within the development work area.

 6. Export the visual model to the desired presentation format (Flash/HTML, PowerPoint, or PDF).

Features are built in to various versions of Crystal Xcelsius that enable extensive Web-centric capabilities, such as retrieving and sending XML information, utilizing Web Services, and implementing collaboration services. The use of these extra facilities doesn't really entail changing the basic design and deployment cycle.

Cost of ownership

You might notice that the word *development* is conspicuously absent from the preceding section. This omission is intentional. At no point is it necessary for programmers to code an application.

Think of what is generally involved in preparing a Visual Basic application that has the sophistication and interactivity of the dashboards and visual models. Think of the many lines of programming code, the level of testing and validation, and the overall amount of time and cost for a development project.

Removing the requirement for customized programming lowers the total life-cycle cost. As with any software application, a learning curve is involved with designing and deploying professional quality visual models and dashboards when using tools like Crystal Xcelsius. However, other than following best practices and acquiring basic knowledge, there is no need (and actually no provision) for programming when using Crystal Xcelsius. These best practices are essential to keeping the cost of ownership low.

Concluding Remarks

Every now and then, a technology comes along and completely revises how you do things. Visual modeling and dashboards are mind-expanding technologies that unlock the computational facilities of a spreadsheet. We can't predict with certainty how spreadsheets are going to evolve, but it's a good bet that Microsoft's next generation technology will be strongly influenced by products like Crystal Xcelsius.

Reprinted with permission
(c)2006 Evolving Technologies Corporation - All rights reserved.
Loren Abdulezer is the CEO of Evolving Technologies Corporation
and the author of Excel Best Practices for Business *and*
Escape from Excel Hell *(Wiley, both).*
He also happens to be the technical editor of this book,
Crystal Xcelsius For Dummies.

Index

• G •

• Y •

• Z •

BUSINESS, CAREERS & PERSONAL FINANCE

0-7645-5307-0

0-7645-5331-3 *†

Also available:

- Accounting For Dummies †
  0-7645-5314-3
- Business Plans Kit For Dummies †
  0-7645-5365-8
- Cover Letters For Dummies
  0-7645-5224-4
- Frugal Living For Dummies
  0-7645-5403-4
- Leadership For Dummies
  0-7645-5176-0
- Managing For Dummies
  0-7645-1771-6

- Marketing For Dummies
  0-7645-5600-2
- Personal Finance For Dummies *
  0-7645-2590-5
- Project Management For Dummies
  0-7645-5283-X
- Resumes For Dummies †
  0-7645-5471-9
- Selling For Dummies
  0-7645-5363-1
- Small Business Kit For Dummies *†
  0-7645-5093-4

HOME & BUSINESS COMPUTER BASICS

0-7645-4074-2

0-7645-3758-X

Also available:

- ACT! 6 For Dummies
  0-7645-2645-6
- iLife '04 All-in-One Desk Reference
  For Dummies
  0-7645-7347-0
- iPAQ For Dummies
  0-7645-6769-1
- Mac OS X Panther Timesaving
  Techniques For Dummies
  0-7645-5812-9
- Macs For Dummies
  0-7645-5656-8

- Microsoft Money 2004 For Dummies
  0-7645-4195-1
- Office 2003 All-in-One Desk Reference
  For Dummies
  0-7645-3883-7
- Outlook 2003 For Dummies
  0-7645-3759-8
- PCs For Dummies
  0-7645-4074-2
- TiVo For Dummies
  0-7645-6923-6
- Upgrading and Fixing PCs For Dummies
  0-7645-1665-5
- Windows XP Timesaving Techniques
  For Dummies
  0-7645-3748-2

FOOD, HOME, GARDEN, HOBBIES, MUSIC & PETS

0-7645-5295-3

0-7645-5232-5

Also available:

- Bass Guitar For Dummies
  0-7645-2487-9
- Diabetes Cookbook For Dummies
  0-7645-5230-9
- Gardening For Dummies *
  0-7645-5130-2
- Guitar For Dummies
  0-7645-5106-X
- Holiday Decorating For Dummies
  0-7645-2570-0
- Home Improvement All-in-One
  For Dummies
  0-7645-5680-0

- Knitting For Dummies
  0-7645-5395-X
- Piano For Dummies
  0-7645-5105-1
- Puppies For Dummies
  0-7645-5255-4
- Scrapbooking For Dummies
  0-7645-7208-3
- Senior Dogs For Dummies
  0-7645-5818-8
- Singing For Dummies
  0-7645-2475-5
- 30-Minute Meals For Dummies
  0-7645-2589-1

INTERNET & DIGITAL MEDIA

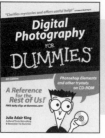

0-7645-1664-7

0-7645-6924-4

Also available:

- 2005 Online Shopping Directory
  For Dummies
  0-7645-7495-7
- CD & DVD Recording For Dummies
  0-7645-5956-7
- eBay For Dummies
  0-7645-5654-1
- Fighting Spam For Dummies
  0-7645-5965-6
- Genealogy Online For Dummies
  0-7645-5964-8
- Google For Dummies
  0-7645-4420-9

- Home Recording For Musicians
  For Dummies
  0-7645-1634-5
- The Internet For Dummies
  0-7645-4173-0
- iPod & iTunes For Dummies
  0-7645-7772-7
- Preventing Identity Theft For Dummies
  0-7645-7336-5
- Pro Tools All-in-One Desk Reference
  For Dummies
  0-7645-5714-9
- Roxio Easy Media Creator For Dummies
  0-7645-7131-1

* Separate Canadian edition also available
† Separate U.K. edition also available

Available wherever books are sold. For more information or to order direct: U.S. customers visit www.dummies.com or call 1-877-762-2974.
U.K. customers visit www.wileyeurope.com or call 0800 243407. Canadian customers visit www.wiley.ca or call 1-800-567-4797.

SPORTS, FITNESS, PARENTING, RELIGION & SPIRITUALITY

0-7645-5146-9

0-7645-5418-2

Also available:
- Adoption For Dummies
  0-7645-5488-3
- Basketball For Dummies
  0-7645-5248-1
- The Bible For Dummies
  0-7645-5296-1
- Buddhism For Dummies
  0-7645-5359-3
- Catholicism For Dummies
  0-7645-5391-7
- Hockey For Dummies
  0-7645-5228-7

- Judaism For Dummies
  0-7645-5299-6
- Martial Arts For Dummies
  0-7645-5358-5
- Pilates For Dummies
  0-7645-5397-6
- Religion For Dummies
  0-7645-5264-3
- Teaching Kids to Read For Dummies
  0-7645-4043-2
- Weight Training For Dummies
  0-7645-5168-X
- Yoga For Dummies
  0-7645-5117-5

TRAVEL

0-7645-5438-7

0-7645-5453-0

Also available:
- Alaska For Dummies
  0-7645-1761-9
- Arizona For Dummies
  0-7645-6938-4
- Cancún and the Yucatán For Dummies
  0-7645-2437-2
- Cruise Vacations For Dummies
  0-7645-6941-4
- Europe For Dummies
  0-7645-5456-5
- Ireland For Dummies
  0-7645-5455-7

- Las Vegas For Dummies
  0-7645-5448-4
- London For Dummies
  0-7645-4277-X
- New York City For Dummies
  0-7645-6945-7
- Paris For Dummies
  0-7645-5494-8
- RV Vacations For Dummies
  0-7645-5443-3
- Walt Disney World & Orlando For Dummies
  0-7645-6943-0

GRAPHICS, DESIGN & WEB DEVELOPMENT

0-7645-4345-8

0-7645-5589-8

Also available:
- Adobe Acrobat 6 PDF For Dummies
  0-7645-3760-1
- Building a Web Site For Dummies
  0-7645-7144-3
- Dreamweaver MX 2004 For Dummies
  0-7645-4342-3
- FrontPage 2003 For Dummies
  0-7645-3882-9
- HTML 4 For Dummies
  0-7645-1995-6
- Illustrator CS For Dummies
  0-7645-4084-X

- Macromedia Flash MX 2004 For Dummies
  0-7645-4358-X
- Photoshop 7 All-in-One Desk Reference For Dummies
  0-7645-1667-1
- Photoshop CS Timesaving Techniques For Dummies
  0-7645-6782-9
- PHP 5 For Dummies
  0-7645-4166-8
- PowerPoint 2003 For Dummies
  0-7645-3908-6
- QuarkXPress 6 For Dummies
  0-7645-2593-X

NETWORKING, SECURITY, PROGRAMMING & DATABASES

0-7645-6852-3

0-7645-5784-X

Also available:
- A+ Certification For Dummies
  0-7645-4187-0
- Access 2003 All-in-One Desk Reference For Dummies
  0-7645-3988-4
- Beginning Programming For Dummies
  0-7645-4997-9
- C For Dummies
  0-7645-7068-4
- Firewalls For Dummies
  0-7645-4048-3
- Home Networking For Dummies
  0-7645-42796

- Network Security For Dummies
  0-7645-1679-5
- Networking For Dummies
  0-7645-1677-9
- TCP/IP For Dummies
  0-7645-1760-0
- VBA For Dummies
  0-7645-3989-2
- Wireless All In-One Desk Reference For Dummies
  0-7645-7496-5
- Wireless Home Networking For Dummies
  0-7645-3910-8

HEALTH & SELF-HELP

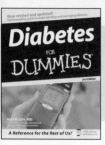

0-7645-6820-5 *†

0-7645-2566-2

Also available:

- Alzheimer's For Dummies
  0-7645-3899-3
- Asthma For Dummies
  0-7645-4233-8
- Controlling Cholesterol For Dummies
  0-7645-5440-9
- Depression For Dummies
  0-7645-3900-0
- Dieting For Dummies
  0-7645-4149-8
- Fertility For Dummies
  0-7645-2549-2

- Fibromyalgia For Dummies
  0-7645-5441-7
- Improving Your Memory For Dummies
  0-7645-5435-2
- Pregnancy For Dummies †
  0-7645-4483-7
- Quitting Smoking For Dummies
  0-7645-2629-4
- Relationships For Dummies
  0-7645-5384-4
- Thyroid For Dummies
  0-7645-5385-2

EDUCATION, HISTORY, REFERENCE & TEST PREPARATION

0-7645-5194-9

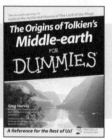

0-7645-4186-2

Also available:

- Algebra For Dummies
  0-7645-5325-9
- British History For Dummies
  0-7645-7021-8
- Calculus For Dummies
  0-7645-2498-4
- English Grammar For Dummies
  0-7645-5322-4
- Forensics For Dummies
  0-7645-5580-4
- The GMAT For Dummies
  0-7645-5251-1
- Inglés Para Dummies
  0-7645-5427-1

- Italian For Dummies
  0-7645-5196-5
- Latin For Dummies
  0-7645-5431-X
- Lewis & Clark For Dummies
  0-7645-2545-X
- Research Papers For Dummies
  0-7645-5426-3
- The SAT I For Dummies
  0-7645-7193-1
- Science Fair Projects For Dummies
  0-7645-5460-3
- U.S. History For Dummies
  0-7645-5249-X

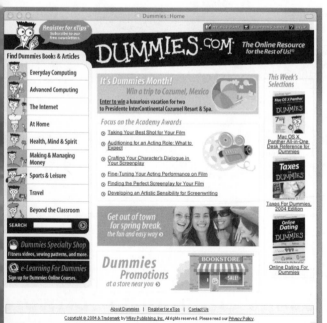

Get smart @ dummies.com®

- **Find a full list of Dummies titles**
- **Look into loads of FREE on-site articles**
- **Sign up for FREE eTips e-mailed to you weekly**
- **See what other products carry the Dummies name**
- **Shop directly from the Dummies bookstore**
- **Enter to win new prizes every month!**

Separate Canadian edition also available
Separate U.K. edition also available

Available wherever books are sold. For more information or to order direct: U.S. customers visit www.dummies.com or call 1-877-762-2974.
U.K. customers visit www.wileyeurope.com or call 0800 243407. Canadian customers visit www.wiley.ca or call 1-800-567-4797.

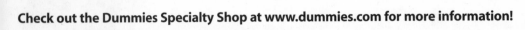